EVERY WOMAN WORKS

EVERY WOMAN WORKS

A COMPLETE MANUAL FOR
WOMEN RE-ENTERING THE JOB MARKET
OR CHANGING JOBS

BONNIE GRAY
DOROTHY LOEFFLER
ROBIN KING COOPER

Psyche, Inc. and the University of Minnesota

LIFETIME LEARNING PUBLICATIONS
A division of Wadsworth, Inc.

Belmont, California

London, Singapore, Sydney
Toronto, Mexico City

Developmental Editor: Lorraine Anderson
Text Designer: Marie Carluccio
Cover Designer: Benedict Norbert Wong

Printed in the United States of America

1 2 3 4 5 6 7 8 9 10---86 85 84 83 82

LIBRARY OF CONGRESS CATALOGING IN PUBLICATION DATA
Gray, Bonnie, 1946–
    Every woman works.

    Bibliography: p.
    Includes index.
    1. Vocational guidance for women. I. Loeffler,
Dorothy, 1925–   . II. Cooper, Robin King, 1950–   . III. Title.
HD6057.9.G7   650.1'4'088042   81-8238
ISBN 0-534-97981-5   AACR2

CONTENTS

5   SETTING ACTION GOALS   43

You *can* state and achieve your intentions. Break goals down into manageable action steps. Plan for success.

SECTION III   DISCOVERING YOURSELF   51

6   IDENTIFYING YOUR ROLES   53

You derive your identity from the roles you play. Past roles: your unique lifeline. Current roles: are you postponing defining your identity? Future roles: planning for increased satisfaction.

7   UNCOVERING YOUR VALUES   63

The way you spend your money and your time, the people you admire, the places you prefer, are clues to your values. Clarify your work values to insure that you end up using your skills in a setting that's congenial.

8   ARTICULATING YOUR INTERESTS   73

What do you like to do? Discover your interest profile. You will find the greatest satisfaction in work and non-work activities that interest you. Ways to cultivate interests.

9   RECOGNIZING YOUR ABILITIES   89

Have some of your valuable talents and potentials been latent for years? Why some abilities stay hidden. How to begin unearthing yours so you can turn them into skills.

10   SURVEYING YOUR SKILLS   95

You have hundreds of skills, though you may not realize it. The trick is to look for three different types of skills, in five areas of your life. Checklists help you analyze your accomplishments.

SECTION IV   DISCOVERING WORK OPPORTUNITIES 119

11   IDENTIFYING JOBS TO INVESTIGATE 121

How careers are built on skills. The Job Possibility
Guide: a rich source of job ideas based on your
interests and skills. Using forecast information and
knowledge of fields in which women are underrepresented.

12   LEARNING TO RESEARCH A JOB   141

You have more than enough information about jobs
readily available to you, if you know where to look.
Learn to effectively use printed material and information
interviews.

13   BRIDGING THE "EXPERIENCE WANTED" GAP   155

"But do you have experience?" need never stop you again.
Use a goal-oriented approach to building experience in
volunteer work, internships, apprenticeships.

14   RETURNING TO SCHOOL   169

If you decide to, you'll be in good company. Some good
reasons for doing it. How to get around the financial
hurdle and revive rusty study skills (you *can* expect to
outperform younger students).

15   INVESTIGATING ALTERNATE WORK SCHEDULES   185

Nine to five is no longer your only choice. How about
flexitime, a compressed work week, permanent part-time
jobs, job sharing, temporary work, consulting?

16   GOING INTO BUSINESS FOR YOURSELF   197

Should you do it? Find out if you have what it takes.
What kind of business? Start thinking about practical
considerations: checklists and resources to help you do so.

EXERCISES

With thanks to my family: Darwin Hendel, my husband, and Jessie and Adam, my children. BG

To Rose and Ewald Loeffler, *sine qua non;* Connie Clark who has always believed me capable of more than I believed; and Jackie Lynn Loeffler who every day reminds me of the worthiness of the goals toward which every woman works. DRL

To my husband Michael, for your consistent support and encouragement, and to my son, Jonathan, for providing balance in my life. RKC

PREFACE

Ever get that boxed-in feeling?
It might come over you when you answer "no" to such questions as:

- ☐ Am I using the skills I want to use?

- ☐ Do I know what my values, interests, skills, and abilities are?

- ☐ Do I know what job options might fit those values, interests, skills, and abilities?

- ☐ Do I know how to go after those jobs?

- ☐ Do I know how to evaluate my current work as well as other job choices?

- ☐ Do I have a sense that I'm getting somewhere?

Every Woman Works offers a sequence of practical strategies you can use to independently make and implement new choices for your work and your life. It is based on the premise that one thing women share is *we all work. Every woman works.* For work is much more than what we get paid to do. To be a student is work, to mother is work, and to continuously bring vitality and growth into any long-term relationship is work.

In these pages we have combined our expertise as psychologists, vocational counselors, job placement specialists, and women to teach you a process of discovery, assessment, and planning, building on whatever your previous work experience has been. Once you learn this process and begin using it, you will start to gain a new measure of independence and control over the direction of your life, and start to answer "yes!" to the questions above.

WHO THIS BOOK IS FOR

This book is for every woman who works (whether as a mother, student, wife, or member of the paid labor force) and who wants or needs to make a change in the kind of work she does. You will find this book particularly helpful if you're curious about exploring the new opportunities and roles that have been previously unavailable or uninteresting to you. Or if you have been thrust into a set of circumstances that impatiently demand that you abandon your comfortable roles and former choices. You may be

- ☐ a homemaker no longer able to make ends meet with one paycheck, or no longer willing to stay at home
- ☐ a mother whose children have left the nest
- ☐ a woman who finds herself unexpectedly widowed or divorced
- ☐ a wife who has decided not to have children
- ☐ a single woman working in a job that is no longer interesting or challenging

Whatever your situation, working your way carefully down the path we have marked for you in this book will help you focus your skills, interests, and enthusiasms in a direction that will best meet your unique needs and goals.

HOW THIS BOOK IS ORGANIZED

This book is organized to take you step by step through a process for exploring yourself and your opportunities, and making crucial choices to build a more satisfying life. Each section builds on the knowledge, skills, and strategies you have gained in the preceding ones.

In Section I, we will help you prepare for the work ahead by acknowledging your fears and feeding your enthusiasms.

In Section II, we will help you polish self-management skills you will use throughout the process and for the rest of your life. Managing your time and tasks, coping with being a parent, gaining the active support of others, making realistic decisions, and setting goals for action are the valuable skills you will learn or revitalize in this section. Applying these skills should gain you the time, support, and motivation you need to move on through the book.

In Section III, you will take stock of your present roles, values, and interests, and the assets you possess—your abilities and skills. The self-knowledge you gain here will help you move out into your environment on a firmer footing.

In Section IV, we will teach you how to go about investigating an expanded variety of work alternatives. You will collect and evaluate essential information about these alternatives.

In Section V, you will learn creative, practical skills for finding and landing the job you want.

And in Section VI, we will tell you how you can continue to apply throughout your lifetime the sequence of strategies you have learned.

HOW TO USE THIS BOOK

We believe you will derive the greatest benefit from this book if you are able to complete each chapter and exercise in sequence, taking the time you need for daydreaming, exploring, investigating, and planning. However, if you have previously done self-assessment or job-assessment in any of the areas we cover, you may choose to skip those chapters, reading only the chapter Highlights to retain the thread of the process.

Or if you would like to accelerate your work, you can do a chapter in Section III, Discovering Yourself, while also doing a chapter in Section IV, Discovering Work Opportunities. The information you get from your work in these two sections fits together to enable you to move out into your job search. Our only caution to you is that you should do both self- and job-assessment before you actually start looking for work. Our experience has shown that women who know what they want and what they do well, and know where to find it, are most successful in locating employment.

WHAT IF YOU NEED A JOB IMMEDIATELY?

If you have been thrown by circumstances into the necessity of finding a job immediately, we suggest that you start by reading and completing Chapters 8 and 10. Once you have thus identified your interests and skills, go to Chapter 11 to identify job fields that will use them. Then read Chapters 17, 18, and 19 and use those tools to locate and secure an interim job. This is a job which, while not ideal, offers a paycheck while you are putting together your long-term goals and career strategy.

For example, Wendy McCullem chose to work as a personnel secretary following an unexpected divorce while she finished the coursework for a degree in accounting and began a job search for a management position. Cheryl Bradley went to work for a temporary employment agency because it helped her build contacts in a variety of employment settings and allowed her the flexible time to explore her career interests. Maria Hernandez found that teaching full-time critically limited her ability to reach potential job contacts during the work week. She negotiated a half-time job as a resource teacher to free her time to look into jobs outside of education that would utilize her teaching skills.

THE EXPLORING THAT LIES AHEAD

The exploring and planning that lies ahead of you will be hard work, but you can accomplish it step by step. And if you approach it with an open and flexible attitude, you are bound to find enjoyment and rewards along the way. Remember that you are a different person than you were ten, twenty, or thirty years ago, and the work you choose to do in the future does not need to be the same as your past work or educational experience. Set yourself free to think creatively; be open to those wild and crazy ideas. *You* are the chief architect of your life, and only you have the answers to your questions. We think you will find this book a valuable guide; your investment of time and energy in it may be the best investment you'll ever make.

Bonnie Gray
Dorothy Loeffler
Robin King Cooper

ACKNOWLEDGMENTS

Our thanks

- ☐ to all the women who have shared of their time and experiences in our classes, workshops and counseling sessions,

- ☐ to our friends and associates at Psyche, Inc., the University of Minnesota, and in our professional associations,

- ☐ to our editor, Lorraine Anderson, whose fine suggestions helped shape the final manuscript,

- ☐ to all the women in our lives, our mothers, sisters, and daughters, who have known, or will know, the truth that Every Woman Works. We hope that our book will help make that work more satisfying, more fulfilling, more rewarding.

CREDITS

Ideas on eliminating, delegating, simplifying in Chapter 3 adapted and reprinted with permission from Dr. Vera M. Schletzer of the University of Minnesota.

List of decision strategies in Chapter 4 adapted and reprinted with permission from DECIDING by H. B. Gelatt, Barbara Varenhorst, and Richard Carey, copyright © 1972 by the College Entrance Examination Board, New York.

"Things I Love to Do" exercise in Chapter 8 adapted and reprinted by permission of A&W Publishers, Inc. from VALUES CLARIFICATION: A HANDBOOK OF PRACTICAL STRATEGIES FOR TEACHERS AND STUDENTS by Sidney B. Simon, Leland W. Howe, and Howard Kirschenbaum, copyright © 1972, copyright © 1978 by Hart Publishing Company, Inc.

Explanation of theory behind "Chart Your Vocational Interest Pattern" exercise in Chapter 8 adapted by permission of Prentice-Hall, Inc., Englewood Cliffs, NJ from John L. Holland, MAKING VOCATIONAL CHOICES: A THEORY OF CAREERS, © 1973. Items for the exercise are based on Holland; David Campbell, IF YOU DON'T KNOW WHERE YOU'RE GOING YOU'LL PROBABLY END UP SOMEWHERE ELSE, © 1974 by Argus Communications, Niles, IL; and David Campbell, MANUAL FOR THE SVIB-SCII, second edition, © 1977 by the Stanford University Press, Stanford, CA.

The creative job search stategy described in Chapters 17 and 18 is based on the ideas of Richard Bolles, WHAT COLOR IS YOUR PARACHUTE?, © 1978 by Ten Speed Press, Berkeley, CA.

"List of Assertive Rights" in Chapter 19 adapted and reprinted with permission from RESPONSIBLE ASSERTIVE BEHAVIOR by Arthur J. Lange and Patricia Jakubowski, copyright © 1976 by Research Press, Champaign, IL.

The common interview questions listed in Chapter 20 were adapted from THE NORTHWESTERN ENDICOTT REPORT by Frank Endicott, Placement Center, Northwestern University; EVERYWOMAN'S GUIDE TO COLLEGE by Eileen Gray, © 1977 by Les Femmes Publishing, Millbrae, CA; and WHO'S HIRING WHO by Richard Lathrop, © 1977 by Ten Speed Press, Berkeley, CA.

EVERY WOMAN WORKS

SECTION I

GETTING STARTED

GETTING STARTED

Once I had set out
I was already far on my way.
Colette

J_{ANE} Hamilton, a forty-year-old divorcee, started by calling her local Displaced Homemaker Center to inquire about career planning and placement services. Beth Simpson, recently widowed, started by talking with a friend who had just returned to college. Clipping a feature article entitled "Women in the Ministry" was the start for Dorothy Green, who had been an elementary school teacher for 17 years. And picking up this book may be the way you have chosen to start planning for work change. If so, you have already taken a crucial first step.

Whether taking this step was easy or difficult for you, you may have found that it triggered a mixture of fears and enthusiasms. Clipping a newspaper article was a simple task for Dorothy Green. But she had to push and pull herself pretty hard to take her next step, calling a local seminary for information on training possibilities. Many women find this experience typical. While exhilarated by the numerous possibilities, you may also feel confused, frustrated, and scared. Taking time to acknowledge these feelings at the start may give you some constructive, motivating energy.

ACKNOWLEDGE YOUR FEARS

We must not misunderstand feelings of discontent, restlessness, doubt, and longing, warns Anne Morrow Lindbergh in *Gift From The Sea*. She tells us that these are the signs that presage growth. "Accept these feelings as growing pains," she writes. "Take them seriously. Follow where they lead. One is afraid. Naturally. Who is not afraid of pure space—that breath-taking empty space of an open door? But despite fear, one goes through to the room beyond."

Can you identify with any of these fears?

- ☐ Am I bright enough, skilled enough, tough enough to re-enter the work place or to succeed in a different kind of work?

- ☐ Is it too late to re-enter or change my work? Will employers or educators react negatively to my age? How will a change affect my retirement benefits?

- ☐ Will I have to take a salary cut to make a change? Will advancement opportunities really materialize?

- ☐ Am I still capable of academic learning?

- ☐ What if I go back to school for retraining and then there are no related jobs when I finish?

- ☐ What if I aim my job search in a particular direction but find nothing?

- ☐ How will important people in my life react to my change? How will my children suffer or benefit? How will household tasks get done? Who will care for my aging parents?

- ☐ How will my change affect my roles as wife, mother, daughter, friend, volunteer?

- ☐ What if I give up the security of my present work and don't like my new choice?

- ☐ Can I make the RIGHT career decision for myself?

We hope to help you find some reassuring answers in the work ahead. Meanwhile, you may find it comforting to recognize that although you are a unique individual, many hundreds of women have experienced the same fears, doubts, and questions as you. Further, we have found that women consistently underrate their skills and abilities, so realize that you have many more than you give yourself credit for. And one more word of encouragement: there are dozens of "right" career choices for you. As you explore, note those sparks of interest; don't wait for the flash of lightening.

There are likely to be several points as you work through this book at which you may feel emotionally blocked by anxiety or the need to evaluate too many choices at one time. You will need to decide if you are experiencing normal, predictable change anxiety or whether there are deeper, more serious issues in your life that you need to confront before you can move on.

This difference will become clearer as you explore the exercises and discussions in the next few chapters.

If you are anxious about change, take a few deep breaths and plunge on. If you are seriously stuck, consult a counselor and explore some methods to free yourself. (See Appendix A for suggestions on choosing a counselor or group.) In either case you may find that some kind of support system— a professional counselor, a small group of women in similar situations, an empathic friend—will ease your passage. It will be a relief to discover that you are not alone with your emotions or your dilemma.

FEED YOUR ENTHUSIASMS

What is stressful to one person may not be stressful to another. It's sometimes the way we view or think about a situation that causes us pain. Despite your fears, you can probably agree with some or all of these positive statements:

- ☐ There are so many more options open to me now. I'm eager to learn about new possibilities.
- ☐ I finally have a little more time for myself. I'm eager to direct my energies.
- ☐ I know my talents are underutilized. I'm ready to consider a change.
- ☐ This is the time to dust off some of my old stored dreams. I'm excited about creating change in my work and life.
- ☐ This is my opportunity to make my own choices and decisions.
- ☐ I feel as though I'm entering a new passage in my life. Now is the time to take some action.

It's important to feed your sense of enthusiasm about the possibilities ahead of you, as it will provide you with motivation. As one way of doing this we suggest that you start an *Idea Box*. This is a device to help you imagine kinds of work or lifestyles you might really enjoy. Along the way you may also unearth some interests you may not have realized or acknowledged you had.

Your Idea Box

The Idea Box is actually a file. You might use a file envelope or accordian-type file pocket, or an actual box that holds 3 × 5 or 5 × 7 cards. Into this file you should stash anything related to the kind of work or lifestyle you might enjoy. Some sources for the contents of your box are:

☐ You meet someone whose work sounds interesting—write it down. Note an approximate job title and a fairly detailed description of what that person does. What elements of this person's work are particularly attractive to you?

☐ You are browsing through the want ads in the newspaper and see some interesting possibilities. Clip or copy them.

☐ A magazine does a feature on women with unusual occupations. Save the article and circle the job and lifestyle elements that appeal to you.

☐ While watching TV you see or hear of some person, job, or idea you find fascinating. Record it in your Idea Box.

☐ You are daydreaming that you could do or be anything you want. Write down these dreams in detail and keep them in your Idea Box.

The key to the Idea Box is *interest*. Don't worry about whether you could do that job now or whether it is in a work area traditionally open to women. If your interest is piqued, slip the idea into the box. Daydream a little or daydream a lot. No, you may never be a second Golda Meier but if she's someone you would like to emulate, record it.

The key to the success of your Idea Box is not to evaluate or analyze each piece of data individually, but merely to put it into the Box and evaluate it later. The most value comes from adding to the Box over an extended time period, certainly weeks and perhaps months. In Chapter 8 we give suggestions for evaluating the contents of the Box.

Now that you understand the concept of the Idea Box, obtain your box or file envelope and get started. If possible, use a box or container you have on hand. Start today or at best this week. Plan to maintain your Idea Box the rest of your working future.

BE PATIENT WITH YOURSELF

Above all, as you move step by step through this book and out into your new life, be patient with yourself. It will take time for you to ease into new work and personal roles, and the path will not always be smooth. You may have wishes for an overnight work and life transformation, similar to fantasies about weight loss. But as in weight loss efforts, you'll find you succeed better if you give yourself time to gradually move towards a new identity.

Taking your time will also give time for significant individuals in your life to adjust to a changed you and perhaps a changed relationship with you. So you won't be the block mother, spend Thursday making 180 cookies for the bake sale, have the car keys permanently attached to your hand. There may be mumbling in the ranks, but these people can learn to be supportive of your plans during this period.

So now that you've taken the first step, on to brushing up your self-management skills: managing time, integrating roles, building support, making decisions, and setting goals for action. These tools will be your allies throughout the process of exploring and into your new work life.

LEARNING SELF-MANAGEMENT SKILLS

2

MANAGING
TIME

*"Now here you see, it takes all the running
you can do, to keep in the same place.
If you want to get somewhere else, you must run
at least twice as fast as that."*

Lewis Carroll, *Through the Looking Glass*

*H*OW often have we all said "I didn't have time" or "Where did the time go?" We will never forget the woman, age forty-three, married right out of high school and with nine children, who said to us, "Sometime, before I die, I would like to have a piece of life that is my own."

Time will pass. If you aren't in charge of your time, others will be. Time is like the salary you receive. If you don't plan for its use, it's gone, and you don't know where it went.

Most women find managing their time (and thereby their lives) an eye-opening and also a freeing experience. You may discover that "I didn't have time" is mostly untrue. We do find the time for what's important to us. And controlling your time will help you become more self-confident. As you become more self-confident, you will more easily control your time. It's an upward spiral.

Because it will take a disciplined commitment of your time to complete the exercises ahead in *Every Woman Works,* this is a good place for you to begin managing your time better. In this chapter you will:

☐ assess your current use of time

☐ learn ways to change your time use

☐ start to plan your future use of time

WHERE DOES YOUR TIME GO?

The first step towards more effective time management is analyzing how you spend your time right now. Most of us don't know how we spend our time until we consciously take stock of it; what we find is sometimes quite a revelation.

On the following chart, fill in how you used your time over a week's period. If you remember what you did, use the past week. If not, keep a record over the next week. Include such things as paid work, reading newspapers, cooking and eating, social activities, phone conversations. Be specific.

Look at how you spent your time. There are probably a few surprises. How much time was for you? How much was for others? Is there time for you every day, every other day, or every week, to spend working in this book?

Recognize that changing how you spend time will at first cost you time. Each of us gets into a pattern of time use, and old habits are hard to break. Besides, these habits of time usage make our lives predictable and secure. You may be bored or quite frustrated in your role as chairperson of a community arts board, Girl Scout leader, or accounting major. Yet you know what the next committee meeting, the next Girl Scout activity, your next accounting assignment will be like. It's much more risky to walk into a new life role or activity.

ELIMINATE, DELEGATE, SIMPLIFY

If your completed time analysis chart is as busy and full as many women's, you'll probably need to eliminate, delegate, and simplify current time commitments. We offer you these suggestions, adapted from the ideas of Dr. Vera Schletzer of the University of Minnesota.

Looking over your activities in a typical week, ask yourself: "Does this activity absolutely have to be done?" If the answer is "No," eliminate this in future weeks, whether the task is reading a novel for your literature seminar, entertaining your business associates, or working on a fund raising drive for your child's school.

If you believe the activity must be done, try to delegate all or at least part of the task to someone else. Many of your "must-be-done" activities are probably household tasks. If so, you may be hanging on to a role that does not need to be yours exclusively. You can ask your child, spouse, or neighborhood teenager to clean the bathroom, run to the dry cleaners, plant the garden. See the next chapter for help in involving your family in these tasks.

WHERE DOES YOUR TIME GO?
Week of _____

	Sunday	Monday	Tuesday	Wednesday	Thursday	Friday	Saturday
6–7 A.M.							
7–8							
8–9							
9–10							
10–11							
11–12							
12–1							
1–2							
2–3							
3–4							
4–5							
5–6							
6–7							
7–8							
8–9							
9–10							
10–11							
11–12							

Finally, if you feel YOU must complete the task, simplify your actions. Write a form Christmas letter with added personal notes. Cut your term paper project time in half by zeroing in on a more specific topic. Serve purchased pie and ice cream at your co-worker's retirement party.

If you typically sew your child's Halloween costume, you might consider buying a costume, or supervising your child's concoction out of some rummage sale stuff, or suggesting that your children help each other. If you annually hostess a lavish cocktail party with homemade hors d'oeuvres, limit yourself to wine and cheese, hire a caterer, turn your party into a potluck, or cancel it.

To get started eliminating, delegating, and simplifying, complete these sentences:

Something I could quit doing is _____

_____

Some things I do with my time which others could do instead are _____

_____

Something which I could cut back on or do more simply is _____

_____

I feel good about how I spend time when I _____

_____

RECOGNIZE YOUR TRADE-OFFS

Most of us feel a tug of war between the desire for adventure and growth hoped for in change and the fear that we'll lose our sense of identity. Feeling that you must continue to do all the established activities in your life while making a transition to new life activities may mean you're worried about losing personal significance. "Can it be they don't *really* need me? They can carry on if I'm doing other things?" If you resign or greatly simplify your Girl Scout leadership role, you may have less impact on your daughter's and her friends' personal development. Other parents and your daughter herself may view you as uncaring. You won't enjoy the fun of camping and going on adventurous excursions as "one of the scouts."

It's important to examine potential losses and weigh these against gains from freeing your time. What's the probability your daughter will view you as uncaring? Sometimes the loss we fear doesn't occur.

You may feel a loss when the community arts board obtains a grant to bring theater to the deaf under someone else's leadership. In such a situation of actual loss, you have a right to grieve; take time for this. Recognize that everyone's life is a series of trade-offs.

FREE PRIME TIME FOR YOU

You'll need to free two types of time for your work in this book. Alan Lakein, in his excellent book *How to Get Control of Your Time and Your Life,* calls them internal prime time and external prime time. Internal prime time is when you concentrate best. This is the kind of time you will need to complete exercises in the sections that follow. External prime time is hours when external resources, usually people, are most available for information or consultation. You'll need external prime time for library trips to obtain printed literature about work, school, or finances and to talk with resource individuals about particular kinds of work and training programs.

Your internal and external time preferences are uniquely yours. Betsy Greeler chose to work on self-assessment three times a week in one–hour time slots. Betsy did this from six to seven in the morning since she could concentrate best in this quiet time before her family arose. Sandy Morrison initially scheduled time during her childrens' afternoon naps, but she soon found that the naps were lasting from fifteen minutes to two hours, so that she could not count on accomplishing much. Sandy revised her plan. She got a babysitter three afternoons a week, scheduling two afternoons for exploration assignments and one for playtime. Marcia Sundquist, an elementary music teacher, discovered that she was too tired on school nights to complete the self-awareness exercises, so she scheduled Saturday afternoons for this. The point is you'll need to experiment and discover which times work best for you.

MAKE PLANS

Use results of your time analysis and the above guidelines to plan your next week on the chart that follows. Those of us who say "I don't have time to plan" can benefit the most. Be sure to:

☐ Mark down time to work in this book. Schedule this as a top priority.

☐ Schedule activities you feel committed to do. Include maintenance activities such as overhauling the car, dishwashing, returning phone calls. Focus on priority activities.

☐ Leave yourself time to breathe; avoid scheduling every hour.

☐ Include time daily to review your plans and make needed revisions. Ten minutes at the beginning of your day or the previous evening will be ample.

☐ Schedule time at the end of your week to review your progress. How did you actually spend time? How did this compare with your plans? Which planning strategies worked well for you? Which didn't?

☐ Use what you learned from your successes and mistakes to make a revised, more realistic plan for the next week. Continue to *write down* your plans.

Be patient with yourself. Revise your schedule until it works for you. Suppose that you've scheduled your work exploration assignments for the past six weeks yet rarely accomplished anything. *Call time out.* Clarify your feelings about this.

☐ Are you experiencing ambivalence about giving up activities you typically do during these hours?

☐ Are these low energy hours?

☐ Do you have mixed feelings about finding or changing jobs?

☐ Is your goal too big at this point in your exploration?

You may want to restate a smaller, more specific goal. Try doing assignments twice a week for an hour rather than four times a week for two hours. Building your involvement gradually will probably be more effective in the long run.

There are many possible conflicts which can stand in your way and many possible solutions you can try. List the conflicts you are experiencing. You may want to discuss these with a friend or relative or with a career counselor. Mary Bates, age thirty-nine, came to us for career counseling, but we soon discovered she had to deal with her very understandable resentment at being placed by a divorce in the position of *having* to do this. After that was recognized and worked through she could focus her energies on these new plans for her future.

WHERE WOULD YOU LIKE YOUR TIME TO GO?
Week of _____

	Sunday	Monday	Tuesday	Wednesday	Thursday	Friday	Saturday
6–7 A.M.							
7–8							
8–9							
9–10							
10–11							
11–12							
12–1							
1–2							
2–3							
3–4							
4–5							
5–6							
6–7							
7–8							
8–9							
9–10							
10–11							
11–12							

Your efforts to better manage your time can be helped tremendously if you are able to integrate new roles and build support from people close to you. This is our topic in the next chapter.

Take *your* time!

HIGHLIGHTS

□ Get control of your time by
  — recognizing how you presently spend it
  — delegating, eliminating, simplifying
□ Schedule time for working in this book by
  — freeing prime time for you
  — giving it high priority
  — making a written plan

RESOURCES

Lakein, A. *How to Get Control of Your Time and Your Life.* New York: McGraw-Hill, 1973.

> *A practical, no-nonsense guide to managing your personal and professional time. You will learn how to establish priorities, set short-term and long-term goals, organize a daily schedule, and accomplish what's most important to you.*

Mackenzie, R. A. *The Time Trap: How to Get More Done in Less Time.* New York: McGraw-Hill, 1972.

> *Easy-to-apply techniques for overcoming problems of procrastination, interruptions, decision-making, organization and delegation.*

Winston, S. *Getting Organized: The Easy Way to Put Your Life in Order.* New York: Warner Books, 1978.

> *Winston's organizing principle helps you get it all together—your time and paperwork, money, and your home. You can learn how to maximize storage space, reduce your shopping time and increase your efficiency, make the most of a new home or office, and even teach your child to organize, too!*

INTEGRATING ROLES
AND
BUILDING SUPPORT

*We commute daily, weekly, yearly
between one world and another. Between a life
as a family member that can be nurturing
or smothering. Between life as an individual
that can free us or flatten us.
We vacillate between two separate sets of demands
and possibilities. . . .With any luck the
territory we travel can be a fertile one,
rich with care and space. It can be a place
where the "I" and the "we" interact.*

Ellen Goodman,
The Washington Post 11/24/80

As our roles change and we find that we have the right or the necessity to juggle home and work commitments, we need support and creative suggestions about how to pull off this juggling act. Whatever your situation—in a marriage or other relationship, as a parent or not, or alone—it's no easy task to find the proper balance between roles, the harmonious combination of give and take that will nurture you. There are no clear road maps, only solutions which are unique to each woman and her situation. We hope you will begin evolving some solutions to your own situation in this chapter, as we discuss

☐ combining work and parenting, if you have children

☐ building moral and practical support, so important for every woman

IF YOU HAVE CHILDREN: COMBINING WORK AND PARENTING

As you prepare to enter paid employment, problems may stem not so much from the sheer trick of juggling many roles at once as from trying to cope with others' and your own strong mandates about mothering. You might face directly or in more in-between-the-lines fashion all of these value-laden questions:

> *You're going back to work* ALREADY?
>
> *But who'll be there when the kids come home from school, or when they're sick?*
>
> *Which comes first—your career or your family?*
>
> *But when do you find time for Jackie/Stevie?*
>
> *How do you manage so much—your career, being a wife and mother, taking care of your home?*

You may find these questions hard to answer or ignore because they echo your own concerns. Elaine Heffner addresses this issue well in *Mothering: The Emotional Experience of Motherhood after Freud and Feminism*. She says that each mother experiences an internal conflict between a desire to teach and nurture her children and a desire to create meaning in her life in additional ways. This persistent tug of war may take different shapes and forms, but the conflict is ever–present.

Coping with Conflicts of Conscience

We can suggest several strategies for coping with the inevitable conflict you will feel if you are a mother going back to work. First, you can cultivate the attitude that accepting this conflict as a fact of life, rather than seeking yes or no resolutions, acknowledges your own complexity as a woman and an individual. Each of us has complex needs and desires; parenthood may be an avenue to satisfy some, but not all, of these needs.

Share Psychological Parenting Second, you can clearly recognize mothering as *work*—valuable, skilled work, rather than something women "naturally" do. From this perspective it may be easier for you to modify or share the role which Jean Curtis in her excellent book *Working Mothers* calls "psychological parent":

> *I defined the "psychological parent" as the person who is always mindful of—who always feels a direct personal responsibility for the whereabouts and the feelings of each child. Who knows what's happening inside the head of each child, all the time? Who knows what*

emotional supports they need, what size shoe they wear, what diseases they've been exposed to, who their teachers are, what kind of work the first grade does, what new math is all about, who their friends are, who the parents of their friends are, what the current nightmares are, how the baby lies—on his/her stomach or back— how tightly to bind the blanket in infancy, and so on.

To gradually evolve sharing of this role with your partner or others, you'll need to openly communicate feelings and ideas, listen and extend empathy, and try new behaviors.

If you are a single parent, you may experience more difficulty and tension. You could try to work out some variation of co-parenting with the father. You could choose to involve other family members or good friends in your parenting. Perhaps you could trade parenting responsibilities with others. Parents and children both can benefit from developing an extended family. A key issue for growing children is learning to be responsible for themselves and to share responsibilities for the family. The single parent family is made to order for this.

And then there is the sticky problem of children returning to the supposedly empty nest, and requiring "psychological parenting" by their presence. Jean Ames had gone back to her old job when her husband became too seriously ill to work. She figured she could balance it all. But she wasn't prepared for the return of her youngest daughter when she dropped out of college. This is more than just a rare occurrence for the older woman returning to work. Again, the answers vary, but a firm respect for yourself and the new life you are trying to establish must be part of the solution.

Prepare for Contingencies   Third, you can plan ahead by asking yourself "What do I do if . . ." questions for situations such as:

. . .   *if my child gets sick five minutes before my morning bus to work?*

. . .   *if I have to leave for work before my child has to leave for school?*

. . .   *if my children's day care provider gets sick?*

. . .   *if my spouse and I have overnight business trips simultaneously?*

. . .   *if I get sick, who else will hold this whole package together?*

Write down five or more of your own "What if . . ." questions that target your worst fears or strongest barriers against returning to work. These may be fairly concrete problems such as the examples above, or they may be attitudinal barriers in your mind about what other people, or family members, will think if you return to work. Begin to share these concerns with your family, co-parent, and supportive friends. Make a particular effort to survey working women who appear to be coping with their home/career juggling act and ask them how they deal with these issues.

Making Practical Arrangements

Once you have gotten used to the idea of mixing work and family commitments, you'll need to actively delegate and share your parental responsibilities with others. Your child may need daycare, after school care, summer activities. You'll need to evolve back-up plans for sick days and school vacations. And you'll still need personal breathing space between your parental and other work roles.

Investigate Pre-School Day Care   If you have pre-school children, returning to work means that you will have to arrange for someone to care for them. Some families have worked out flexible schedules which allow the parents to share care, or have relatives nearby who are willing to assume care. A few parents can take their children to work with them or work at home. Others have on-site day care at their workplace. Many turn to babysitters or day care providers. Your own options may be narrow or with investigation may prove to be wider than you had supposed. So much is determined by the individual child and the available options for care that you'll need to do some careful research to find the best situation.

We suggest that you read several articles or books on day care selection (see those listed at the end of this chapter) and talk with other parents. You may find your community has a Day Care Council to help you. In any case, interview day care personnel and observe them with children in the care setting. Remember there are no guarantees against a bad situation; you may need to try a few options to evolve comfortable arrangements.

Arrange After-School Care   There is no magic time when school-age children can take care of themselves after school and during vacations. What do you do with a twelve-year-old who has outgrown Day Club in the summers, but who needs supervision? What do you do with her for two weeks at Christmas, two weeks at Easter?

The answers to these questions vary from family to family. Either you or your partner may decide to take work that allows you to be home when the kids are. Possibly a neighborhood after school or latchkey program, where kids are involved in activities from school dismissal time until parents are able to pick them up, may be an answer. You and your older children will need to exercise some ingenuity to negotiate whatever check-in or supervisory arrangements seem appropriate.

Look Into Solutions at Work   Share your concerns with co-workers and explore using your collective power to create working conditions which support both quality work performance and parenting. As a group you may decide to promote work-site day care, sick leaves to cover children's illnesses, and improved leave policies for new parents. Or you may assist each other in finding or creating alternative work styles (see Chapter 15).

It's important for you to keep in mind that developing a flexible parenting style can facilitate increased competence in your job. And it's important for your employer to realize that flexible job conditions can facilitate your competence as a parent and increase your job productivity, too.

BUILDING MORAL AND PRACTICAL SUPPORT

Whether you are a parent or not, management of your home and work responsibilities is greatly facilitated (and this is an understatement) if your family members and/or friends can become allies, supporters of your process of exploring and your eventual work change. To get support from those closest to you it is critical that you involve them as soon as possible. Tell them about your need to seriously consider change in your life. Let them in on how such a change will benefit you, and perhaps them. Realize that your self-respect and planful career exploration serves as an excellent model for your children and others.

You will probably have qualms about *asking* for support if you, like most women, are used to putting a considerable quantity of time and energy into being supportive of others. You may wish others would "just know" what's obvious (to you): you need encouragement and assistance. But this form of intuition is rare, except in romantic movies and novels. "Supporting others" is a *learned behavior* and you may need to teach the significant people in your life to give you what you need.

Delegate Household Tasks

Even if you live alone, it's important to delegate, eliminate, and simplify household tasks to leave you some time in your life for social contact outside of work. If you are a wife and/or mother, the tasks multiply, but so do the hands available to help. The point is you must acknowledge and confront the problem of getting household tasks done.

If You Are A Family Member   Your partner and children are likely to give you some gung-ho forms of verbal approval until asked to translate their attitudes into action. As a woman you are the "psychological parent" for household tasks as well as the one everyone tends to lean on for support and direction. You will need to renegotiate household chores as well as asking family members to take responsibility for dealing with each other's emotional needs.

Asking your family to help you implies that you own these chores, so shaking the broom closet and tool box of household management is no smooth trick. Besides, it also means that you must let go of *your* tasks and allow others to complete them in their own manner, even if they don't do them in your efficient way. But having family members share a diversity of chores will not only help you, it will more fully develop their independent living skills.

Request concrete support. Start with small, tangible requests. You might ask a child to pack her own lunch, your husband to do the grocery shopping, or a teenager to build shelves for your study area.

Whatever Your Status, Complete the Household Job Inventory   Complete the following Household Job Inventory as an awareness tool about all the jobs that have to get done for your household to keep functioning. If you live alone, this is a critical issue for you to address since you are the only person around to get the jobs done. If you are a family member, urge everyone in the family, including children, to complete this form on their own. Then, get together for a discussion of results.

First, look for areas of agreement. Second, anticipate some disagreement about what the essential tasks are, who actually does what and how well. You will probably differ somewhat on priorities. Avoid making this a battleground. Rather, use this input to negotiate some concrete assignments of tasks. For example, your partner may cook dinner three times a week while you wash clothes and pay bills. Your children may develop a rotating series of chores to accomplish daily or weekly.

Praise each other for learning new jobs and performing old, boring ones well. See what tasks you can eliminate, simplify, or delegate outside the family so that you will have more time to enjoy each other. Pay someone else to mow the lawn, bake coffee cakes, or clean the rugs. Finally, review your new household job system periodically and make needed changes. Flexibility and variety are important.

HOUSEHOLD JOB INVENTORY

List below all the jobs that need to get done for your household to function. Include jobs that have to be completed regularly, if not every day, such as cooking, washing clothes, paying bills, special care of family members, etc. Describe the jobs in *concrete* words so that an outside observer can visualize the task. After you finish your entire list, write answers to the questions outlined in the columns for each job. In the last column, rate the job's importance according to this scale:

1 = survival job   3 = nice to do, if I get time
2 = important to me   4 = think I should do it

Household jobs	Who does this job	How well is the job being done?	Importance rating

Build Your Support Network

Besides help with household tasks, at this time you need active support in the form of direct feedback, suggestions for problem-solving, and empathic listening. Female friends can be extremely supportive as you explore options and change work. Support might involve giving you feedback on your strengths as chairperson of a community arts board, exchanging child care while you attend class, or role-playing a job interview. Or better yet, find a friend who also wants to consider a life change. The two of you can read and complete the exercises in this book together.

Set Up a Support Group Several of you may wish to set up a support group to help each other through the changes of the next few months. You can set up weekly or bi-weekly meetings to share awareness and plan goals. Women who are struggling with their own work decisions are prime candidates for building mutual support. Involvement in a structured career planning work-shop or a support group has many bonuses. You'll get a fresh perspective on your strengths and priorities, which you may not get from old friends or yourself.

Survey Your Interpersonal Supports Take time to complete the following Interpersonal Support Chart, listing specific names of known resource people or at least marking categories of needed individuals. Spell out the ways that particular people are presently supportive of your exploration. You may have more available support than you've acknowledged. Also, list some specific kinds of support or assistance you can request. Ideally, your interpersonal support system will be mutual: they'll support your aspirations and you'll be supportive of theirs.

This is an ongoing list; add resource people throughout your explo-ration. When you're feeling discouraged or stuck in one place, re-survey your people resources. Can someone help you revitalize your energies and get moving? Ask them!

You may still find that in spite of your best efforts you do not receive the practical or moral support you need or want. In this case, don't beat your head against a wall trying to get active support from persons who will not give it or who sabotage your growth. Look for new friends or resource individuals who *will* be supportive. Keep moving forward with determina-tion. Remember we are all pioneers in this effort to integrate new roles, and the way can only get easier.

INTERPERSONAL SUPPORT CHART

Resource individuals	Name	Specific supports I already receive	Specific requests for support I can make
spouse			
children			
parents			
siblings			
other relatives			
friends			
co-workers			

Service Organization	Name	Address	Phone	Available Services
professional assistants (e.g., counselors, librarians, etc.)				
service providers (e.g., child care, housekeeping, etc.)				

Service Organization	Name	Address	Phone	Available Services
career planning center				
library				
daycare center				

HIGHLIGHTS

□ If you have children, integrating work and parenting can be made easier if you

— acknowledge and resolve conflicts of conscience

— make practical arrangements for child care

□ Whatever your situation, you can build moral and practical support by

— involving significant people close to you in your process of exploring

— inventorying and delegating, eliminating, simplifying household jobs

— creating a support network

RESOURCES

Bird, C. *The Two Paycheck Marriage.* New York: Pocket Books, 1979.

This book addresses the issues confronting dual career marriages— housework, money, role reversals, children, and the effects of family life. Does an excellent job of pointing out hidden sexist imperatives and how we can still be down even when we think we are moving up. Excellent discussion of how working women are changing American life.

Boston Women's Health Collective. *Ourselves and Our Children.* New York: Random House, 1978.

This book carefully and empathically explores these issues: 1) deciding about parenthood, 2) being a parent during the child's beginning, middle, teenage and grown-up years, 3) shared parenthood between mothers and fathers and for single parents, 4) how diverse families work and live, and 5) what parents are doing to promote social change. Special attention is given to how you can help yourself and how to find help from formal and informal sources. This reference book is exceptionally readable and has excellent annotated bibliographies, including many references about day care.

Catalyst special bibliographies. Write for a bibliographies listing and order blank from Catalyst, 14 East 60th St., New York, New York 10022.

Bibliographies are available on topics such as: "Dual-Career Families," "Home-Career Conflicts" and "Child Care Deductions." Catalyst is a national organization which promotes career opportunities for women with family responsibilities.

Curtis, J. *Working Mothers*. New York: Simon and Schuster, 1975.

Based on 200 in-depth interviews with working women, this book empathically describes the dilemmas of women coping with each stage of parenting and paid work. Case illustrations help the reader identify with these issues: when is the best time to go back to work, what will happen to the children, child care, housework, relating to husbands, defining personal success.

Glickman, B. M. and Springer, N. B. *Who Cares for the Baby? Choices in Child Care*. New York: Schocken Books, 1978.

This book presents guidelines for selecting child care based upon individual needs. An objective but comforting approach that leaves the decision to each family.

Greenleaf, B. K. *Help: A Handbook for Working Mothers*. Berkeley, CA: Berkeley Publishing Company, 1980.

This book is filled with practical, easy-to-try solutions for the everyday problems of working mothers. Issues include: what to do when your child wakes up ill on a work day, how to create an "action house" with a minimum of fuss and upkeep, how to streamline gift shopping. Greenleaf also tackles core issues such as whether you can be a top achiever in your field while also being a good mother (yes) and whether it's worth it (maybe).

Heffner, E. *Mothering: The Emotional Experience of Motherhood After Freud and Feminism*. New York: Doubleday, 1978.

This book focuses on the emotional experience of motherhood as it has been influenced by psychoanalytic theory of child rearing and the women's movement.

Levine, J. A. *Who Will Raise the Children? New Options for Fathers (and Mothers)*. Philadelphia: J. B. Lippincott, 1976.

A major step toward getting fathers more involved in parenting, this book profiles the thoughts and actions of men who deliberately choose to care for children. Based on interviews with househusbands, single adoptive fathers, men who have custody of their children, and men who voluntarily work part time to spend time with their children.

Scott, N. *The Balancing Act: A Handbook for Working Mothers.* Kansas City, Kansas: Sheed Andrews and McNeel, Inc., subsidiary of Universal Press Syndicate, 1978.

Helpful advice, sympathy, and shared knowledge on numerous daily stress situations that arise for women who work for pay and try to carry on a "normal" life as well. Almost every woman will recognize herself at some point in this book and realize that many of her struggles are shared by others.

U. S. Department of Health and Human Services. *A Parent's Guide to Day Care.*

This 75-page pamphlet provides material to help parents select a day care center and develop confidence in the center, to help improve the day care arrangement, and to provide information on what day care should offer children. To obtain the pamphlet, write to the Day Care Division, Administration for Children, Youth and Families, HEW, P. O. Box 1182, Washington, DC 20013.

U. S. Department of Labor, Women's Bureau. *Employers and Child Care: Establishing Services Through the Workplace,* pamphlet 23, 1981.

This excellent monograph includes information about existing employer-related child care services and practical guidelines for planning child care services.

Magazines

The following three excellent magazines contain articles on numerous professional and personal issues faced by working women:

Working Mother, published bi-monthly, available on newsstand or write McCall Publishing Co., 230 Park Ave., New York, New York 10017.

Women's Work, published bi-monthly, write Women's Work, 1302 18th St., N.W., #203 Washington, D.C. 20036.

Working Woman, published monthly by Hal Publications Inc., 600 Madison Ave., New York, New York 10022, available at newsstand.

4

MAKING
DECISIONS

Along with other recent freedoms,
we now have the freedom to be confused.
Options—was that what we were saying we wanted?
Okay, here they are, in profusion:
home or office, long skirt or Levi's,
chopsticks or fork, kids this year or next or never,
my place or yours, bridal showers or
graduate school or abortions or custody fights,
take your pick or try to take it all.
Jane Howard, in *Life Special Report: Remarkable American Women 1776–1976*

*Y*OU picked this book up because you are facing a major decision in your life. We believe that if you have a method for making this decision, you will see more clearly what input you need, and will be happier with the outcome. So in this chapter you will

- ☐ learn a planning strategy for making decisions
- ☐ state your major decision to be made
- ☐ preview how you will use the information you gather in the chapters ahead to make your decision

DECISION-MAKING STRATEGIES

Making decisions, particularly those which are important to us, is rarely easy. We may tell ourselves, "I'd better make the right choice the first time—I won't get any second chances!" or "It's not really fair for me to subject others to my anxiety and indecision." We are concerned about how the important others in our lives will react to our decisions.

All of us have probably used a number of the following strategies (adapted from *Deciding* by Gelatt, Varenhorst, and Carey) in making past decisions.

Delaying: Taking a moratorium, postponing thought and action. "I'll cross that bridge later."

Fatalistic: Letting the environment decide, leaving it up to fate. "It's all in the cards."

Compliant: Letting someone else decide, following someone else's plans. "Anything you say, dear."

Impulsive: Giving little thought, taking the first alternative. "Don't look before you leap."

Intuitive: Making a mystical, preconscious choice, based on "inner harmony." "It feels right."

Planning: Using a procedure to predict which end result will be most satisfying, a rational approach with a balance between cognition and affect. "Weighing the facts."

Agonizing: Getting lost in all the data, getting overwhelmed with analyzing alternatives. "I don't know what to do."

Paralysis: Accepting responsibility but being unable to approach it. "I can't face up to it."

What combination of these strategies have you used to make major personal decisions? From your present perspective, what were the advantages and disadvantages of the strategies you tried?

Obviously, some of these strategies (particularly the last two) are less effective than others. But actually, most of these strategies have both advantages and disadvantages and some are more appropriate for certain kinds of decisions. None are absolutely right or wrong. If you delay, a better alternative may come into existence, yet some present alternatives may be lost. If you choose what feels right intuitively, you may hit a good one or may miss a better but momentarily uncomfortable one.

Even planning, with all its pluses, has minuses. It takes considerable time and effort. Still, we believe the planning strategy outlined here is worth your time and effort. After all, you are making an important decision.

Whichever strategy you employ, remember:

☐ *Few* decisions are irreversible.

☐ Many things which we fear are seldom as painful as we anticipate.

☐ *No* decision is perfect.

☐ A good decision is one that uses all the *available* information.

USING A PLANNING APPROACH

You probably already employ a planning approach in making everyday decisions, although it may be at a subconscious level. In a quick moment you may think through what you want to achieve, what your alternatives are, and the possible gains and losses associated with each choice, as you decide

☐ what to wear to work

☐ how to cope with a child's sudden illness

☐ what to have for dinner

☐ how to spend leisure time on the weekend

☐ whether to say "no" to a co-worker's request

The steps to using a planning approach to decision-making are:

Step 1: State your decision to be made

Step 2: List and rank your criteria

Step 3: Generate and explore alternatives

Step 4: Evaluate risks

Step 5: Make a tentative decision

Step 6: Set goals and take action

This book is arranged to enable you to use a planning approach in making your major decision about work. You will state your decision to be made in this chapter. In Section III, Discovering Yourself, you will be clarifying what's important to you so that you can list and rank your criteria. In Section IV, Discovering Your Opportunities, you will be generating and exploring alternatives in the work world. In Section V, Going About Your Job Search, we will show you how to synthesize the information you've gathered as you evaluate risks and decide on a job objective for your search. You'll want to employ the planning approach once again as you decide which job offer to accept.

State Your Decision to be Made

You will find you can achieve greater clarity about your situation if you make a written statement of the decision you want to make. Instead of swimming around in your head, it will be on paper where you can refine it and look at it a little more objectively. Getting it down on paper will also enable you to determine whether you actually have a decision to make, or whether you have a goal to implement.

To make a decision you must have more than one option from which to choose. For example, suppose you say "I want to decide whether to return to college full-time or to stay in my present job and not go to school." This is a decision; there are two if not more alternatives. However, "I want to go to college" is a goal statement. If you have chosen to attend college, you may really have another set of decisions to make, like how to finance your education or how to request your family's support. Again, these are decisions *if* there are alternatives.

As part of your decision statement you should set a target deadline, the date by which you must choose an alternative. You can use your target date to pace information gathering and synthesis.

For example, Shirley Zimmerman was beginning to feel burned out in her job as a junior high school English teacher. She had heard about several other jobs she thought she might find more satisfying. She stated her decision to be made as follows:

I want to decide whether to leave my current job. I will make this decision by April 1.

Take time now to write your own decision statement and target deadline, perhaps about a decision you face that motivated you to read this book.

I want to decide _____

_____

_____

_____

I will make this decision by (date) _____

Rank Multiple Decision Statements   You may be facing multiple decisions simultaneously. For example, suppose you're wondering whether to get a job, change something about your present job, have another child, move out of your neighborhood, return to school. Decisions do tend to come at us like that, and these decisions do interact. However, your decision-making will be more effective if you state each decision separately. Later on, you can deal with how various choices fit together.

For now, list each decision separately and then rank them first, second, and so on. Perhaps you'll see a fairly obvious sequencing in terms of urgency or time deadlines. Or, dealing with one problem may give you insight or confidence to handle a more difficult one.

Shirley Zimmerman ranked her decisions as follows:

2 Choose new living arrangements
1 Decide whether to leave current job
3 Choose new child care service

List and Rank Criteria

Next, you will need to discover what's important to you so that the alternative you choose will satisfy these criteria. In choosing a job, you'll want to know the following:

- ☐ What skills and abilities do I want to use?

- ☐ What values and interests do I want to express?

- ☐ What type of work setting do I want or need?

- ☐ How do I want to balance my work and personal life?

- ☐ What type and amount of contact do I want to have with people?

- ☐ What salary and benefits do I need?

- ☐ How close to home do I want or need to work?

- ☐ What kind of opportunities for advancement or on-the-job training do I want?

- ☐ Do I want to work in a field where there will be plenty of job openings, even though the job may be a little less desirable?

You may already know what your requirements and preferences are regarding some of these decision factors. If so, jot them down now. After you have worked carefully through Section III you will be able to answer more of these questions for yourself.

Generate and Explore Alternatives

By the same token, you may already have an idea of some of the alternatives available to you. To expand your awareness and gather more information about alternatives, you'll want to pay particular attention in Sections IV and V, as you discover and investigate work opportunities.

Right now, you might begin to fantasize about options, holding off judgment for the moment about their practicality. Use a structured fantasy aid if you find fantasizing difficult. For example, if you're making a decision about paid work imagine that you've been guaranteed a very desirable salary *if* you write a job description and then follow what you've outlined. What kind of job would you select or create?

Brainstorming with others can be another helpful way to generate alternatives. Share the decision you are facing with others in your support network, and see how many options you can come up with together.

Evaluate Risks

Encountering possible risks, losses, or obstacles is part of all major personal decisions. While there are times when we'd all prefer to avoid risks, taking some can be challenging and growth-producing. Wanting more challenge and growth is often what motivates a career change in the first place.

Writing down specific risks can be helpful. You can clearly see what risks you're anticipating, estimate their probability, and can plan stand-by action steps. Then you can decide how willing you are to accept these risks. In Chapter 17 you'll learn how to list and evaluate risks associated with each of your job objective alternatives.

Make a Tentative Decision

Once you have reached that point you will choose job objective alternatives that fit what's important to you *and* that have acceptable risks. Your decision will be tentative because, as we pointed out earlier, no decision is perfect or irreversible, and you may find that in implementing it you need to re-evaluate and adjust.

Set Action Goals

The last step of the planning approach to decision-making, setting goals and planning for action, is so important and so useful as a tool in many situations that we devote the next chapter to an expanded discussion of it.

HIGHLIGHTS

□ Making decisions is seldom easy, and there are any numer of strategies you can use.

□ Using a planning approach takes time and effort, but it can be an effective way to make satisfying choices. The steps are:
 — state your decision to be made
 — list and rank your criteria
 — generate and explore alternatives
 — evaluate risks
 — make a tentative decision
 — set goals and take action

RESOURCES

Cammaert, L. P. and Larsen, C. C. *A Woman's Choice: A Guide to Decision-Making*. Champaign, IL: Research Press Company, 1979.

Useful exercises, well written text, and case examples assist a woman in surveying work and life alternatives, in making decisions and setting goals. Alternatives are weighed in terms of personal values.

Gelatt, H. B., Varenhorst, B. and Carey, R. *Deciding*. New York: College Entrance Examination Board, 1972.

Written primarily for high school students, this guide contains helpful exercises for any adult, especially concerning decision-making styles and risk-taking.

Scholz, N. T., Prince, J. S. and Miller, G. P. *How to Decide: A Guide for Women*. New York: College Entrance Examination Board, 1979.

This is an excellent guide for any woman facing important life decisions. Myths and blocks to decision-making are examined and well-researched alternatives are weighed in terms of personal values and risk-taking.

5

SETTING
ACTION GOALS

*"Would you tell me, please, which way
I ought to walk from here?"
"That depends a good deal on
where you want to get to," said the Cat.
"I don't much care where—" said Alice.
"Then it doesn't matter which way you walk,"
said the Cat.*
Lewis Carroll, *Alice in Wonderland*

ONCE you've made a decision, you need some way to take action on it. Setting goals can be a powerful way to motivate yourself to the constructive action necessary to implement your decisions. And setting and attaining goals can be an assertive way to take charge of your future.

In this chapter we show you how to

☐ turn a decision into a goal

☐ break this goal into manageable action steps

☐ set yourself up to succeed by planning rewards, supports, and progress evaluations

STATE YOUR DECISION AS A GOAL

When you first decided to explore new work options, you also made another decision: how to go about it. You may have considered and chosen some of these alternatives: seek individual career counseling, enroll in a career planning workshop, read and work through a career planning manual. As part of your decision, you chose to read and work through *Every Woman Works*.

You may have already turned this decision into a goal by setting a deadline for completing the book and envisioning the end result of the process: a confident you receiving a number of job offers. And you may have broken this goal into manageable units by promising yourself you would complete a chapter a week, and designating time in your schedule to do that.

On the other hand, if once you made the decision to read this book you immediately got sidetracked and put it down for six months, you will benefit by paying careful attention in this chapter.

Write It Down

State your decision as a goal by writing it down as a positive statement ("I will . . .") following these guidelines:

- ☐ Your goal should be *appropriate*. It should be something you want to do and that you have chosen for yourself.

- ☐ Your goal should be *specific*. You should state a target date for its achievement and state behaviors you will exhibit when you have reached your goal. These behaviors should be within your capabilities and should be easy to describe. For example, "I will go to the library on Thursday night and make a list of sources of occupational information."

- ☐ Your goal should be *definite*. It should be stated with no "if's" or "but's." This does not imply that you must be inflexible, since you can always adapt to changed circumstances by establishing a new, definite, goal.

- ☐ Your goal should be *productive*. It should be something you know you can do, and that is within your control. It should be something that will produce positive results.

Now write down a current goal, following these guidelines. (It may well have to do with completing this book.)

I will _____

_____

_____

BREAK YOUR GOAL INTO MANAGEABLE UNITS

The more long-range and general your goal statement is, the harder it is to implement. By the same token, the simpler and more specific you can make your goal statement, the easier it will be for you to accomplish.

Break Long-Term Goals Into Short-Term Goals

While there is no magic formula about what size goals are best, you need goals that seem manageable to you. If many aspects of your life are in transition, you may feel most comfortable breaking the goal you wrote down above into smaller goals you can accomplish in a week or a day. On the other hand, if your self-confidence is high, you may aim for goals that take a month or six months to complete.

Break your goal of completing this book into week-sized goals: "I will spend two hours every Monday morning and three hours every Thursday night working in *Every Woman Works*." Or if the goal you wrote above has to do with something else, think now about how you can break it into week-sized goals.

My week-sized goal is _____

_____

_____

_____

Break Short-Term Goals Into Action Steps

You may find brainstorming, alone or with a friend, to be a good way to come up with actions steps to complete each of your short-term goals. In the work ahead we will often set goals for you, having to do with completing exercises, doing library research, attending meetings, or talking to people. You will probably find it easier to accomplish these goals if you list action steps for yourself for each goal. Take ten minutes or so to make a detailed to-do list, without worrying at first about the sequencing or timing of the steps.

Right now, jot down some steps you can take to help you accomplish your week-sized goal. While you should attempt to list all the specific steps you can, don't expect yourself to think of everything. You can add or delete steps as you proceed. Sometimes you can't anticipate the need for certain steps until you've tackled a few preliminary ones. Just focus on steps that will get you moving, that you believe you can accomplish, and that are self-enhancing.

Here are some examples of steps you might list to accomplish a week-sized goal of starting to think about a work change:

- ☐ Call the YWCA for information about career planning workshops
- ☐ Teach my son how to pack his lunch.
- ☐ Ask a friend to tell me about her new job and how she found it.
- ☐ Write for a brochure on financial aid for returning students.
- ☐ Spend two hours next Wednesday reading and working in this book.
- ☐ Ask my spouse, child, or roommate to do the weekly grocery shopping.
- ☐ Read a magazine article on "Single Parents and Their Careers."
- ☐ Plan a quiet reading/working space in my home.

ACTION STEPS   DEADLINES

_____   _____

_____   _____

_____   _____

_____   _____

Next, plan what you'll do first, second, third and so on, and indicate this by putting 1, 2, 3 next to your listed action steps. Perhaps some action steps must be completed before you can tackle others. Or perhaps you can start with a fairly easy step and then move on to a more difficult one. Consider the other expected events in your life. Is this a good time for you to take this particular action step?

Set time deadlines for each action step, being as specific as possible. If you feel apprehensive or just plain scared, set a date to complete the step. For example, "Next Monday at 10 a.m. I'm filling in this financial aid application." Write down deadlines for each action step you listed above.

You'll be more likely to follow through if you set firm, but flexible, deadlines. You may decide to revise these targets with changing circumstances, but you can avoid procrastination by stating definite deadlines in your initial plan. While you may believe that all these deadlines will take the spontaneity out of your life, this is farthest from the case. Following an organized, timely action plan will leave you more time to be spontaneous.

PLAN FOR SUCCESS

How can you maintain motivation to actually carry out listed action steps, especially if certain steps are difficult, boring, or quite lengthy? One effective strategy is planning to reward yourself after completion of each action step. Concrete, anticipated rewards can help maintain your enthusiasm as you move gradually toward goal attainment.

Decide on Rewards

Look over your list of action steps. Perhaps some steps have natural, intrinsic rewards, such as the satisfaction of learning something new or enjoyable. On the other hand, many of your action steps may be far from intrinsically rewarding. If this is the case, select something totally unrelated to the action step, a special treat like going for a leisurely hike or taking yourself out for lunch.

Interim self-rewards should be:

☐ pleasant or satisfying to you.

☐ readily accessible.

☐ provided as soon after completing the action step as possible. This way, you'll associate the reward with doing the desired action step.

You might want to decide right now on some special rewards you'll give yourself after you've completed each chapter ahead.

Preview Possible Obstacles and Support

When you think of your goal and imagine it becoming reality, ask yourself:

☐ Who or what might help you in the process?

☐ What obstacles, fears, limitations might hinder you?

Think of people, things, ideas, or activities that may operate to support or restrain you in reaching this goal. You may want to review your Interpersonal Support Chart in Chapter 3 to jog your memory. Don't forget tangible environmental forces, such as money, transportation, a home work area. Be as specific as possible. In considering your goal:

☐ Are there supports you need to add, develop, utilize more effectively?

☐ Are there restraining forces you would like to eliminate or handle more effectively?

Completing this sentence may help you organize your thoughts:

Something I will do within the next two weeks to help build support for my

goal is _____

_____

And you may want to make back-up plans for handling major obstacles that might occur. Consider: What's the *worst* thing that could happen if this restraining force takes effect? And, what's the *most probable* thing that could occur? Think about how you could handle both of these situations. While you don't need intricate plans for handling every conceivable obstacle, it's a good idea to anticipate how to handle major threats.

Evaluate Your Progress

Make some specific dates with yourself to evaluate progress towards your goal. This step is essential; it's easy to lose perspective without periodic evaluation. Often individuals focus on what they have not done and lose track of actual accomplishments. Keeping your progress in mind can motivate you to keep going.

While you're at it, review and perhaps revise upcoming action steps. Does new information imply a need to add some action steps, request another source of support, deal with an unanticipated obstacle? Do you see ways to speed progress toward the goal? It may help you follow through on your plans if you share your goal with a supportive person, a friend, family member, or counselor.

Now you're ready to take that first step. It may be to complete the next section in the book, so . . . onward!

HIGHLIGHTS

- ☐ To take action on a decision
  - —state it as a goal
  - —break long-range, general goals into short-term, specific goals
  - —break short-term goals into action steps
- ☐ Encourage success in achieving your goals by
  - —setting deadlines
  - —planning rewards and support
  - —anticipating obstacles
  - —reviewing your plan periodically

RESOURCES

Campbell, D. C. *If You Don't Know Where You're Going, You'll Probably End Up Somewhere Else.* Niles, IL: Argus Communications, 1974.

An easy-to-read, practical book about personal goal-setting, inspiring the reader to plan for success while keeping a humorous perspective.

Ford, G. A. and Lippitt, G. L. *Planning Your Future: A Workshop for Personal Goal Setting.* La Jolla, CA: University Associates, 1976.

Step-by-step exercises for planning attainable personal goals. Helpful examples of how others have responded to the exercises are given for comparative purposes.

DISCOVERING YOURSELF

6

IDENTIFYING

YOUR ROLES

"Whatever happened to Edith?"
one of the women asked.
"What do you mean?" I inquired.
"Well, she used to be so . . ."
"Invisible?"
"That's it! She used to be Bill's wife."
Iris Sangiuliano, *In Her Time*

OUR identities are largely defined by the roles we play. Thus, looking carefully at the roles we choose, as well as those we are required to play, is an opportunity to come to a better understanding of ourselves. In this chapter you will begin to expand your self-awareness as you learn

☐   how roles change over time

☐   how to chart your past roles and identify your unique lifeline

☐   how to evaluate your current roles and begin evolving more desirable future roles

HOW ROLES CHANGE OVER TIME

All women play many roles over time. At birth we immediately take on the role of daughter; perhaps we are also sisters. Later we may become mother's helper, daddy's girl, class poet, star performer, Girl Scout, tomboy, best friend, student, employee, wife, mother, dutiful daughter, volunteer, den mother, teacher, chauffeur, gourmet cook, lover, director, politician, innovator, organizer. As we mature, roles we once relished may begin to feel burdensome or outgrown. This is part of our predictable evolution as individuals.

We May Postpone Roles

While adolescence is commonly thought of as the time to resolve many of our "Who am I?" crises and confusions, by and large, women are late bloomers. Iris Sangiuliano, author of *In Her Time,* emphasizes that women tend to postpone forging more complete identities, including career commitment, until after they have resolved the question of personal relationships. While men typically focus early on shaping and achieving their identities through career choice and commitment, then move on to the consideration of personal relationships, women are often victims of the "after" syndrome:

- ☐ "I'll apply to graduate school *after* my husband gets his degree."

- ☐ "I can't think about a career until *after* I get married and I know where my husband's job will take me."

- ☐ "I'll stay with this clerical job *until* we have enough money to buy a house."

- ☐ "I don't want to get a job until *after* my youngest child is in junior high school."

- ☐ "I didn't decide to commit myself to my career until *after* I found that I couldn't have any children."

Thus many women do not begin a process of vocational exploration and commitment until after they become aware that relationships are an incomplete, and often unsatisfying, manner of defining their identities.

Disruptions May Force Role Changes

Some women grow into an awareness of the need to broaden their horizons. Many are forced into it by disruptions in life (divorce, the death of a loved one, the loss of a dream, relocation, illness and injury) or disruptions in philosophy (a raised consciousness). Iris Sangiuliano advises that if we view these jolts and endings as the seeds of new beginnings, rather than remaining sorrowful and embedded in our losses, we can grow into richer roles and enlarged identities. It is through our jolts that we come to the awareness of ourselves as special, unique, and precious.

CHARTING YOUR LIFELINE

Often we can more comfortably contemplate role changes in the future, if we can see in black and white how our roles have changed in the past and how these role changes have led to growth. Take a moment now to draw your own lifeline on a large sheet of paper. Start at birth and draw the line to now, projecting it off into the future in any direction and to any length that seems appropriate to you. Let your line reflect critical events and experiences with peaks, loops, and dips. Label your significant events and add dates, names of important people, and feeling words. Following are the lifelines drawn by Joyce Rosner and Clare Jenkins. It's apparent that each woman's lifeline is uniquely her own.

Both Joyce and Clare discovered that their real highs were when they attained something and took charge of their lives. Lows were often broken or lost relationships coupled with feelings of worthlessness and insignificance. A clear pattern seemed to develop for both women that others controlled their ups and downs until they took charge.

As you look at the lifeline you have drawn for yourself, notice how the necessity or the choice to change roles has given you the impetus for growth. And although you may wish your lifeline reflected a smooth and orderly progression, this is seldom the reality for any of us. More often we

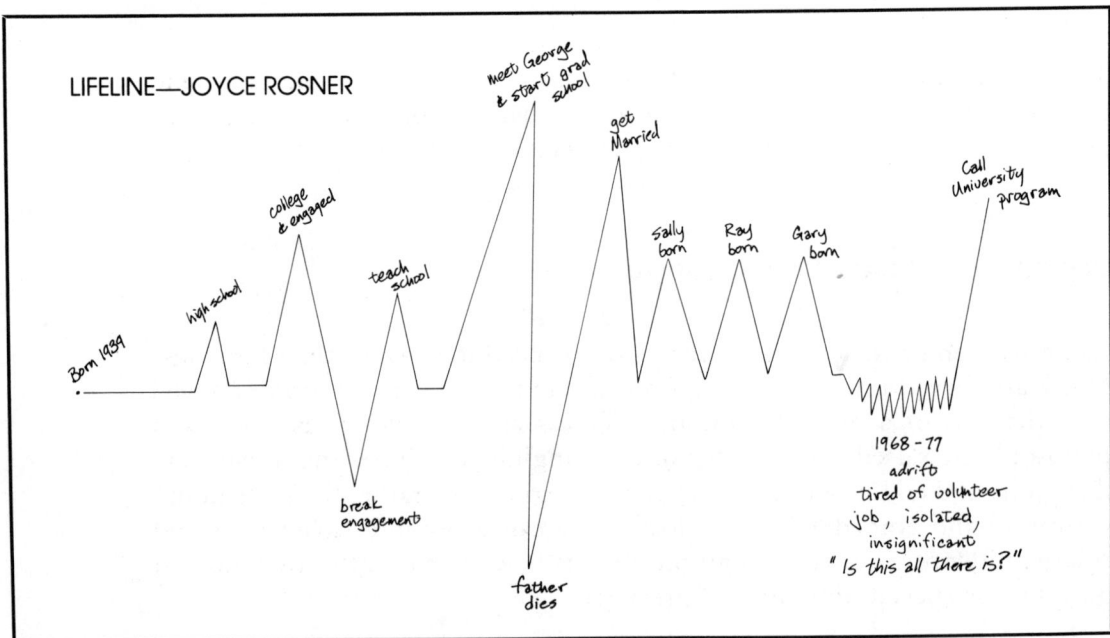

LIFELINE—JOYCE ROSNER

Born 1939
high school
college & engaged
teach school
break engagement
meet George & start grad school
father dies
get Married
Sally born
Ray born
Gary born
1968-77 adrift tired of volunteer job, isolated, insignificant "Is this all there is?"
Call University program

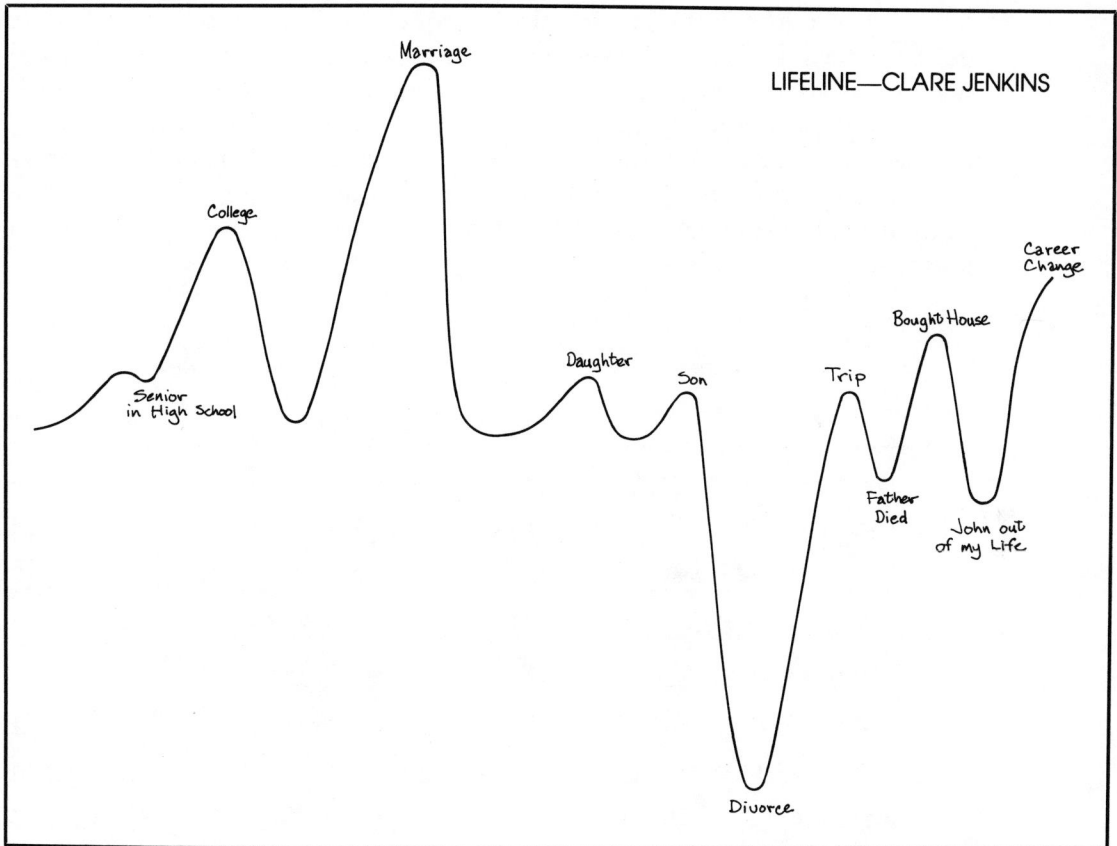

LIFELINE—CLARE JENKINS

mature through a process of ups and downs and switchbacks and backtracks. Accepting the uniqueness of your own path in the past can free you to see more clearly where you are right now.

EVALUATING CURRENT ROLES

Who Are You?

You probably have many answers to the important question "Who am I?" You carry on a variety of roles simultaneously. Listing those roles may help you appreciate your complexity as an individual, and identify facets of yourself that are ripe for change.

Joyce Rosner taught social studies before she returned to college to get a master's degree in counseling. She married during graduate school and her first child arrived at the same time as her diploma. A professional volunteer and part-time teacher, she chooses to emphasize her roles of wife, mother, and Christian before her role of counselor/teacher. Now, at forty-one, she recognizes that she is ready to turn another corner in her life as she hears herself asking "Is this all there is?" She listed the following roles in response to the question "Who am I?":

Joyce Rosner		*Clare Jenkins*	
wife	1	mother	1
mother	2	student	3
friend	6	teacher	6
Christian	3	daughter	7
enabler	7	Friend	2
musician	8	sexual partner	8
organizer	9	Presenter / speaker	4
contributor	10	consultant	5
counselor / teacher	4	singer	9
traveler	5		

Clare Jenkins, whose list appears next to Joyce's, has recently divorced and is in the process of questioning and redefining her career as well as facing a number of difficult issues of personal identity. A thirty-eight-year-old high school teacher and mother of two, she wants to achieve and make up for many lost years. But at the same time she feels that achievement will be meaningless unless she is also able to value her role as mother and to maintain close relationships with friends.

On your own "Who am I?" chart write in up to ten answers which describe you as you are today in terms of your personal and work-related roles, your responsibilities, your personal qualities, group affiliations, family, beliefs, or needs and feelings which are important to your sense of self. Take no more than about ten minutes to complete your list.

WHO AM I?

———————————————————————— ☐
———————————————————————— ☐
———————————————————————— ☐
———————————————————————— ☐
———————————————————————— ☐
———————————————————————— ☐
———————————————————————— ☐
———————————————————————— ☐
———————————————————————— ☐
———————————————————————— ☐

Which Roles Are Most Important to You?

It's easy to get caught up in the activities of our various roles and not take the time to think about which ones are most important to us. After completing your list, ask yourself:

☐   Which role would I never choose to give up?

☐   Which role would it be a relief to change or drop, assuming I could?

☐   Which of my roles complement each other?

☐   Which roles conflict?

☐   Which of my roles would I like to give less time to?

After reviewing these questions, think about the order of importance of your roles. Using the box to the right of each line on your chart, write in a ranking from 1 to 10, with 1 representing top importance and 10 being of lowest importance, and all others falling in between. Force yourself to assign priorities but allow yourself the flexibility of giving tied ranks when the roles seem to be truly of equal importance to you.

Which Roles Would You Like To Change?

Often we find ourselves stuck in outgrown roles because while we know what we *don't* want, we are less clear about what we do want. Looking more closely at which roles we want to change and how we might go about it can stimulate us to face the risks and glean the rewards.

Joyce Rosner wanted to change her role of volunteer organizer and contributor. She planned to begin by seeking new avenues of employment which would allow her to use her professional training as well as build on her extensive volunteer experience. She decided the worst outcome would be, quite simply, that she wouldn't find anything, which would leave her back where she started. But if her plans worked out, she expected the reward of achieving her goal and using her skills in a paid job.

Clare Jenkins chose to focus on the more personal goal of changing her role as sexual partner. As she was breaking out of her current relationship, she anticipated that she might have to cope with loneliness, but looked forward to the opportunity to come more alive sexually.

Complete these sentences for yourself:

I want to change my role of _____

I will do this by (action steps) _____

_____

The worst that could happen if I do this is _____

_____

The good things that could happen if I do this are _____

_____

IMAGINING FUTURE ROLES

Using fantasy is a good way to begin exploring possible future roles. Free yourself to try out and reject different roles as you follow this exercise.

Live Through a Day in the Future

Find a place where you can relax undisturbed. Close your eyes, and pick a time three, five, eight, ten, or fifteen years into the future. How old will you be then? What year will it be?

Imagine yourself waking up in the morning. See yourself lying quietly in bed, and allow your awareness to drift around the room and around your home. Where are you? What time is it? Who is there with you? Fill in the details of your environment—the colors of the room, the sounds of morning, the smells from inside and outside your home. Now, still lying quietly, or perhaps while making yourself a cup of coffee, begin to review your plans for the day. Think about where you will go, what you will wear, and how you will travel.

What are the pleasures today holds for you? What are the challenges, responsibilities, and ordeals? Follow yourself through the day like a shadow noting what you do and who you see. Do you stay at home or do you leave? Are you alone or with someone? Notice how you feel. What are your emotions at different times during the day?

As you imagine the day turning to dusk, think about how you plan to spend the evening. What leisure, family, or work activities do you choose to do? As you see yourself finally climb into bed, allow your mind to drift back over the events of the day.

Then permit your thoughts to float further into the past. What pleases you about the changes you have made since that day you were reading Chapter 6 in *Every Woman Works*? What goals have you implemented and how have they impacted your life? What have you learned to do well? What have you given up? What has caused you pain? What directions have you grown from your experiences?

Write Your Fantasy Down

Now write down what you have imagined. Circle or check parts of the fantasy you really want to come true. Discuss this day in your future with a friend to help clarify what is particularly important to you. Is there one thing you want so much that if you don't get it you will feel cheated? Put a copy of your fantasy in an envelope marked with the date of your day in the future. Look at it now and then, and as you proceed with self-exploration and into your new work role, let your fantasy be your guide.

HIGHLIGHTS

☐ Past role changes add up to your unique lifeline.

☐ Your present identity

—encompasses the many roles you choose or are required to play

—will change as you try on roles you've been postponing

—may be tested and stretched by disruptions in your life.

☐ You can motivate yourself to change roles by evaluating your present roles and imagining future roles.

RESOURCES

Goodman, E. *Turning Points: How People Change through Crisis and Commitment*. Garden City, NY: Doubleday and Company, 1979.

A journalist's description of how adults encounter and deal with turning points in their lives. Special attention is paid to changing male/female roles and the real-life anxieties and emotional losses associated with major changes. Well-written case studies will hold your attention.

Sangiuliano, I. *In Her Time*. New York: William Morrow and Company, 1978.

A practicing psychotherapist examines the unpredictable crises that jolt women into growth. An intensive study of how women's adult lives are shaped by upheavals and their resolutions. You will undoubtedly identify with many of the women's stories and gain insight into your own patterns of development.

Sheehy, G. *Passages: Predictable Crises of Adult Life*. New York: E. P. Dutton and Company, 1976.

Citing 115 in-depth interviews, this journalist plots the personality changes common to each stage of adult life from the years 18 to 50. She compares the developmental rhythms of women and men, which she finds strikingly unsynchronized. In light of this, she describes the crises that couples can anticipate.

7

UNCOVERING YOUR VALUES

A woman wants work equal to her gifts,
work worthy of her time, work that trusts
she has something to say instead of
parroting. . . . To be oneself, especially in
relation to work, is the most emancipated
thing any of us can do.
Alexandra Johnson, *Christian Science*
Monitor 2/15/79

V*ALUES* are basic, strongly-held be-
liefs which run through and under our interests, abilities, and skills. I may
be interested, able, and skillful in organizing networks of people. Does it
matter to me if I am the Godmother of the local numbers racket or chief
fund raiser for the new wing on the children's hospital? You bet it does! My
values determine which it will be.

In this chapter you will:

□ learn techniques for uncovering your values

□ identify the values that are most important to you in work

□ recognize your work setting preferences and needs

VALUES SHOW UP IN EVERYTHING YOU DO

Everytime you make a choice, you express values. The values you express
may be your own or they may be those imposed by societal or cultural
norms. For example, many women feel they *should* value social service and
nurturing in making work choices, even though these values may not really
be at the tops of their lists. And many women who learned as children that
they *should not* be competitive find when they enter work that they do value
competition, pitting their talents against others' or their own standards. For

this reason it's important to find out what *your* values really are, if you are to make satisfying work choices.

Fruitful Places to Look for Values

There are a variety of places where you can look to start identifying your values. We suggest a few here. If you are not clear about what values are, skip ahead to the Work Values Chart and review those listed.

Your Lifeline Look at the lifeline you drew in the last chapter. What values were you expressing as you made critical life and work decisions? Undoubtedly, your values have evolved since then, but you will probably find a few very basic values still intact.

Your Time Plan Look at the time plan you completed in Chapter 2. What values are reflected in the way you chose to spend your time that week?

Your Idea Box Pull out the file or box you started in Chapter 1, and sort through your idea gold mine. You are probably attracted to people, places, and things on the basis of values. What common threads do you see, and what specific values can be inferred? Do you see indications of conflicts between values?

Your Spending Habits How you choose to spend your money also reflects your values. Get out your financial records and identify major areas of expenditure. Which of your values dictate where you put your dollars?

Your Journal You may already keep a journal, but if you don't, consider starting one. Record everyday experiences and feelings. Christina Baldwin's book *One to One* can guide you in initiating a meaningful journal. After writing in it for a couple of weeks, re-read your entries. What values underlie these personal events and reactions?

People You Admire Identify three individuals you admire. These people may be living or dead, people you've met on the street or in books. What are their values? Which key values do you share with them, and which of your values conflict?

Others' Work Chat with friends and acquaintances about the everyday details of their work. Or meet diverse new acquaintances in Suzanne Seed's *Satur-*

day's Child or Terry Wetherby's *Conversations: Working Women Talk About Doing a "Man's Job."* What values are represented in these individuals' work? Fantasize about doing their work for a day. What satisfactions or dissatisfactions would you experience?

IDENTIFY IMPORTANT WORK VALUES

Now that you have some idea of what your values are, it will help you clarify your thinking even further to discover what you do *not* value or which values

---

YOUR WORK VALUES

For each factor below, circle the number that best describes how much you value this factor in your ideal work.

        1 = do not value
        2 = value slightly
        3 = value somewhat
        4 = value very much
        5 = value to an extreme extent

Achievement: see the results of my efforts	1	2	3	4	5
Advancement: have my work lead to better opportunities.	1	2	3	4	5
Artistic Creativity: do creative work, involving one or more art forms	1	2	3	4	5
Autonomy: plan and carry through my own work, without a lot of orders and directions from others	1	2	3	4	5
Benefits: have substantial health, retirement, and other fringe benefits	1	2	3	4	5
Challenge: apply my energies thoroughly to difficult or complex tasks	1	2	3	4	5
Compatibility: be with people at work who share my interests and values	1	2	3	4	5
Constructive Feedback: have the quality of my work judged critically by colleagues, clients, or customers	1	2	3	4	5
Creative Problem-Solving: come up with new ways to solve problems, or to implement more effective/efficient approaches	1	2	3	4	5
Competition: work in situations in which I pit my talents against those of others or against my own standards	1	2	3	4	5
Decision-Making: have the power to make decisions about policy, course of action, etc.	1	2	3	4	5

Economic Independence: know that I can depend on myself for a decent living wage	1	2	3	4	5
Energizing Atmosphere: work with people who are energized by the challenge of their work	1	2	3	4	5
Ethics: not perform work activities which violate my personal beliefs	1	2	3	4	5
Expertise: be a recognized expert in my field	1	2	3	4	5
Face-to-Face Social Service: help others in direct, visible ways, either individually or in groups	1	2	3	4	5
Fast Pace: work in situations where there is a fast pace of activity	1	2	3	4	5
Friendship: develop close personal relationships as a result of my work	1	2	3	4	5
Influencing Others: be in a position to change the attitudes, opinions, or actions of others	1	2	3	4	5
Location: work and live in a location (i.e., geographical area, type community) which affords me opportunities to do the things I enjoy most	1	2	3	4	5
Money: earn large amounts of money or other material gain	1	2	3	4	5
Organizational Ethics: work only for an organization/employer which treats its employees honestly & fairly	1	2	3	4	5
Organizational Prestige: be recognized as a member of a well-known organization.	1	2	3	4	5
Precision: work in situations where there is little tolerance for error	1	2	3	4	5
Prestige: work at an occupational level that signifies influence and evokes respect	1	2	3	4	5
Public Contact: have lots of day-to-day contact with many new people, rather than just working with a few familiar individuals	1	2	3	4	5
Recognition: have my work valued and acknowledged by others	1	2	3	4	5
Risk-Taking: work on assignments that require frequent risk-taking	1	2	3	4	5
Security: be able to keep a job a long time	1	2	3	4	5
Self-Enrichment: learn new ideas, skills, and tasks at work	1	2	3	4	5
Social Contribution: use my energies and talents to make the world a better place in which to live	1	2	3	4	5
Stability: work in a situation where the work routine is fairly predictable	1	2	3	4	5
Teamwork: work in a team toward common goals	1	2	3	4	5
Time Freedom: work according to my own time schedule	1	2	3	4	5
Time Pressure: work under time pressure or deadlines	1	2	3	4	5
Variety: have a variety of experiences or challenges, rather than a single area of concentration	1	2	3	4	5
Work Alone: work at tasks which I can accomplish by myself	1	2	3	4	5

are less important than others. By completing the Work Values Chart you will get an idea of how your values compare among themselves. While filling it out, consider which values you would like to express in your *ideal* work, the kind of work you would most like to do. As you read each statement, feel free to reword the item so that it is meaningful to you, and to add items that are not listed.

As you fill out the chart, you may find that you feel very strongly about your need for certain values in your ideal work, while your reaction to other values is "It would be nice, but not necessary." If so, you've already separated your top values from your preferences.

On the other hand, if you find you've given a preponderance of high ratings, you may need to prepare yourself to view your next work situation as a compromise in which you will meet some but not all your work values. In reality, almost all work choices are compromises.

In either case, weighing your values will make it easier for you to eventually compare jobs you may be considering against what's most important to you.

Pick Five Key Work Values

If your work could only satisfy five values, which values would you choose? Madge Johnson, a fifty-year-old widow preparing for re-entry into the paid labor force, answered that question as follows.

> *For the past three months I've been struggling with what I want to get out of work for myself, in this new part of my life. Oh, it's not easy! I've gotten out of the habit of thinking just in terms of me. I want a decent wage; heaven knows, now I just plain need it. Looking over my many years of community activities, I've realized that using my creative problem-solving talents is very special to me. I like to lay all the facts and feelings out on the table and then look for innovative, unusual solutions. I really valued this aspect of my contributions to our arboretum, and to the school board. I also know that variety—lots of different experiences or challenges—is important to me. And when it comes right down to it, I'd like work to give me opportunities to develop some new friendships with people of all ages.*

She listed and ranked her five key values like this:

1 Economic independence
2 Money
3 Creative problem-solving
4 Variety
5. Friendship

It may help you to pick your top five work values if you remember that these are not cast in concrete. Your values will evolve further as you gain more experience, and your needs and preferences will change in the future. This is just a tentative list for now. Go ahead and list your five key values now in the Values Synopsis Chart at the end of this chapter.

RECOGNIZE WORK SETTING NEEDS

Your eventual work choice will be made easier if you know what your needs and preferences are with regard to your tangible work environment, as well as which intangible work values you wish to express. Use the following Work Setting Needs Chart to stimulate your thinking about your require-ments and preferences. Your situation may dictate that you work in a certain setting, or you may have a lot of latitude as far as these factors go. Knowing which factors are negotiable and which are not will help you think more clearly about job choices.

YOUR WORK SETTING NEEDS

In the blank space before each item, put a letter "n" if it describes a situation you _need_ your work to provide. Put a letter "p" if it describes a situation you would _prefer_ your work to provide. Put a letter "a" if it describes a situation you want to _avoid_ in your work setting. Leave it blank if it doesn't matter to you one way or the other.

n = need
p = prefer
a = avoid

Where in the state, country, or world do you want to work?

_____ present community

_____ metropolitan area

_____ medium size city

_____ small town

_____ rural area

_____ other _____

YOUR WORK SETTING NEEDS *(continued)*

Where in terms of everyday working context do you want to work?

_____ in own home
_____ large organization/corporation
_____ small business
_____ self-employed
_____ profit structure
_____ nonprofit structure
_____ indoors
_____ outdoors
_____ one centralized workplace (e.g., one office, one forest)
_____ changeable, varied workplace
_____ travel outside local community
_____ travel within local community
_____ other _____
_____
_____

_____ self-regulated schedule
_____ other _____
_____
_____

How much monetary reward do you want?

_____ 0–$5000
_____ $5000–10,000
_____ $10,000–20,000
_____ $20,000–30,000
_____ $30,000–50,000
_____ $50,000 and up
_____ predictable salary
_____ full commission
_____ partial salary and partial commission
_____ other _____
_____
_____

When do you prefer to work?

_____ full-time
_____ part-time
_____ weekdays
_____ weekends
_____ mornings
_____ afternoons
_____ evenings
_____ nights
_____ year round
_____ certain seasons
_____ same schedule all the time
_____ changeable schedule
_____ scheduled by employer

With whom do you want to work?

_____ people who share my values/ interests
_____ people with varied values/interests
_____ same people most of time
_____ many different people
_____ in-depth contacts with small number of people
_____ brief contacts with large number of people
_____ member of working team
_____ complete work assignments on my own
_____ other _____
_____
_____

SUMMARIZE VALUES IMPORTANT TO YOU IN WORK

By filling in the following Values Synopsis Chart with information gleaned in this chapter, you will have a ready reference to review when you are faced with several job choices. How closely does each job fit your values and work setting needs? This does not preclude your accepting trade-offs when the time comes. Remember that if some of your needs are not met in the job you choose, you can meet them outside of regular paid work in activities with your family and friends, religious group, labor union, neighbors, city government, professional organization, or hobby. The key to your satisfaction is knowing what *you* value.

YOUR VALUES SYNOPSIS

My five key work values, ranked according to importance, are:

_____

_____

_____

_____

_____

I *need* the following factors in my work setting: _____

_____

_____

I would *prefer* the following factors in my work setting: _____

_____

_____

I would like to *avoid* the following factors in my work setting: _____

_____

_____

HIGHLIGHTS

☐   Values underlie your interests, abilities, and skills.

☐   You can find a job that fits you better if you
  — uncover your values by noting your everyday choices and
    reactions
  — list and rank your key work values
  — recognize what you need, prefer, and want to avoid in your
    work setting.

RESOURCES

Baldwin, C. *One to One: Self-Understanding through Journal Writing.* New
    York: M. Evans and Co., 1977

*Many practical tips for initiating a journal to expand self-under-
standing.*

Renwick, P. and Lawler, E. E. "What You Really Want From Your Job,"
    Psychology Today, May 1978.

*Results of an extensive September 1977 survey reveal how some
Americans feel about work. Many want more opportunities for self-
growth, including opportunities to develop skills and abilities, to
learn new things, to accomplish something important.*

Seed, S. *Saturday's Child: 36 Women Talk about Their Jobs.* Chicago, IL:
    O'Hara, 1973.

*Thirty-six women are interviewed about their jobs in the arts and
communication, trades, services, business, science and medicine, and
government. In short vignettes these women tell how they became
interested in their field, difficulties encountered, and satisfactions they
achieved.*

Simon, S. B., Howe, L. W. and Kirschenbaum, H. *Values Clarification: A
    Handbook of Practical Strategies for Teachers and Students.* New York:
    A & W Visual Library, 1978.

*These seventy-nine personal values exercises are excellent for indi-
vidual or group use.*

Wetherby, T. *Conversations: Working Women Talk about Doing a "Man's Job."*
    Millbrae, CA: Les Femmes, 1977.

*Conversations held in 1976 with 22 women holding jobs typically
held by men, e.g., pesticide inspector, mechanic, butcher, bank president, truckdriver, chaplin, etc. Topics range from early influences,
how they started, what they do, problems and accomplishments,
advice to other women.*

8

ARTICULATING
YOUR INTERESTS

To love what you do and feel that

it matters—how could anything be more fun?

Katherine Graham, quoted in "The Power
That Didn't Corrupt," by Jane
Howard, *Ms* magazine, October 1974

*I*DENTIFYING your interests is as
simple (and as difficult) as answering the question "What do I like?" Interests
are preferences for activities. Your interests are expressed in what you do
for fun, the subjects you choose to explore, and the experiences you find
exciting. They also are reflected in what you dislike. The probability that
you will find satisfaction in your life and work increases with the amount
of your involvement in activities which are related to your interests. So in
this chapter we will help you:

- □ search out and articulate your interests

- □ identify your interest patterns

- □ explore ways you might pursue your interests in work and non-
  work activities

WHAT DO YOU LIKE TO DO?

You may be a woman who likes just about everything and engages in a wide
range of activities. If you are this type of natural dilettante or Renaissance
woman, you may find it difficult to rank and choose between options. You
can use the exercises that follow to clarify where your strongest interests and
the best uses of your energy lie.

Or you may be someone who likes only a few things and engages in a narrow range of activities. If this is a result of having had limited options or experiences in the past, you can use the exercises that follow to unearth potential interests and ways to pursue them.

Whatever your present range of interests, you may feel, like so many of us, that you have spent your time doing what you believe you *have* to do or have no choice about, or what others have told you is "appropriate" for a woman. Now is the time to let go of any and all constraints and barriers. As you work through this chapter, erase the words "should" and "can't" from your vocabulary and substitute instead the words "I enjoy," "I want to," "I am enthusiastic about," "I am fascinated by," "I relish." These are the keys to truly satisfying experiences.

Don't feel obligated to do all the exercises that follow. Feel free to focus on those which hold the most meaning for you, and skip those that do not seem to pertain to you.

Search Your Past for Clues

While some aspects of your personality may change over time, your pattern of interests is likely to become more stable. As a result of your experiences in childhood and youth, you probably learned to prefer some activities over others. Over time and with continued practice these activities can develop into strong interests. To focus on these interests, it might help you to think back and answer the following questions.

- ☐   What kinds of activities did I enjoy as a child? (Active or passive, alone or with others, as a leader or a follower?)

- ☐   What did I daydream about growing up to be? (Evaluate these daydreams for sex role stereotypes and look for the beginnings of interest patterns.)

- ☐   Who did I pretend that I was? What were my favorite games?

Look at Your Lifeline   To see how your interests have developed over time, refer back to the lifeline you drew in Chapter 6. What interests were you expressing in your significant experiences and accomplishments? Take a few moments to think about your favorite activities, school subjects, role models, hobbies, and extracurricular activities.

Joyce Rosner found it helpful to prepare an interest lifeline to trace her development. Notice that many of her activities related to a few early interests. Prepare one of these lifelines for yourself if you think it would be helpful.

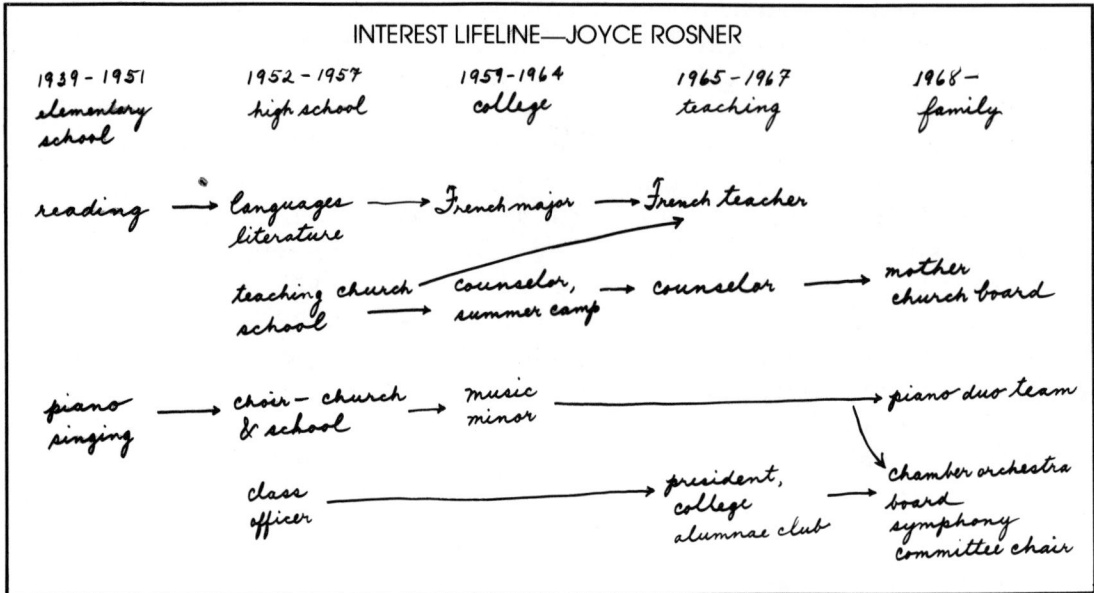

INTEREST LIFELINE—JOYCE ROSNER

1939 – 1951 elementary school	1952 – 1957 high school	1959 – 1964 college	1965 – 1967 teaching	1968 – family
reading	→ languages literature	→ French major	→ French teacher	
	teaching church school	→ counselor, summer camp	→ counselor	→ mother church board
piano singing	→ choir – church & school	→ music minor		→ piano duo team
	class officer		→ president, college alumnae club	→ chamber orchestra board symphony committee chair

Focus on the Present

Your everyday life is rich in clues about your interests. To stimulate your thinking, ask yourself these questions:

- ☐ What do I like to do with my spare time?
- ☐ What types of people do I enjoy being around?
- ☐ What do I like to do on my vacation?
- ☐ What kinds of books and magazines do I read?
- ☐ If I were to sign up for a course, what would I take?
- ☐ What hobbies do I enjoy?
- ☐ What kinds of social activities do I enjoy?

Or, if it's easier for you to identify what you *don't* like:

- ☐ What job would I really hate?
- ☐ What would I never do, if I could possibly avoid it?
- ☐ What types of people do I feel I have nothing in common with?

- [ ] What were my least favorite subjects in school?

- [ ] What's the last kind of book or magazine I would read?

List Things You Love to Do   Now that you're warmed up, make a list of at least fifteen activities that you love to do. Some of these may be rusty interests that you haven't had the time or the opportunity to indulge recently. Think of school or work experiences, leisure activities, hobbies, and so forth. These can be major undertakings or small five-minute pleasures.

THINGS I LOVE TO DO	Last time	Alone	People	Risk	Cost	N5	MT

Now, in the first column note the date when you last engaged in this activity. Place a check mark under the column labelled "Alone" beside those activities you prefer to do alone, and under the column labelled "People" beside those activities you prefer to do with people. Check both columns if you enjoy the activity both ways.

Check the column labelled "Risk" beside those activities that have an element of risk to them. This can be physical, emotional, or intellectual risk. Put a check in the column labelled "Cost" beside any activity that costs money to do. This should pertain to the actual activity and not the circumstances leading up to the activity, such as transportation required.

Check the column labelled "N5" next to any activities you were not doing five years ago. And place a check mark in the last column, labelled "MT," beside any activities you want to devote increasingly more time to in the years to come.

Now circle or check your five best-loved activities. Do you see any patterns emerging from the check marks you placed beside these activities? Do you see any patterns in the fifteen things you love to do?

Sift Through Your Idea Box   Now is a good time to go through your Idea Box. Quickly read the contents and then brainstorm answers to these questions:

☐   What common themes run through the items? You may discover general interest trends such as a desire to influence people or an interest in artistic expression. Or you may find quite specific interests, such as computer programming or teaching dance to senior citizens.

☐   How could you express these interests in your own work or non-work activities?

You can gain even more insight from your Idea Box if you enlist the assistance of friends or acquaintances. Other people can often see common themes that you might miss entirely. So ask a couple of people to sift through your box and respond to the same two questions. And keep adding to your box. It will help you stretch your imagination.

CHART YOUR VOCATIONAL INTEREST PATTERN

You will be more satisfied in your work if you seek out an occupation which will let you take on problems and roles and use skills which fit with your interests, and where you share similar interests and attitudes with your co-workers. Indeed, it's been found that people who find satisfaction in their vocation share similar and predictable sets of interests with their coworkers and flourish in work environments which provide the kinds of opportunities and rewards they prefer. This is the principle behind John L. Holland's widely-known theory of careers. He proposes that most people and work environments in our culture can be described as one, or more likely a combination of, six model occupational interest personality types: *realistic, investigative, artistic, social, enterprising, or conventional*.

Holland's formulation provides a useful structure to help you think about your interests. You can estimate which types you most resemble by completing the following exercise based on Holland's theory. The statements on these lists broadly describe some of the characteristics of each of Holland's types. Whether you have taken the time to do the preceding exercises or not, *do* take time to complete this one, as it will give you important input you will use in Chapter 11.

As you read each statement, feel free to reword the item so that it is meaningful to you. When several adjectives are listed or two similar statements are linked together, you may feel that you would rate some parts of the statement differently than others. In this case, circle the parts of the statement that best describe you, and rate them.

YOUR VOCATIONAL INTEREST PATTERN

Read each statement, and check the column that indicates how well it describes you.

Realistic

	very much unlike you	somewhat unlike you	neither like nor unlike you	somewhat like you	very much like you
I like to operate powerful or precision machinery.					
I enjoy physically challenging and outdoor activities.					
I like to work with tools or with animals.					
I prefer to solve problems in a practical, hands-on manner rather than in abstract ways.					

Realistic *(continued)*

	very much unlike you	somewhat unlike you	neither like nor unlike you	somewhat like you	very much like you

I would describe myself as practical, physically robust, conforming, honest, and persistent.

I have mechanical ability and good physical coordination.

I would be interested in working in skilled trades, agricultural or technical occupations.

I dislike social and intellectual situations.

I value conventional political and economic goals.

Investigative

I like to observe and investigate physical, biological, and cultural phenomena.

I like to work independently on open-ended problems and ambiguous tasks.

I have a need to understand the physical world and like to analyze data or information.

I prefer to solve problems by thinking them through in a rational manner.

I would describe myself as analytical, curious, scholarly, independent and reserved.

I have intellectual and academic abilities and can focus on tasks that involve long periods of intellectual effort.

I would enjoy working in a scientific, research, or academic occupation.

I dislike repetitive work, persuasive and social activities, and highly structured situations with many rules.

I value theoretical and speculative ways of viewing the world.

Artistic

	very much unlike you	somewhat unlike you	neither like nor unlike you	somewhat like you	very much like you
I like to work in an unstructured and innovative environment where I can express myself.					
I like music, art, drama, or writing activities.					
I relish the opportunity to create original art forms or products.					
I prefer to use intuition, feeling, and imagination to deal with problems.					
I would describe myself as original, expressive, imaginative, independent, unconventional, and introspective.					
I would score high on a test of creativity or originality.					
I would be interested in occupations involving music, art, drama or writing.					
I dislike highly structured problems and situations, political and economic matters, and physical activities.					
I value individuality, creativity and artistic expression.					

Social

I like group activities and enjoy being central in a group.					
I like to teach, inform, advise, heal, and develop others.					
I like to work closely with others in a helping way.					
I prefer to solve problems through feelings and relationships with others.					

Social *(continued)*

I would describe myself as humanistic, sociable, cooperative, insightful, responsible, understanding, and idealistic.

I have good verbal and human relations skills.

I would enjoy working in social service and educational occupations.

I dislike intellectual, physical, and highly ordered activities.

I value interpersonal relationships and ethical activities and problems.

very much unlike you	somewhat unlike you	neither like nor unlike you	somewhat like you	very much like you

Enterprising

I like to sell products, services, or ideas to people.

I like to achieve organizational goals and economic aims.

I like to work in groups where I can have some influence over what the group is doing.

I prefer to solve problems through persuasion and humor.

I would describe myself as ambitious, energetic, competitive, enthusiastic, outspoken, self-confident, persuasive, and entrepreneurial.

I am a good leader and speaker who can influence and organize others.

I would enjoy working in sales, political, public relations, and supervisory occupations.

I dislike scientific activities, long periods of intellectual effort, and detail work.

I value power, status, and material wealth.

Conventional

	very much unlike you	somewhat unlike you	neither like nor unlike you	somewhat like you	very much like you
I like carrying out well-defined tasks.					
I like detail work and keeping a lot of data and tasks efficiently organized.					
I like to prepare careful reports and statements.					
I solve problems by adhering to structure and following through in a methodical fashion.					
I would describe myself as dependable, moderate, efficient, cautious, orderly, and practical.					
I am good at detail work and have clerical and arithmetic ability.					
I would like to work in clerical and computational jobs or in other occupations in which the work is carefully organized.					
I dislike ambiguous and unstructured situations, leadership positions, and activities that require a lot of creative thinking.					
I value material possessions and status.					

The categories in which you rated the most statements "somewhat like you" or "very much like you" reflect the Holland types you most resemble. Most people find they resemble two or three categories most strongly, although some resemble fewer or more. List the categories here that appear most descriptive of you, in descending order. If two categories are very close, list both as one category, such as artistic/social.

_____

_____

_____

What Your Interest Pattern Means

Your interest-personality pattern is best described by an integration of the items and categories you rated most highly.

If you resemble two or three of the Holland categories, as most people do, this means you share characteristics with people in several areas of work and should look for an occupation in fields and settings that cut across these categories. If you rated all six categories highly, you have a wide range of interests and are likely to find many different activities attractive and rewarding. You may experience some difficulty in making choices or alloting time in your life for all the activities you would like to do.

If the statements you rated most highly are scattered and do not seem to form a cluster or pattern, you may be happy in any of several types of work. It may be that the employment setting or other characteristics of work apart from its intrinsic content are most important to you. Or perhaps you have had limited opportunities to become familiar with a variety of occupational activities and settings.

In Chapter 11 we will cover more specifically how you can identify jobs that match your interest pattern. For now, we'll describe generally the types of work corresponding to each Holland category, and initial ways you can go about exploring your interest and building your experience in these types of work.

Realistic   These are usually technical or skilled trades, jobs which require mechanical or physical skills. Work is often outdoors. Often called "blue collar" positions, they involve the use of tools, machines, and work with animals. The tools might be large, powerful machines, precision machinery, or small hand tools.

New federal laws have opened up the skilled trades to women more than ever before. Learning about skilled crafts and tools will help you better understand these jobs. Tuning up your car, remodeling the plumbing and electrical systems in your home, repairing your sewing machine, working on a farm, caring for animals in a zoo, an internship as a forester, or building stage sets for your community theater, are ways to build your experience and skills in these areas.

Investigative   These are usually scholarly, scientific, or laboratory jobs where people investigate, explore, and examine cultural, scientific, and mathematical problems.

You can get experience in these areas by pursuing hobbies such as astronomy, experimenting with chemistry sets, or going on field trips to gather biological or geological specimens. Get a job in a laboratory, take a course in computer operations, indulge yourself with a telescope for stargazing, or volunteer to collect water samples for your local environmental protection agency.

Artistic These are creative jobs where people have many possibilities for expressing themselves with words, music, or art.

You can gain relevant experience by acting in a community theater production, entering your pottery, photography, or sketches in an art show, joining a chamber music group, or working in an art gallery.

Social These human relations jobs are chosen by people who like to work closely with others—helping, healing, teaching, informing, and entertaining them.

More volunteer opportunities are available in this than any other area. You can seek experience working with old people or young people, in hospitals, schools, or churches, with the physically handicapped or the emotionally disturbed. You can work on a one-to-one basis, with a group, or on the telephone. You can help others as you determine whether this type of work or these settings appeal to you.

Enterprising These are persuasive or leadership jobs—political, sales, merchandising, management, and public relations positions. You may sell ideas, services, or products and may work to attain organizational or economic goals.

You can gain relevant experience by working in a political campaign or running for office yourself, managing a fund-raising campaign or representing a local organization to the media. A job as a sales clerk or selling door-to-door can let you know if you have a real interest in or aptitude for selling.

Conventional These are usually administrative or office jobs which involve methodical and ordered use of information and business detail.

Gather useful experience by serving as treasurer of your club or organizing records and data for a political campaign. Look for opportunities to gain skills such as typing, running a calculator, keeping both books and records, using a dictaphone, or operating data processing machines.

HOW ELSE CAN YOU SATISFY YOUR INTERESTS?

While it would be nice if your job allowed you to pursue every one of your interests, this is seldom the reality. But there are many ways for you to realize and act on your interests. Building a satisfying lifestyle is a process of integrating interesting activities, whether in your occupation or in your leisure time, as a hobby, a volunteer or community activity, or a family project.

Charlotte Bronstein, a nurse and the mother of a school-age daughter, discovered a latent interest and used it to enrich her leisure time:

> *I enrolled my daugher in ballet classes which I was sure would be really fun for her. I know that I've always regretted not having the choice as a child to develop any talent I might have had in dance or music. As recital time approached, Susan's teacher pointed out to me that she seemed to be balking about the show. Susan kept saying that I really didn't need to work so hard on her costume since she wasn't going to be in the show anyway. I assured her that it was just stage-fright. Well, she didn't say much of anything until a few days later when she announced that she wanted to quit the ballet classes in order to devote more time to being on the gymnastics team. 'Mom' she said, 'why don't you take the dance classes? I'll bet you'd like them.' I was flabbergasted, but you know what—I did and I do! I don't think I'll give up nursing to become a gypsy on the big stage, but I may try out for the chorus line the next time the community theater does a musical.*

Take Time to Brainstorm and Fantasize

Take some time to brainstorm alternative ways of pursuing interests you've uncovered. It can be helpful to remove the constraints of reality and allow yourself to dream as you did when you were a child. While many factors may ultimately intrude on your fantasies and affect the reality of how you pursue your interests, your dreams can serve as important guideposts to where you would like to go. Learn to trust your insides, your gut reactions.

Take a deep breath, close your eyes, and ponder these questions:

☐ If I had the time and the money to pursue my interests any way I wanted to, how would I go about it?

☐ If I had every opportunity to follow whatever career I wanted, what would I do?

Now take a few moments to jot down your ideas in the following chart. Charlotte Bronstein listed after her interest in dancing these possibilities: "Taking classes; performing with the community theater; buying season tickets to the dance theater; being a teaching assistant with the Park Board." Edith Johnson listed her interest in carpentry and woodworking, and after it noted, "Get a job in a cabinetry shop; invest in good tools for my own workshop; make wooden toys and cannisters for craft fairs; take classes at the community college; teach adult community education classes; open my own custom cabinet shop."

MAJOR INTERESTS	ALTERNATIVE WAYS OF PURSUING MY INTERESTS

Now we proceed to looking at your abilities and skills, the tools you develop and use to pursue your interests.

HIGHLIGHTS

☐ Past and present activities that you enjoy provide clues to your interests, as you
— forget the "shoulds"
— trust your gut feelings

☐ Your pattern of vocational interests points the way to work that you will enjoy, with co-workers similar to you.

☐ You can pursue your interests in a variety of ways both during and outside of paid work.

RESOURCES

Holland, John L. *Making Vocational Choices: A Theory of Careers.* Englewood Cliffs, NJ: Prentice-Hall, 1973.

Outlines Holland's theory of vocational behavior. Includes his Vocational Preference Inventory and Self-Directed Search which the reader can fill out and interpret using the theory presented in the text.

9

RECOGNIZING YOUR ABILITIES

First, she bore ten children and raised
the five who survived, working
hard farmwife days until she was 78.
Only then, in 1938, did she have leisure to
hearken again to her girlhood yearning to paint.
On panels of Masonite, using paints
she found out in the barn, working on
several pictures at once to make the
pigments go further, she brought alive the
warm world of the past as brightly
as it lived in her mind.

Description of Grandma Moses, in
Life Special Report: Remarkable
American Women 1776–1976

*A*BILITIES are those things you have
the natural potential to do, while skills are learned behaviors which may or
may not be built upon natural abilities. Because the skills you use in everyday
life may not tap all your real abilities, some talents and potentials may lie
latent for years, undiscovered and undeveloped. Many women do not unearth
valuable abilities until middle or later years; we all know of women who
became painters or writers or musicians in their 50s, 60s, and 70s. There are
also women in every community who rediscover their ability for leadership,
for working with mechanical objects and machines, or for cultivating plants,
shrubs, and trees.

It is only when you recognize your abilities that you can gain the
learning experience you need to turn them into skills. In this chapter we look
at:

□ blocks that may keep you from recognizing your abilities

□ some ways to start discovering your abilities

WHY SOME ABILITIES STAY HIDDEN

Many of us were brought up to be modest and warned not to "toot your own horn." If you are overly modest, though, you run the risk of overlooking many important abilities. So free yourself to brag a little as you think about what some of your hidden abilities may be. And recognize that there are probably a couple of other factors operating if you have a hard time discerning what your natural talents are.

Sex Role Stereotypes

If there was little opportunity or encouragement in your early environment to gain experience in particular areas, by the time you're older you're likely to decide that you have no ability in those areas. You may hang a label around your neck that reads, "I'm not artistic," or "I'm not mechanical," or "I'm not musical," or "I'm not mathematical." Indeed, it may be that you're not. But on the other hand, you may just have lacked positive experiences in those areas.

Without your knowing it, sex role stereotypes may have stamped out your opportunity for experience in certain areas. Some of the more common stereotypes are that females can't handle money, are no good with numbers, are bewildered by anything with moving parts.

Pat Schuman, now forty-one, traced her aversion to math back to her freshman year in high school. She recalled her algebra teacher focusing most attention on the male students. "After all, boys really need math for their eventual careers. How much math does a homemaker, nurse, teacher, or secretary use, anyhow!" In addition, while Pat's parents encouraged her to work for As and Bs in English and social studies, they felt her low Cs in math were okay. Throughout high school and college Pat's aversion to math became more pronounced. Her choice of a college major, English, was partially a way to avoid math requirements. When she took an entry-level position two years ago in an expanding marketing research division, she was forced to confront her "I'm not mathematical" label.

Her boss urged her to complete a Master's of Business Administration degree as a ticket to job advancement. Yet she had to complete college algebra, calculus, and statistics courses as entrance requirements into an MBA. Her math anxiety was seriously blocking her desired career path.

Deciding to give math one more try, Pat enrolled in a math anxiety curriculum in a returning students' program at a local junior college. She started at her current math level, eighth grade arithmetic, and worked at her own pace through higher levels of algebra. A math anxiety support group taught her specific strategies for dealing with her anxieties and polishing her study skills. She consulted an encouraging math tutor when she was stuck.

Struggling painfully through the first two school terms, Pat eventually began to actually enjoy math. Now enrolled in calculus, Pat has a strong B in the course and is finding that she has more math ability than she ever thought!

It's Hard to See Behind the Ordinary

For most of us, the *really* tough part of defining our abilities is that we tend to take for granted and overlook some of our best abilities. We say "Oh, it's just something I've always had a knack for." Or, "It's been so much a part of me since early years that I didn't realize that not everyone else has it too!"

Recognize that ordinary accomplishments can be clues to hidden abilities. You do not have to be *the best*—in your department, athletic team, or neighborhood—to acknowledge an ability. Saying you have a certain ability simply means you have a potential that not everyone else has.

HOW TO UNEARTH YOUR ABILITIES

Look to Early Experiences

When people show ability we often say they are "gifted" or "naturally endowed," or "a natural." Some people are "born athletes." Some take to reading like a "duck to water." Others have a "real ear for music." "Her vocabulary as a child used to startle people." "Her mother always knew she could find her playing bookstore with her friends." "Class prophecies at sixth grade graduation said she'd be a librarian."

Since many abilities are "born," they show themselves early in our lives. It can be helpful to recall what others said about you as you were growing up. Complete the following sentences:

People said about me, "That child has a real talent for _____

_____ ."

"It's amazing how well she can _____

_____ ."

"With ability like that she could be a _____

_____ ."

Abilities also show up in competition—races, spelling bees, oratory contests, art projects, school grades, 4-H projects, Girl Scout projects. Perhaps you were given a ribbon, a certificate, or a prize for an accomplishment. What do you remember winning? What subjects did you get your best grades in? Think about your teens and youth as well. Enjoyment of any particular events or experiences could also point to abilities. What abilities have shown up in activities since then?

Start to fill in your Abilities List.

YOUR ABILITIES

_____

_____

_____

_____

_____

_____

_____

_____

_____

_____

Try New Experiences

You may need to try an experience in order to find out if you have any ability in that area. If you are blocked by the idea that you don't have an ability in some area, it may help you to think about why you've hung that label around your neck. What specific evidence do you have that you're "not _____"? Can you trace this label back to its early source?

What are your hunches about your hidden abilities? How can you gain more input about these abilities? Susan Simpson, a computer programmer, enrolled in a jewelry making class in a community education center. Having described herself as "not artistic and clumsy with my hands," she still wondered if she'd ever given herself a fair chance to learn creative skills. "So why not, I'll give it a try. What do I have to lose?" Within three years she saw jewelry making as an involving hobby. Satisfactions in this creative pursuit were quite different from those in her paid work; her life felt more balanced.

Some day jewelry making may become part of Susan's paid work, like Pat's math skills. Or it may be her part-time career in retirement. Yet again, she may decide that an engrossing hobby is special enough.

Discovering and developing a hidden ability can add an energizing dimension to your life. Add to your Abilities List as you accumulate experiences. In the next chapter you'll learn how to turn abilities into skills.

HIGHLIGHTS

☐ You may be kept from recognizing your abilities by
— modesty
— sex role stereotypes
— the difficulty of seeing anything you do as special

☐ You can unearth abilities by
— recollecting childhood talents or awards
— trying new experiences

10

SURVEYING YOUR SKILLS

I was not a soldier or a philosopher
or a politician; I could cure
no disease, solve no economic problems,
or lead any revolution. But I could dance,
I could sing. I could make people laugh.
I could make people cry.
Shirley MacLaine, *You Can Get There From Here*

S*KILLS* are the basic building blocks of careers. They are the learned behaviors we use to accomplish tasks in every area of life. Thus, those we possess can be inferred from our past accomplishments, and those we wish to possess can be gained through experience.

Many of us feel we have few marketable skills, when in fact what we really lack is the ability to recognize skills in the things we do every day. So in this chapter you will

- □ learn how to recognize skills
- □ describe key accomplishments
- □ inventory skills and skill patterns
- □ synthesize the self-knowledge you've gained in this section

YOU HAVE HUNDREDS OF SKILLS

"Women tend to underestimate themselves, particularly their abilities and performance, to 'assume incompetence' compared with their own abilities," write Rosalind Barnett and Grace Baruch in *The Competent Woman*. The really tough part of surveying our skills, as in recognizing our abilities, is that we tend to take for granted and overlook some of our best skills just because they're all in a day's work. To overcome this, we urge you to think boldly, immodestly, and confidently as you complete the exercises that follow. And involve an objective observer, a friend or family member who might be able to see skills you've overlooked in yourself.

Look for Skills in Every Area of Your Life

Every task you perform, in every area of your life, involves the use of a number of skills. You have undoubtedly developed numerous valuable skills in the course of home and family duties, volunteer work, school and educational activities, recreational and leisure pursuits, and paid work. A complete assessment of your skills acknowledges your accomplishments in all of these areas.

For example, in the course of your homemaking duties you have developed competencies in child care, home design and maintenance, horticulture, clothing and textiles, nutrition, and financial management. The many skills underlying these competencies are all in demand in the paid labor market. In volunteer work you may have developed skills that will enable you to enter paid work as an administrator or manager, trainer, advocate/change agent, public relations communicator, researcher, fundraiser, counselor, youth group leader, museum assistant, or teacher's aide.

Look for Three Types of Skills

It may help you to begin thinking in terms of three different types of skills. First, there are *basic, transferable skills*. These are skills which cut across tasks and jobs, are applicable in the widest variety of work situations, can be learned almost anywhere, and are retained a long time. They seldom become obsolete and can be applied in many more than the obvious situations. For example, Sandy Smith learned basic, transferable skills in supervision, public relations, and financial management as a homemaker and volunteer fund raiser. She was able to use the same skills in her new position in the communications department of a wildlife zoo. Alena Epstein, who had taught nursing in a junior college, became a successful real estate broker. "I've found skills I used as a teacher invaluable as a broker. I listen carefully to clients, help them do a needs assessment, instruct them about structural details and financial options, and use persuasive communication skills."

Then there are *personal skills,* or *traits.* These are attributes of your personality that you carry into most life situations, and that given the proper setting can help you advance your career. Traits such as cooperativeness, enthusiasm, and curiosity can be valuable if you are part of a scientific research team, for example. Personality attributes are a major factor employers consider in determining who will be hired and retained on a job.

And finally, there are the skills that apply to a specific work situation. Usually these skills can only be learned in the setting in which they are used. These are *work content skills.* A work content skill for a teacher is writing a lesson plan; for a nurse, taking blood pressure; for a statistician, doing a multiple regression; for a homemaker, using a multi-purpose food processor; for a portrait photographer, operating a studio camera.

If you feel you have few marketable skills, you may be thinking only of work content skills. The exercises that follow are designed to expand your thinking to include all three types of skills in five areas of your life.

DESCRIBE KEY ACCOMPLISHMENTS

A logical way to begin your skills survey is by detailing and analyzing selected accomplishments from the past. For each of the areas listed below, take five or ten minutes to complete a short description. Recall something you enjoyed doing and felt you did well. It need not be a monumental accomplishment, just something, however small, that felt good to you. You may find it helpful to refer back to your lifeline, list of roles, or lists of values and interests to remind you of past accomplishments. Describe each situation in a sentence or two; then describe what you did as specifically as possible.

Home and Family   This accomplishment could involve some homemaking activity, planning an outing or vacation, an activity with children, parents, or relatives, remodeling the kitchen, landscaping the yard. For example:

> *My husband and I are gourmet cooks. Our kitchen was extremely small, inefficient. We were constantly tripping over each other as we cooked. I got the idea to add on to the kitchen. First, I got several books from the library on kitchen remodeling. I shared some of my better "finds" with my husband. Next I made a list of features I*

wanted in an ideal kitchen. I went to the bank to investigate home improvement loans and refinancing. After getting the financial go-ahead, I talked with an architect who drew up detailed plans and helped me find two contractors. Each contractor placed a bid and then my husband, the architect, and I weighed the pros and cons of each bid to pick a contractor. I outlined specific materials to be used in the construction and went over this in detail with the contractor. Construction went fairly smoothly, although I found I needed to get out of the house (and out of town!) occasionally to cope with the stress of dirt and noise. On two occasions I had to assert myself with the workers—they had purchased windows different from my spec-ifications. But finally our kitchen was done. It's a joy.

Now write your accomplishment here:

_____

_____

_____

_____

_____

_____

_____

_____

_____

_____

Volunteer Work   This could involve work for your church, school, or community agency. It could be planning events, raising money, teaching children or adults, visiting shut-ins, staging a play. For example:

Two years ago I became a volunteer at our local arboretum. Since my days as a Girl Scout I have enjoyed nature, flowers, and trees. And I thought volunteering would give me opportunities to learn more about nature and help others gain appreciation, too. I started with a six-week orientation class for nature guides. I learned so much in those six short lessons about perennials, wildflowers, and trees.

Then I spent five months guiding groups of school children around the major garden spots. After a few spins around the garden with children more energetic than myself, I proposed "breaks" in our hikes during which the kids sketched their favorite nature scenes. The kids and I both enjoyed our hikes more! Eventually some of these sketches were organized into a little show in the arboretum building—what fun I had sorting through those humorous, colorful drawings! I thought it would be fun to capture my perceptions of nature, too, but I had never had a knack for drawing. I knew there was a 35 mm camera available to guides, but I'd never operated one. So I asked a fellow guide, a delightful seventy-five-year-old woman, to show me the basics of the camera. I've been improving my photography for a year now, and one of my wildflower shots was recently chosen for our new arboretum brochure.

Write your accomplishment here:

_____

_____

_____

_____

_____

_____

_____

_____

_____

_____

School/Education   This could be anything you did in school or in a class that you remember feeling good about. Perhaps you were one of the sisters, cousins, or aunts in *H.M.S. Pinafore* in tenth grade. Did you work on the school paper? Help tutor other students? Were you voted best girl athlete in sixth grade? Did you figure out another way for the school to do something? Were you in student government? Were you a stand-out in geometry? Did you get high praise on your first college term paper after being out of school fifteen years? Did you organize a dorm party? Were you a teaching assistant as a graduate student? For example:

> *In tenth grade English we were asked to write an autobiography. It was great enjoyment to do. I organized it by ancestors, early years, grade school. I talked to my grandfather about his early days in Germany and in this country. I interviewed my parents, aunts, and uncles. I jotted down incidents as I remembered them in my life. I especially liked writing up those I remembered as having humorous aspects. I put them all together and used my new typing skill to put them on paper. My family enjoyed reading it. My teacher read parts to other classes as good examples of content and writing.*

Write your accomplishment here:

_____

_____

_____

_____

_____

_____

_____

_____

_____

Recreation/Leisure   Did you pick up and polish those old piano skills? Have you started a regular exercise program, learned to play tennis, earned a hiking medallion, run a race, begun a plant or bird identification program, started a garden, begun painting? For example:

> *In my younger days I had always been physically active (and physically fit!). But over the years I had become "too busy." I decided to find a time to go to a nearby health club. The best time was 6 a.m. I started my own running and exercise program. Some mornings I*

had to push myself but I got there! I've been doing this for two years and I find myself more energetic. Others have become interested also since I was so enthusiastic. My mother at seventy-two has an exercise program. My daughter runs with me some days. I feel good about my increased vitality.

Write your accomplishment here:

_____

_____

_____

_____

_____

_____

_____

_____

_____

_____

Paid Work   This is any paid work, any time. Did you work after school or weekends in high school or college? Or drop out of school to work? Are you working now? Pick something you did in any job that you felt good about. For example:

About ten years ago I worked as an office manager for a law firm downtown. The firm had twelve lawyers and ten clerical employees. I interviewed and hired the clerical personnel and oriented them to the various procedures and responsibilities of our office. Since there was no one lawyer "in charge" of the partners, I also oriented new lawyers to our firm. Besides everyday supervision of the clerical staff, I coordinated the requests (and DEMANDS!) of the twelve partners for clerical work. Each partner thought his/her work was THE top priority. So I learned how to juggle an incredible amount of paper-work, to play politics between various lawyers, to negotiate and be tactful with both the lawyers and clerical staff, and to use a sense of humor. I actually began to like the time pressure and the challenge to coordinate detailed work and manage complex people. At the end of my third year I put together an office policies and procedures manual which spelled out a lot of guidelines for getting our work done.

Write your accomplishment here:

_____

_____

_____

_____

_____

_____

_____

_____

_____

Any Other Accomplishment   You may be thinking of something you felt good about which really doesn't fall into any of the five areas above. Perhaps you lost ten pounds, quit smoking, negotiated a divorce, cut down involvement in volunteer activities, organized your high school reunion, planned and carried out a ten-day backpacking trip, bought a condominium, re-negotiated your job description with your boss. If so, write your accomplishment here:

_____

_____

_____

_____

_____

_____

_____

_____

_____

INVENTORY YOUR SKILLS

Now you will inventory the basic transferable skills, the personal traits, and the work content skills that show up in your key accomplishments. This should be a rewarding process of discovery; remember to think boldly, immodestly, and confidently!

Your Basic Transferable Skills

Transferable skills can be grouped into the same six categories you became familiar with as you uncovered your interest patterns: Realistic, Investigative, Artistic, Social, Enterprising, and Conventional. Grouping your transferable skills into these categories will make it easier for you to see how your skills relate to particular jobs and job fields.

This is a rather time-consuming exercise, so you may want to break it down into manageable parts rather than doing it all at once. Start by scanning the checklists that follow to get an idea of their scope. Next, reread your accomplishment description for the Home and Family area. Then go down each checklist and think about whether you used each skill listed in the course of that particular accomplishment. If so, place a check mark in the appropriate space. A good way to break this exercise down is to analyze one accomplishment a day.

Next, reread your accomplishment description for the Volunteer Work area, and go down the checklists with it in mind. Do this for each accomplishment. Remember, each skill had to be only a *small* part of your accomplishment to receive a check mark. Give yourself credit here!

These are not meant to be exhaustive lists of skills, but rather strong skill words and descriptions which you can use to clearly represent your skills in an interview situation or to write an achievement-oriented resume.

When you have completed each checklist, note the skills you have checked that you did well or very well. List these at the bottom of each list after "My highlight skills are. . . ." On any particular checklist, you may have low to high frequencies of checked skills and highlight skills. Notice which categories contain most of your check marks and highlight skills. These are your strongest basic skill categories.

You may consider making a photocopy of the checklists and asking a friend or co-worker to complete them according to their perceptions of you.

Your Basic Skills

Realistic

Skills involve the use of things, tools, machines, animals, and your body. These skills lead to competencies in farming, skilled trades, mechanical and technical occupations, and physical activities and sports. Activity examples: tuning up a car, driving a tractor, constructing kitchen cabinets, installing a shower, canoeing a wild river, cultivating tomato seedlings or planting 100 acres, competing on a volleyball team, participating in a survival skills course.

	home & family	volunteer work	school/education	recreation/leisure	paid work	other
CONSTRUCTING: putting together parts, assembling, building (a mechanism, a meal, a building)						
CULTIVATING: raising growing things (plants, animals)						
DESIGNING: creating furniture, models, patterns, buildings and devices						
HANDLING: lifting, balancing, carrying, unloading, moving						
INSPECTING: appraising, examining, determining state of plants, animals, equipment, buildings						
INSTALLING: positioning for use, putting in						
MAINTAINING: maintaining optimal condition of plants, animals, equipment, buildings						
MANUAL/HAND COORDINATION: showing eye-hand coordination, ability to do precision work with dexterity and speed						
MOTOR/PHYSICAL COORDINATION: demonstrating physical skills, agility, endurance, strength						
OPERATING: controlling a tool, machine, or vehicle, mechanical devices and instruments, scientific equipment						
PROTECTING: guarding, overseeing people, property, animals, grounds						
REPAIRING: fixing, refinishing						
TESTING: measuring and evaluating equipment, materials, plant or animal tissues						
USING SENSORY FACULTIES: smelling, tasting, seeing, hearing						

My highlight skills are _____

Investigative

Skills involve observing, exploring, investigating, and examining ideas and phenomena from a scientific perspective. These skills lead to competencies in scholarly, mathematical, and scientific occupations. Activity examples: doing thought-provoking word and number games, reading technical reports on environmental pollution, researching day care options, reading science fiction, taking a course in calculus.

	home & family	volunteer work	school/education	recreation/leisure	paid work	other
ANALYZING: critically examining, studying, and appraising						
CONCEPTUALIZING: getting a general notion or idea based on what you have learned and stating it in a precise form						
DIAGNOSING: investigating and analyzing the cause or nature of a phenomena						
EVALUATING: assessing or judging information and alternatives						
EXAMINING: looking over and exploring						
INFORMING: presenting information through oral or written communication						
INTERPRETING: explaining or assigning meaning; translating into familiar language or terms						
PREDICTING: anticipating or foreseeing future events						
PROBLEM SOLVING: identifying possibilities and alternatives and developing answers or solutions						
QUESTIONING: interrogating, interviewing, challenging						
RESEARCHING: gathering data and information, systematically investigating, getting expert advice and assistance						
SYNTHESIZING: combining and integrating information						
THINKING: using logic and reason; formulating creative possibilities						
UNDERSTANDING: perceiving meaning; learning						

My highlight skills are _____

Artistic

Skills involve creating art forms or products through materials, music, drama, or writing. These skills lead to competencies in artistic and creative occupations. Activity examples: writing a poem or short story, preparing a special meal, performing in a one-act play, exhibiting your photographs, designing a piece of jewelry, attending a concert.

	home & family	volunteer work	school/education	recreation/leisure	paid work	other
APPRECIATING: evaluating highly or admiring; being critically and emotionally aware of aesthetic value						
COMPOSING: arranging or forming by uniting parts and elements						
CREATING: bringing into being from thought or imagination, originating, inventing						
DECORATING/CONSULTING: advising others on artistry, color, form, arrangement of interiors, clothing and accessories						
DESIGNING: conceiving and planning, jewelry, graphics, models, patterns for self or others to produce						
DRAWING: portraying people, scenes, or events by sketching, painting, illustrating, lettering, graphics						
ENTERTAINING: performing before an audience, diverting, amusing						
EXHIBITING: displaying, demonstrating						
EXPLORING: seeking new experiences, showing perpetual curiosity						
EXPRESSING: conveying thoughts and feelings through an artistic medium						
IMAGINING: visualizing, forming mental images						
PRODUCING: making a product in art or craft form, written material, or performance						
SPEAKING/SINGING: using voice to entertain, inform, tell a story, dramatize						
WRITING: using words to tell a story, describe a product, critique an artistic event, convert a story to a script						

My highlight skills are _____

Social

Skills involve working with people to help, teach, inform, train, and heal. These skills lead to competencies in educational, social service, humanitarian, and religious occupations. Activity examples: facilitating a personal growth group, counseling runaway teenagers, interviewing applicants for a job, supervising playground activities, teaching an adult education class, caring for a sick person.

	home & family	volunteer work	school/education	recreation/leisure	paid work	other

ADVISING: giving information, consulting, aiding decision making

COLLABORATING: cooperating, working as a team member

COMMUNICATING: about personal issues, exchanging thoughts and information, interviewing, informing

COORDINATING: synchronizing relationships, acting as a liason, putting others in touch with useful resources

COUNSELING: guiding or mentoring others

ENCOURAGING: motivating and developing the capabilities of others

FACILITATING: assisting the progress of a person or a group

GIVING/GETTING FEEDBACK: conducting appraisals of others, asking for and giving supportive and critical feedback

LISTENING: attending to others actively and accurately and with openness and concern

PLANNING: arranging meetings, social occasions and activities

REHABILITATING: restoring to healthy functioning

RELATING: meeting and associating easily with all kinds of people, developing trust and rapport

SERVING: anticipating and attending to the needs of others

TEACHING: instructing, tutoring, coaching, and training others

My highlight skills are _____

Enterprising

Skills involve persuading and leading people and organizations to attain goals or economic gains. These skills lead to competencies in public relations, political, business, and sales occupations. Activity examples: campaigning for a seat on the Park Board, organizing a fundraiser, starting your own business, lobbying for a state clean air act, selling Girl Scout cookies.

	home & family	volunteer work	school/education	recreation/leisure	paid work	other

ADMINISTERING: managing people and projects by setting goals and standards, choosing priorities, assigning activities, and evaluating progress

DELEGATING: giving responsibility to others appropriately

IMPLEMENTING: establishing and executing policies and procedures

INFLUENCING: exerting power and authority, advocating a course of action

LEADING: taking initiative, advancing ideas, directing action

MOTIVATING: prompting action, providing incentive, inspiring and encouraging others

NEGOTIATING: promoting resolution of conflict, arbitrating, mediating, bargaining

PERSUADING: winning acceptance and approval for ideas or products, selling, advocating, raising funds

PLANNING/FORECASTING: designing long-range strategies based on predictions of the direction of growth and opportunities

RISKING: hazarding change, promoting alternatives, troubleshooting

SPEAKING: communicating publicly and persuasively, representing or acting as a spokesperson

STAFFING: recruiting, interviewing, selecting, placing, promoting, and transferring personnel

SUPERVISING: overseeing the performance of others, disciplining, setting priorities

TEAM BUILDING: recognizing and utilizing the skills of others, organizing and supporting cooperative efforts

My highlight skills are _____

Conventional

Skills involve gathering, organizing, and evaluating numerical and written data, attention to detail, systematic procedures, and operating business and data processing machines. These skills lead to competencies in clerical, computational, data processing, and business system occupations. Activity examples: developing a filing system, computing your income taxes, serving as club treasurer, plotting the route for a vacation trip, setting up a library system, budgeting carefully.

AUDITING: examining and verifying accounts and records

CALCULATING: using numbers and performing accurate computations

CLASSIFYING: cataloging information, coding, filing

COLLECTING: gathering data and information

DEVELOPING: designing systematic procedures

EVALUATING: assessing the effectiveness of procedures, accuracy of information, and compliance with standards

FOLLOWING PROCEDURES: attending to detail, following through on the details of a plan

INVENTORYING: counting, listing, and assigning value to articles

KEEPING RECORDS: carefully recording and listing; keeping books

MANAGING RESOURCES: planning and managing finances, time, personnel, and materials

OPERATING: running business and data processing machines

ORGANIZING: organizing information, procedures, tasks

PREPARING: producing budgets, written reports, correspondence, maps, charts, and tables

PURCHASING: finding and buying resources and materials

My highlight skills are _____

	home & family	volunteer work	school/education	recreation/leisure	paid work	other

Write down your top three skills categories here:

_____

_____

_____

Your Personal Traits

Now it's time to take stock of your personal traits, in much the same fashion as you inventoried your basic skills. Preview the following checklist to get an idea of its scope. Review your first accomplishment and run down the list of traits, checking those that describe you. Review each accomplishment in turn and check off the appropriate traits. After you're done, total the number of check marks opposite each trait.

Again, you may want to make photocopies of this list and ask friends and family to check off those they believe describe you. This gives you the benefit of comparing your opinions to those of people important to you. It is also a way to involve them as you make decisions about work.

YOUR PERSONAL TRAITS

	home & family	volunteer work	school/education	recreation/leisure	paid work	other	TOTAL
accurate							
adventurous							
ambitious							
analytical							
assertive							
athletic							
attractive							
calm							
caring							
cautious							
clever							
competent							

	home & family	volunteer work	school/education	recreation/leisure	paid work	other	TOTAL
competitive							
confident							
considerate							
cooperative							
courageous							
creative							
curious							
dependable							
discreet							
easygoing							
efficient							
empathic							

YOUR PERSONAL TRAITS *(continued)*

	home & family	volunteer work	school/education	recreation/leisure	paid work	other	TOTAL
energetic							
enterprising							
entertaining							
enthusiastic							
expressive							
farsighted							
firm							
flexible							
forceful							
friendly							
gentle							
helpful							
honest							
humorous							
imaginative							
independent							
intelligent							
inventive							
logical							
loyal							
mature							
meticulous							
optimistic							
organized							
original							

	home & family	volunteer work	school/education	recreation/leisure	paid work	other	TOTAL
patient							
persistent							
planful							
poised							
practical							
precise							
punctual							
quick							
realistic							
relaxed							
resourceful							
responsible							
sensitive							
sociable							
spontaneous							
stable							
strong							
tactful							
thorough							
thoughtful							
tolerant							
trustworthy							
versatile							
warm							
Others?							

Now select ten high-scoring personal traits which you believe describe you well, and enter them here:

_____   _____

_____   _____

_____   _____

_____   _____

_____   _____

Your Work Content Skills

For each accomplishment, identify skills you used that were specific to the situation. For example, work content skills used by the woman whose story appeared under "Home and Family" above were arranging for a home improvement loan, soliciting bids, compiling lists of desired features and construction materials, choosing an architect, and overseeing labor. Remember, these skills have to do specifically with the content of the situation.

Note the work content skills you used in each of your accomplishments.

YOUR WORK CONTENT SKILLS

Home and Family: _____

_____

_____

_____

Volunteer Work: _____

_____

_____

_____

YOUR WORK CONTENT SKILLS *(continued)*

School/Education: _____

_____

_____

_____

Recreation/Leisure: _____

_____

_____

_____

Paid Work: _____

_____

_____

_____

Any Other Accomplishment: _____

_____

_____

_____

PUT IT ALL TOGETHER:
YOUR SELF-KNOWLEDGE SYNOPSIS

In the last five chapters you've collected a tremendous amount of valuable information about yourself. You have produced lists of roles, values, interests, abilities, and skills. Here we provide a place for you to summarize that information, and some suggestions as to how you might begin to synthesize and use what you've learned about yourself.

After you've filled it in, quickly review all the information contained in the Self-Knowledge Synopsis and form an intuitive impression of the type of job and lifestyle that would fit you. Ideally, the work you do should integrate your skills and interests in settings that match your values. Are there some abilities that might be turned into skills in your interest areas?

SELF-KNOWLEDGE SYNOPSIS

Enter here the three roles you prefer most from those listed in Chapter 6 (pg. 59).

_____

_____

_____

Enter here the major interests you listed at the end of Chapter 8 (pg. 87).

_____

_____

_____

_____

_____

_____

Enter here the highlight skills you listed at the end of each checklist in the "Basic Skills" section of this chapter:

_____

_____

_____

_____

_____

_____

_____

_____

_____

_____

Enter here, in rank order, the five key work values you listed in Chapter 7 (pg. 71).

_____

_____

_____

_____

_____

Enter here the abilities you listed in Chapter 9 (pg. 93).

_____

_____

_____

_____

_____

_____

_____

Enter here your top three interest categories from Chapter 8 (pg. 83).

_____

_____

_____

Enter here your top three basic skills categories from this chapter:

_____

_____

_____

To imagine new roles that might facilitate or complement a work choice, return to the "Live Through a Day In The Future" exercise at the end of Chapter 6. Try it again with your new understanding of yourself. Free yourself to get in touch with your deepest intuitions.

Now we move out into an exploration of the opportunities that await you as you seek to fulfill the self you have discovered. Take a breather, congratulate yourself on what you've accomplished so far, and then plunge on!

HIGHLIGHTS

- ☐ Skills are the basic building blocks of careers.

- ☐ Your skills are of three types:
  — basic transferable skills
  — personal skills or attributes
  — work content skills

- ☐ They show up in all areas of your life:
  — family and home
  — volunteer work
  — school and education
  — leisure and recreation
  — paid work

- ☐ You can create new roles for yourself by turning abilities into skills in areas that interest you and match your values.

RESOURCES

Barnett, R. C. and Baruch, G. K. *The Competent Woman: Perspectives on Development.* New York: Irvington Publishers, 1978.

Competence, the ability to interact effectively with the environment, is the focus of this book which includes a review of literature on women's struggles to develop and exercise competence. The authors, both psychologists, discuss the nature of competence, what is known about successful women, family influences, the influences of the schools, and the literature on attribution theory. They present both the costs and rewards of accomplishment.

Bolles, R. N. *The Quick Job-Hunting Map (advanced version).* Berkeley, CA: Ten Speed Press, 1975.

This small booklet has a transferable skills inventory, a prioritizing grid, and six principles for helping people narrow down their focus. Also has guides for information interviews. It can be ordered separately from the publisher, or found in Appendix A of What Color Is Your Parachute?*, 1979 edition.*

Bolles, R. N. *The Quick Job-Hunting Map (beginning version).* Berkeley, CA: Ten Speed Press, 1975.

A simpler skill-list than found in the advanced version. Even though called "quick," these maps do take considerable time to complete. This beginning version can be ordered from the publisher, or found in Bolles' The Three Boxes of Life.

Ekstrom, R. B., Harris, A. M. and Lockheed, M. *How to Get College Credit For What You Learned as a Homemaker and Volunteer.* Princeton, NJ: Educational Testing Service, 1977.

This book not only gives information for turning life experiences into college credit, it also lists skills typically found in homemaking and volunteering activities.

DISCOVERING WORK OPPORTUNITIES

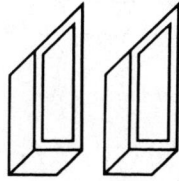

IDENTIFYING JOBS TO INVESTIGATE

In a world where there is so much
to be done, I felt strongly impressed
that there must be something for me to do.

Dorothea Dix,
Letters From New York

*N*OW that you have established a firm foundation of self-knowledge, you are ready to move with confidence into the task of identifying opportunities to express your strengths in useful and fulfilling work. If you approach this section with openmindedness, you may discover possibilities for yourself that haven't occurred to you before.

Most of us are limited in our knowledge about jobs and job fields. We've expanded our awareness beyond the old jump rope rhyme, "Doctor, lawyer, merchant, chief; tinker, tailor, beggar, thief," but almost all of us need to explore more widely than we do. The purpose of this chapter is to give you a chance to do just that. Specifically, you will learn

- ☐ how careers are built on skills
- ☐ which of a wide variety of jobs match your interests and skills
- ☐ how to use trend forecasts and information about fields which are especially opening up for women

CAREERS ARE BUILT ON SKILLS

How do you go about translating the skills you've discovered you have (or would like to develop) into a career? You can think about careers as building on skills in the following manner. A number of *skills* are used in performing a *task*. A number of tasks must be completed in performing a *job*. A wide variety of jobs can be performed relating to one *field* of human endeavor. Your career starts when you choose a field and locate a job within that field whose tasks require the skills and interests you possess.

For example, suppose you are interested in a writing career. First you must choose a field. Are you more interested in creative writing, in which case the field of arts and entertainment might yield a satisfying job, or in realistic, factual writing, in which case the field of communications might fit you better? Then you must find a job within your chosen field: if communications, will you work for a journal, book publisher, newspaper, magazine, public relations department? The types of tasks you will perform depend on the job: if you take a job as a newspaper reporter assigned to the business and financial news, you will be attending meetings, contacting business leaders, studying financial trends, and writing articles. Each of these tasks will engage a number of your skills: writing articles uses the skills of analyzing, researching, conceptualizing, synthesizing, informing, and operating a typewriter.

From this scheme you can see that if you overlook some fields in considering your possibilities, you will not explore a large number of potential jobs and will narrow your options unnecessarily. For this reason we encourage you at this point to be open to identifying possibilities that extend beyond the range of your everyday experience. To stimulate you to do this we have designed a device called the Job Possibility Guide.

HOW TO USE THE JOB POSSIBILITY GUIDE

The Job Possibility Guide will help you identify fields and jobs which may best match your skills and interests. We have broken it down into the six categories you became familiar with in the interests and skills chapters. Within each category we have listed fourteen job fields which we believe map the work world. Within each field we have listed a number of jobs corresponding to the particular interests/skills category under consideration.

Actually, few people or jobs correspond to pure code types. For example, in the writing example used above, the job of a business/financial news reporter is neither purely investigative nor purely artistic but requires skills and interests from both categories. Some of the tasks of a reporter also rely on conventional skills.

An adequate description of either a person or a job usually requires a combination of three codes. The lists in the Job Possibility Guide are mainly common sense, are based on averages among people, and must not be seen as absolute truth. You should therefore use the Guide to suggest a number of possibilities for further investigation while realizing these will be approximations and that your fit with a particular job will depend upon the specifics of that job.

Search Your Top Categories

To use the Job Possibility Guide, first enter your top interests and skills categories from the Self-Knowledge Synopsis at the end of Chapter 10 here:

	Interests	Skills
Highest		
Second Highest		
Third Highest		

Now read through all the jobs listed in the Job Possibility Guide under your top interests/skills category. If your top interests category is different from your top skills category, as it may well be, you will want to scan the lists under both categories in the Guide. Underline those jobs that you want to explore further. Notice if the jobs in your top category or categories tend to cluster in just a few fields. If so, circle these fields to remind yourself to investigate them further for additional related jobs not listed in the Job Possibility Guide.

Then repeat this process for your second and third highest interests/skills categories. As you skim the fields and job titles, keep in mind the reality factors of your situation, taking into account your educational background, your family, financial, geographical, and community resources and constraints. You can't be a ticket agent if the train doesn't stop in your town (but you could be a ticket agent at the bus depot).

Remembering that your objective here is to select those jobs that you want to research further, we suggest that you focus on those categories in which you are most interested. If your skills categories don't match, concentrate on those interest categories in which you have abilities that you can develop into skills through further education or training. For example, Elizabeth Hilton, a forty-three-year-old homemaker who was eager to re-enter paid work, completed her categories chart as follows:

	Interests	Skills
Highest	Investigative	Investigative
Second Highest	Artistic	Conventional
Third Highest	Social	Social

Since her strongest interests/skills category was Investigative, she scanned that section of the Guide. When it came to her second highest category, she realized that she had strong interests, but not strong skills, in the Artistic category. She thought she might consider training in an Artistic skill, especially writing, if she could combine this with her Investigative interests and skills. Therefore, she wrote down jobs in the Communications field, such as technical writer, journal editor, reporter, free-lance writer, media specialist.

If you find it difficult and frustrating to resolve mismatches in your skills and interests by yourself, we suggest you consult a counseling psychologist or vocational counselor. This person can give you an objective assessment of the self-knowledge you have gained thus far, and can suggest vocational tests and inventories to compare with your subjective self-assessments. Refer to Appendix A for suggestions on selecting individual or group counseling.

Consider a Variety of Possibilities

Among the 900 different jobs listed in the Job Possibility Guide, you'll find opportunities corresponding to the whole range of educational backgrounds, in the professions and trades, in traditional jobs and non-traditional jobs. These are not all the existing jobs, but they are broadly representative of jobs across all fields.

As you underline the jobs that sound appealing to you in light of all you've discovered about yourself, be sure to include a broad range of possibilities. Your inclination may be to do just the opposite, to stick to a small number of possibilities in "safe" fields. When you do this you unnecessarily restrict your options and run the risk of omitting from consideration jobs that may prove very interesting once you get further information about them. Recognize that feeling some anxiety about exploring a broad range of possibilities is normal.

Be especially careful not to rule out non-traditional jobs just because you know nothing about them or have an unpleasant stereotype of them.

The more you learn about them, the more appealing they may sound. As you underline job titles you may be doing a lot of guessing about job content, but that's okay at this point. Right now it's better to err in the direction of including too many jobs rather than too few.

JOB POSSIBILITY GUIDE
Realistic

ARTS/ENTERTAINMENT/MUSIC:

museum technician, commercial artist, display worker, industrial designer, sound effects technician, sign painter, string instrument repairer, band instrument repairer, fitter, teleprompter, jeweler, weaver, knitter, drafter, art restorer

BUSINESS RELATIONS/OFFICE:

office machine operator, postal clerk, shipping and receiving clerk, stock clerk, stenographer, typist, computer operator, file clerk, bill collector, repossessor, employee benefits approver, billing machine operator

COMMUNICATIONS:

printing press operator, photoengraver, lithographic worker, photographic laboratory worker, motion picture projectionist, broadcast technician, radio operator, telephone communications technician, bookbinder, film processor, offset plate-maker, technician, telephone servicer, offset cameraperson

CONSTRUCTION:

asbestos and insulating worker, bricklayer, carpenter, cement mason, construction laborer, electrician, floor covering installer, glazier, lather, marble setter, machinery operator, painter and paperhanger, plasterer, housepainter, plumber and pipefitter, roofer, sheet metal worker, stonemason, structural/ornamental and reinforcing iron worker, rigger, machine mover, building inspector, dry wall finisher, dry wall taper, electrical wirer, shipfitter

EDUCATION/SOCIAL SERVICE/SOCIAL SCIENCE:

driving or flying instructor, masseur, individual or group sports instructor, physical education teacher, vocational agriculture teacher, industrial arts teacher, vocational school teacher

ENGINEERING/SCIENCE/TECHNICAL:

forester, cartographer, city planner, forestry aide, broadcast technician, engineering and science technician, food processing technician, tool designer, aerial photographer, cheese maker, taxidermist, recycling operator, water treatment plant operator, mechanical tester, engineer (aeronautical, civil, industrial, mechanical, metallurgical, agricultural, mining), airplane navigator, airplane pilot, electronic technician, wood technologist, engineering aide

FARMING/OUTDOOR/FORESTRY:

farmer, tree surgeon, tree trimmer, landscaper, bee keeper, technician, gardener, plant health technician, plant "sitter," diver, crop duster, water well driller, commercial flower producer, hunting and fishing guide, prospector, groundskeeper, blacksmith, parking meter collector, wildlife attendant, animal groomer, range manager, horticulturist, park naturalist, fish and game warden, zookeeper, nursery manager, naturalist, forester

HEALTH/MEDICINE:

medical laboratory technologist, medical records administrator, x-ray technologist, pharmacist, sanitarian, veterinarian, occupational therapist, dental hygienist, dentist, physical therapist, medical laboratory worker, medical record technician/clerk, veterinary assistant, respiratory therapy technician, nurse (LPN), electrocardiograph technician, electroencephalograph technician, medical assistant, optometric assistant, occupational therapy assistant, physical therapy assistant, operating room technician, embalmer

HOSPITALITY/RECREATION/SPORTS:

lifeguard, karate instructor, physical fitness instructor, athlete

INDUSTRIAL/MACHINE/REPAIRERS/OPERATORS:

safety supervisor, machine tool worker, set up worker, tool and die maker, instrument maker, assembler, auto painter, blacksmith, electro–operator, furniture upholsterer, inspector, power truck operator, stationary engineer, waste water treatment plant operator, telephone installer and repairer, air conditioning/heating/refrigeration mechanic, appliance repairer, auto body repairer, auto mechanic, boat motor mechanic, business machine repairer, farm equipment mechanic, industrial machine repairer, instrument repairer, jewelry repairer, locksmith, maintenance electrician, motorcycle mechanic, piano and organ tuner and repairer, TV and radio service technician, truck and bus mechanic, vending machine mechanic, watch repairer, welder and oxygen arc cutter, airplane mechanic, typewriter repairer, kiln attendant, watch repairer, computer service technician, diesel mechanic, electric sign repairer

MANUFACTURING/CRAFTWORK:

patternmaker, molder, coremaker, inspector, millwright, sewing machine operator, dental technician, shoe repairer, watch repairer, clock maker, taxidermist, furniture refinisher, wood finisher, cabinetmaker, bookbinder, upholsterer, apparel presser, mapper, plant attendant, dressmaker, garment cutter, model maker, weaver, knitter

MARKETING AND SALES:

auto parts salesperson, gasoline service station attendant, automobile sales worker, marker, labeler

SERVICE, PUBLIC/PERSONAL:

building custodian, pest controller, cook and chef, private household worker, firefighter, mail carrier, telephone operator, beautician, bartender, animal trainer, hair transplanter, electrologist, caretaker, meat cutter, baker, appliance demonstrator, maid, postmaster, meter reader, manicurist, cafeteria worker, caterer, trash hauler, security guard, solid waste systems manager, attendant (hat check), highway patrol officer, detective, police officer, armed services officer

TRANSPORTATION:

aircraft mechanic, auto mechanic, air traffic controller, flight engineer, pilot, co-pilot, brake operator, bridge and building worker, locomotive engineer, locomotive firer, telegrapher, telephone and tower worker, inter-city bus driver, local transit bus driver, local truck driver, long distance truck driver, parking attendant, taxi driver, locomotive conductor, station agent, chauffeur, drivers license examiner, delivery person, messenger, elevator operator, route driver, shuttle service driver

Investigative

ARTS/ENTERTAINMENT/MUSIC:

scriptwriter, dramatic reader, gag writer, motion picture narrator, art critic, music critic, theater critic, book critic, comedy writer, picture editor, scientific photographer

BUSINESS RELATIONS/OFFICE:

abstract writer, publisher, law clerk, law librarian, patent lawyer, probate lawyer, real estate lawyer, literary agent, patent examiner, legal assistant

COMMUNICATIONS:

technical writer, language interpreter, newspaper reporter, journal editor, biographer, collaborator, columnist, essayist, manager of news/special events/public affairs, news analyst, public lecturer, public relations director, free lance writer, translator, proposal writer, organizational newsletter editor, book reviewer, commercial writer, specification writer

CONSTRUCTION:

EDUCATION/SOCIAL SERVICE/SOCIAL SCIENCE:

research assistant, social scientist, English teacher, anthropologist, economist, geographer, historian, political scientist, sociologist, archivist, librarian, genealogist, social psychologist, college professor, experimental psychologist, counseling psychologist

ENGINEERING/SCIENCE/TECHNICAL:

statistician, job analyst, biostatistician, chemical engineer, electrical engineer, biomedical engineer, biophysicist, electronics technician, biologist, mathematician, physical scientist, experimental psychologist, scientific researcher, chemist, geologist, metallurgist, geophysicist, meteorologist, oceanographer, biochemist, soil scientist, physicist, zoologist, botanist, spectroscopist, entomologist, geneticist, inventor, airplane navigator, astronomer, food scientist, geographer, seismologist, environmental analyst, veterinarian

FARMING/OUTDOOR/FORESTRY:

agronomist, forest ecologist, horticulturist, plant breeder, soil conservationist, animal breeder

HEALTH/MEDICINE:

public health nurse, speech pathologist, medical librarian, physician, bacteriologist, endocrinologist, hospital pharmacist, internist, pathologist, dentist, pediatrician, optometrist, physician, medical technologist, surgeon, registered nurse, chiropractor, osteopathic physician, anesthesiologist, clinical psychologist, nurse practitioner, veterinarian, medical technologist, medical laboratory technician

HOSPITALITY/RECREATION/SPORTS:

sports announcer, sports editor

INDUSTRIAL/MACHINE/REPAIRERS/OPERATORS:

MANUFACTURING/CRAFTWORK:

MARKETING AND SALES:

book seller, direct mail specialist, market research analyst, marketing researcher

SERVICE, PUBLIC/PERSONAL:

detective, polygraph examiner

TRANSPORTATION:

Artistic

ARTS/ENTERTAINMENT/MUSIC:

interior decorator, theater stage manager, floral designer, composer, artist, entertainer, actor/actress, musician, singer, dancer, clothes designer, costume designer, fashion model, sculptor, musical arranger, photographer, potter, film maker, makeup artist, scenic designer, portrait painter, fabric designer, art restorer, calligrapher, spinner, gift wrapper, pet photographer, fashion design sketcher, style consultant, choreographer, puppeteer, repairer and restorer of art pieces, greeting card designer, needlecraft worker, orchestra conductor, lyricist/composer, playwright, novelist, poet, short story writer, clown, magician, jewelry designer and maker

BUSINESS RELATIONS/OFFICE:

advertising executive, art museum director, curator, cataloger, commercial artist, florist, antique dealer, advertising layout artist, decorating consultant, concert manager, store window designer, display designer, art director, creative director

COMMUNICATIONS:

scientific illustrator, author, librarian, reporter, producer, illustrator, free-lance writer, media specialist, photographer, fashion reporter, TV and radio caster, TV and radio programmer, TV and radio promotor, voice-over performer, TV cameraperson, TV and radio announcer, children's book writer, screen writer, copywriter, critic, cartoonist, photojournalist, disc jockey, narrator

CONSTRUCTION:

metal sculptor, historic house preservationist, hand carver

EDUCATION/SOCIAL SERVICE/SOCIAL SCIENCE:

dancing teacher, sewing teacher, craft teacher, makeup application teacher, music librarian, music historian/recorder, art teacher, language teacher, music teacher, educational film maker, media specialist, dramatics coach, choral director, art or music therapist, English teacher

ENGINEERING/SCIENCE/TECHNICAL:

model builder, graphic designer, sign letterer and designer, technical artist and illustrator, compositor, architect, landscape architect

FARMING/OUTDOOR/FORESTRY:

flytier, landscape gardener, taxidermist, naturalist

HEALTH/MEDICINE:

medical illustrator, medical photographer, occupational therapist, orthotist/prosthetist technician, occupational therapist assistant, music therapist

HOSPITALITY/RECREATION/SPORTS:

sports photographer

INDUSTRIAL/MACHINE/REPAIRERS/OPERATORS:

industrial designer, industrial photographer, engraver, typesetter, typographer, linotype operator, printmaker

MANUFACTURING/CRAFTWORK:

drafter, leather craftsperson, weaver, wood craftsperson, dressmaker, glassblower, knitter, tailor, product designer, metal craftsperson, toy designer, game inventor

MARKETING AND SALES:

music salesperson, artists' agent, literary agent

SERVICE, PUBLIC/PERSONAL:

cake decorator, personal shopper, theatrical dresser, interpreter for the deaf

TRANSPORTATION:

flight attendant

Social

ARTS/ENTERTAINMENT/MUSIC:

music instructor, dramatic coach, tour guide

BUSINESS RELATIONS/OFFICE:

hotel front office clerk, receptionist, bank teller, customer relations expert, information giver, social secretary, industrial tour director, employee counselor

COMMUNICATIONS:

page

CONSTRUCTION:

EDUCATION/SOCIAL SERVICE/SOCIAL SCIENCE:

teacher aide, caterer, dormitory director, homemaking skills teacher, adult education teacher, vocational/technical teacher, art therapist, music therapist, dance therapist, home demonstration agent, physical education teacher, Christian education director, elementary teacher, teaching nun, home economics teacher, rehabilitation counselor, marriage counselor, school psychologist, teacher of handicapped, community health educator, chemical dependency counselor, correspondence school instructor, director of religious activities, home economist, minister, rabbi, priest

ENGINEERING/SCIENCE/TECHNICAL:

vocational training instructor

FARMING/OUTDOOR/FORESTRY:

county agricultural agent, Four H-Club agent, extension service specialist

HEALTH/MEDICINE:

public health nurse, registered nurse, hospital patient representative, medical social worker, recreational therapist, occupational therapist, physical therapist, physical therapy assistant, nurse (LPN), nursing aide/orderly, occupational therapy assistant

HOSPITALITY/RECREATION/SPORTS:

restaurant manager, hostess, tour guide, travel counselor, usher, social director, physical fitness instructor, sports instructor (skating, swimming, skiing, etc.), ski patroller, caterer, camp counselor, recreation leader

INDUSTRIAL/MACHINE/REPAIRERS/OPERATORS:

MANUFACTURING/CRAFTWORK:

MARKETING AND SALES:

SERVICE, PUBLIC/PERSONAL:

social worker, parole officer, welfare worker, case aide, case worker, correction officer, residence counselor, employment counselor, hotel housekeeper, waitress/waiter, barber, beautician, child care assistant, bellhop, bellcaptain, foster parent, homemaker, domestic, wedding consultant, governess, paid companion, houseparent, travel companion, day care provider

TRANSPORTATION:

flight attendant

Enterprising

ARTS/ENTERTAINMENT/MUSIC:

museum director, museum education director, interior designer, art dealer, stage director, disc jockey, fashion show producer, entertainer's agent, fashion coordinator, TV hostess, literary agent

BUSINESS RELATIONS/OFFICE:

corporation lawyer, personnel worker, FBI special agent, florist dealer, Chamber of Commerce executive, department store manager, personnel consultant, director, employment manager, agribusiness manager, banker, manager, public relations worker, industrial relations consultant, small business owner, business broker, business agent, training director, criminal lawyer, interviewer, bank officer, corporate community service director, women's style shop manager, receptionist, hotel/motel manager, beauty shop manager, food service manager, courtroom stenographer, credit manager, political campaign manager, press agent, funeral director, restaurant proprietor, personnel clerk, store detective, resort owner, fund raiser, apartment house manager, lobbyist, investment fund manager

COMMUNICATIONS:

literary agent, publicity director, telephone solicitor, foreign correspondent, TV or radio announcer, legislative lobbyist, television producer, trainer in writing and speaking, news commentator

CONSTRUCTION:

building superintendent, apartment house manager, general contractor, sales representative (building equipment and supplies)

EDUCATION/SOCIAL SERVICE/SOCIAL SCIENCE:

college student personnel worker, school principal, superintendent, vocational counselor, YWCA staff, guidance counselor, social science teacher, home economics teacher, business education teacher, college career planning and placement counselor, missionary, training director, program director

ENGINEERING/SCIENCE/TECHNICAL:

industrial psychologist

FARMING/OUTDOOR/FORESTRY:

extension agent, outdoor leader/guide, agricultural sales representative

HEALTH/MEDICINE:

hospital administrator, food service administrator, embalmer, pharmacist, volunteer coordinator, natural foods salesperson, natural cosmetics salesperson, pharmaceutical salesperson, dental and medical equipment and supplies salesperson

HOSPITALITY/RECREATION/SPORTS:

athletic director, playground director, recreation leader, professional athlete, coach/instructor, manager of recreation establishment, umpire, camp counselor, party/catering planner, convention planner, demonstrator, sports official

INDUSTRIAL/MACHINE/REPAIRERS/OPERATORS:

sales representative (computer and edp systems, industrial machinery, precision instruments)

MANUFACTURING/CRAFTWORK:

production coordinator, salary and wage administrator

MARKETING AND SALES:

buyer, purchasing agent, securities salesworker, property rental agent, insurance sales, real estate sales, life insurance agent, real estate agent, retailer, computer sales, manufacturer's representative, sales manager, department store sales clerk, wholesale trade salesworker, sales promoter, auctioneer, sales director, market researcher, sales support staff

SERVICE, PUBLIC/PERSONAL:

manager child care center, public administrator, legislator, consumer protection agent, safety educator, elected official, army officer, police officer, highway patrol officer, waiter/waitress, funeral director, beautician, executive housekeeper, child caretaker, consumer advocate, court baliff, personal shopper, institutional beautician, personal hairdresser, make-up technician, estate planner

TRANSPORTATION:

travel agent, reservation agent, travel bureau manager, traffic agent, guide, traffic clerk, club travel arranger .

Conventional

ART/ENTERTAINMENT/MUSIC:

film editor, film librarian, script reader

BUSINESS RELATIONS/OFFICE:

accountant, bookkeeper, bank cashier/teller, computer operator, keypunch operator, office clerk, office manager, statistical clerk, quality control manager, payroll clerk, cashier, computer programmer, accountant (CPA), systems analyst, actuary, claim examiner, underwriter, credit official, purchasing agent, budget reviewer, financial analyst, cost estimator, bank examiner, tax expert, mortgage specialist, controller, credit investigator, escrow officer, estate planner, revenue agent, title examiner, stockbroker, trust officer, statistician, court reporter, IRS agent, tax auditor, receptionist, title and contract searcher, secretary, public stenographer, filing clerk, typist, legal secretary

COMMUNICATIONS:

scientific illustrator, science information specialist, radio engineer, index editor, ground radio operator, teletypist, estimator (book publishing), cryptanalyst, book editor, manuscript reader, handbook writer, service publication writer, rewriter, proofreader, copywriter, greeting card editor, editorial assistant, copyreader, communication center operator, radio dispatcher, telegrapher

CONSTRUCTION:

crew scheduler

EDUCATION/SOCIAL SERVICE/SOCIAL SCIENCE:

demographer, math/science teacher, health educator, business education teacher, library assistant, bookmobile librarian, financial aid counselor, eligibility worker, braille transcriber

ENGINEERING/SCIENCE/TECHNICAL:

drafter, surveyor, assayer, biological aide, research aide, mathematical technician, model maker, psychometrist, dietitian, statistician, cartographer

FARMING/OUTDOOR/FORESTRY:

range manager, soil conservationist, park ranger, animal health technician, husbandry specialist, ecology technician, breeder, conservation officer, fire lookout

HEALTH/MEDICINE:

laboratory assistant, respiratory therapy technician, dental assistant, hospital records clerk, optician, optical technician, cytotechnologist, hematology technologist, food inspector, histology technician, dietetic assistant, orthopedic assistant, ophthalmology technician, dental hygienist, pharmacist, audiologist, blood bank technologist, cytologist, biometrist, mortician, hospital admitting clerk, hospital librarian, medical secretary, medical records administrator

HOSPITALITY/RECREATION/SPORTS:

caterer, recreation facility attendant, travel counselor

INDUSTRIAL/MACHINE/REPAIRERS/OPERATORS:

printer, instruction manual writer, typesetter

MANUFACTURING/CRAFTWORK:

production planner, inventory controller, trade or technical editor

MARKETING AND SALES:

property appraiser, agricultural commodities inspector, pharmaceutical salesperson, appraiser, examiner (tariff and schedules), securities trader, market analyst, convention manager, merchandise manager

SERVICE, PUBLIC/PERSONAL:

budget counselor, court clerk, answering service worker, license clerk, registrar, directory assistance operator, telephone operator

TRANSPORTATION:

customs inspector, customs agent, traffic manager, safety program coordinator, station agent (railroad), drivers license examiner, dispatcher, reservations agent

USE TREND INFORMATION

You can use job trend forecasts and information about fields in which women are presently underrepresented to suggest additional job possibilities related to your skills and interests. This type of information can also help you determine which of the possibilities you've underlined in the Job Possibility Guide may have the best prospects for openings, earnings, and advancement.

Job Trend Forecasts

Job openings occur in any industry either as a result of people leaving those jobs or as a result of growth in the industry. Job trend forecasts attempt to predict these changes. Forecasts for the '80s predict that health occupations will enjoy the strongest growth in number of jobs available, followed by technical jobs. If any of the jobs you have underlined are in these fields, they merit your further consideration. If not, you may want to scan again the lists headed "Engineering/Science/Technical" and "Health/Medicine" under your highest categories in the Guide.

Whether or not your skills or interests lie in these areas, consult the *Occupational Outlook Handbook* and the *Occupational Outlook Quarterly,* described in the Resources section of this chapter, for trend information on the fields where you find a fit.

Fields Where Women are Scarce

Fields where a relatively small proportion of the workers are women offer some of the best opportunities today in terms of number of openings for women, possibilities for advancement, and level of earnings. The chart on the next page indicates occupations where women are underrepresented.

Women represent small percentages of the labor force in construction trades, skilled crafts, technical fields, science, law, engineering, medicine, commercial banking, hotel and restaurant management, and in higher-level jobs in many other fields. Because of Affirmative Action quotas, employers are increasingly interested in hiring women for these fields. If any of the jobs you underlined are in these fields, they merit further research. If not, scan your highest categories again with these facts in mind.

The Ripest Jobs and Fields   The ripest jobs and fields for you to research further are those that are growing *and* where women are presently underrepresented. They include the following:

> *Business*
>
> banking, computer programming, word and data processing, health care administration, law, insurance, management, stock brokerage, accounting

Women are underrepresented as managers and skilled craft workers

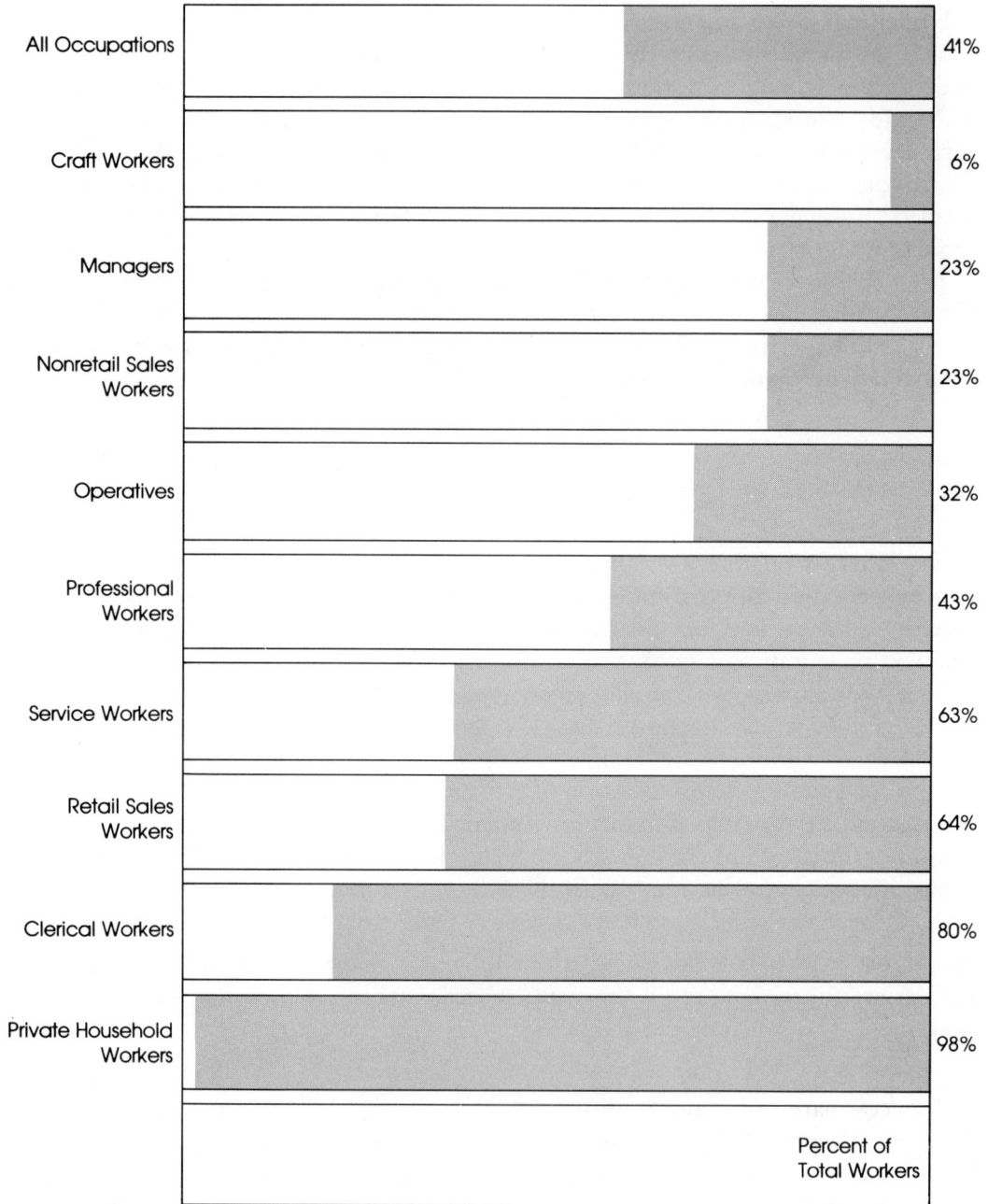

Occupation	Percent
All Occupations	41%
Craft Workers	6%
Managers	23%
Nonretail Sales Workers	23%
Operatives	32%
Professional Workers	43%
Service Workers	63%
Retail Sales Workers	64%
Clerical Workers	80%
Private Household Workers	98%

Percent of
Total Workers

Source: Prepared by the Women's Bureau, Office of the Secretary, from 1978 annual averages data published by the Bureau of Labor Statistics, U.S. Department of Labor.

Engineering/Science/Technical
electronic and environmental engineering, geology, geophysics, soil science, oceanography, marine biology, energy development, computer technology

Health/Medicine
all health professions and services

Marketing and Sales
non-retail sales

Transportation
mass transportation engineering and development

Construction
all skilled trades

If you have marked any of these fields or related jobs in the Guide, be sure to note them for further research in the next chapter. If any of your top interests/skills categories are Realistic, Enterprising, or Investigative, and you haven't included any of the above fields, do scan the lists again and underline some related possibilities.

BEGIN REFINING YOUR LIST

Because your time is limited, you will only be able to do in-depth research on a few of the many jobs you've underlined. So now you need to begin narrowing your list to the five or ten most promising jobs. One way to start is by going through your Idea Box to see if one or a few jobs or fields especially stand out. If so, you have probably underlined related jobs in the Job Possibility Guide and you will want to concentrate your research on some of these.

At this point we suggest you consult a number of survey publications which compare jobs along different factors. We've listed some in the Resources section of this chapter, and you should be able to find them in the reference section of your local library. Particularly comprehensive and useful are the four U.S. Department of Labor works we list. These survey-type guides may provide you with just enough information to eliminate some of the jobs you've underlined, or to suggest related jobs more closely matched to your interests and skills. Spending a few mornings or evenings on this task is well worth your time.

When you've narrowed your list to the five to ten most suitable jobs for further research, jot them down here. You're ready to tackle the next chapter.

JOBS YOU'D LIKE TO INVESTIGATE FURTHER

_____   _____

_____   _____

_____   _____

_____   _____

_____   _____

_____   _____

HIGHLIGHTS

□ A number of skills are used in one task, a number of tasks make up one job, a number of jobs are included in a field, and there are a number of fields to choose from as you pursue your career.

□ You can identify jobs to research further by
— searching the Job Possibility Guide for jobs that match your skills and interests
— using trend information
— skimming survey publications to quickly compare job factors

RESOURCES

Encyclopedia of Careers and Vocational Guidance, vol. II: *Careers and Occupations.* New York: Doubleday, 1978.

Contains descriptions of major kinds of occupations and industries with information on training, demand, and nature of work.

Federal Career Directory: A Guide for College Students. Washington, DC. U.S. Civil Service Commission.

Specific but relevant information about federal careers and the agencies that employ college graduates.

Lederer, M. *The Guide to Career Education.* New York: Quadrangle/New York Times Books, 1974.

Describes 200 occupations that do not require college in terms of a) job duties, b) personal, educational, and training requirements, c) what the occupation has to offer, d) points to consider before selecting this field.

Lembeck, R. *1001 Job Ideas for Today's Woman.* Garden City, NY: Doubleday Dolphin Books, 1974.

Suggests ways to work part-time, full-time, free lance, at home and in the office and as entrepreneur. Contains biographies and illustrations of working women of all ages.

Lieberman, L. *What Can I Be: A Guide to 525 Liberal Arts and Business Careers.* New Rochelle, NY: Martin Bruce, Ph.D., Publishers, 1976.

Lists 525 careers by related majors, level of education, and required competencies working with data, people, and things. Has list of professional associations and government agencies that provide career information.

The U. S. Department of Labor is a valuable source of survey-type publications. The definitive works are:

The Occupational Outlook Handbook

Published biannually, this publication groups occupations in thirteen clusters and describes about 300 jobs. It contains information on the nature of the work, national job trends and forecasts, training requirements, earnings, working conditions, and places to write for additional information.

The Occupational Outlook Quarterly

This contains even more information, especially on new jobs. In the Spring 1980 issue, "The Job Outlook in Brief" summarizes prospects for employment throughout the 1980s in 250 occupations.

The Dictionary of Occupational Titles

> *Contains alphabetically-arranged listings of over 20,000 separate occupations. Training time, aptitudes, interests, temperaments, physical demands, working conditions, industry, and work performed are compared. Be sure to read the introduction before using this volume.*

The Guide for Occupational Exploration

> *This extremely useful book summarizes twelve broad interest areas in the world of work. These twelve areas are broken down into work groups and subgroups under which 12,000 specific jobs are listed and numerically coded and cross-referenced to the Dictionary of Occupational Titles. The body of the book is devoted to describing job requirements in each of the areas, including the aptitudes, skills, and training needed to get into and perform a specific job. Since this and other occupational guides each categorize occupations somewhat differently, be careful to use the instructions given by each resource.*

U.S. Department of Labor, Bureau of Labor Statistics publications. Request a list of minimal cost reprints about job opportunities from: U.S. Department of Labor, Bureau of Labor Statistics Occupational Outlook Service, GAO Building, Washington, DC 20212. Examples include:

> *Jobs For Which High School Education Is Usually Required*
>
> *Jobs For Which A College Education Is Usually Required*
>
> *Health Careers Without a College Degree*

Zambrano, A. L., and Entine, A. D. *A Guide to Career Alternatives for Academics.* New Rochelle, NY: Change Magazine Press, 1976.

> *A 35-page booklet directed to college teachers and administrators, since the supply of PhD's will exceed the demand for the foreseeable future. Briefly discusses transition from academia, writing a resume, where to look, interviewing, and some careers to consider.*

12

LEARNING TO RESEARCH A JOB

We have so many ideas

about things we have never tried.

Maud Younger, *McClure's Magazine* 1907

N*ow* your research shifts into high gear as you focus on those jobs you identified as prime candidates for consideration in the last chapter. The point of researching these few jobs in depth is to equip yourself to start your job search with a firm grasp of which jobs are likely to be available and how well they are likely to fit you. Remember, information is power—the power to make reasonably knowledgeable decisions!

In this chapter you will learn

☐   what type of information to look for

☐   how to go about finding it

WHAT YOU NEED TO KNOW

We provide here a list of basic questions that you should have in mind as you research each job on your list and related jobs that you hear about. Some of these questions will be much more relevant than others to your own situation, so star them and be sure to answer them.

Content of the job

What is the nature of the work in this job? What are the specific job duties performed on a typical day? (If there is a typical day!)

Do employees work primarily with people, data, or things—or some combination of these? What different age groups (or other populations) can people work with in this job?

What are the primary goals which workers in this job are trying to accomplish?

What kinds of skills or abilities are needed in the work? Distinguish between what is desirable and what is indispensable.

What kinds of interests are important for this work?

Are there any physical attributes needed in this work? Distinguish between what is desirable and what is indispensable.

Are there any physical or personal attributes that might make it difficult for you to do the work?

Does the typical worker have a set schedule or are the hours flexible?

Are there part-time job opportunities?

What are the different work settings in which people in this job may work? (e.g., large corporation, public school, retail shop, etc.)

What is the salary range?

Preparation for the job

Which educational programs are recommended preparation? Which specific degree or certificate is necessary and which is desirable?

Which schools or training facilities provide the necessary education and under what conditions (i.e., full-time or part-time, day or evening school, entrance requirements)? How long does this education take to complete?

Which work and/or volunteer experiences are recommended preparation? Distinguish between what is desirable and what is indispensable.

Can an individual enter this job/field solely on the basis of either education or work/volunteer experience or is some combination recommended? Distinguish between what is desirable and what is indispensable.

What steps, besides meeting education and work/volunteer requirements, are necessary to enter this occupation (e.g., union membership, exam, portfolio)?

Opportunities for advancement

What are the opportunities for advancement? Does advancement usually involve changing job positions or adding responsibilities/duties to the same position? Does advancement involve salary increase or change in job title?

What sorts of education, achievements, personal attributes, work experiences are needed for advancement and updating within this field? Distinguish between what is desirable and what is indispensable.

Job prospects

What are the current employment prospects in this job/field? What are the prospects on both a local and national level? Where are the best employment prospects?

What are the employment prospects in this field for the next ten to fifteen years on both a local and national level?

Are there any anticipated future changes in the goals, problems, skill requirements, or technology of this job? How might these changes affect the plans and training of persons interested in this job/field?

What specific difficulties and/or opportunities should a woman in a particular age range entering this field expect to encounter now? In the next ten to fifteen years?

Miscellaneous

Are there related jobs that require more or less education? How are these jobs similar and different? Does coursework completed for a beginning level educational program also apply toward more advanced degrees or does a person have to start all over again to complete a more advanced degree?

What are the names of related jobs or fields to explore?

What are some recent publications, either reprints or references, which tell about this field?

Jot down responses to these crucial questions as you consult the sources we describe next. Record your personal reactions. Making notes will help you keep important points in mind as you later compare jobs and fields.

WHERE TO FIND ANSWERS

There are many sources of information about jobs. The resources available to you may be limited by the size of your community, but no matter how much research you end up doing, you can never hope to have *all* the information about any decision. Chances are you have more than enough information readily available to you, if you know where to look.

As you seek information you may shuttle back and forth between sources, first doing some reading about a particular job, then talking to someone employed in that job, sending for information from a trade association, visiting another person in the work setting. Talking to one person may open up other resource possibilities—more people to talk to, a different set of reading material. Certain jobs may best be researched through one strategy and not others. Mix and match the following sources to meet your own needs.

Things To Read

Printed information about particular jobs is available in a variety of forms—books, magazines, newspapers, pamphlets. Cassettes, filmstrips, movies, and microfilms are also good sources of information. Libraries—public, school, college, agency—are among the best sources of these materials. Be sure to check more than one library since their emphases will vary. And don't forget the library's most valuable resource—its staff. They can direct you to resources you may not discover on your own.

Professional, industrial, and trade associations are an excellent source of current information in their fields. Write to them. There is a listing in Appendix B of 300 such organizations. National associations usually have state associations, and some even have local chapters.

The business section of your newspaper can be a valuable source of current information about jobs. And you may not have thought of your phone book as an information resource, but skimming the yellow pages will provide you with a wealth of information about occupations and employers in your own town.

A Few Tips On Using Printed Materials

Currency: Check the date. Read the most up-to-date resources, since change often comes quickly in the world of work. A statement made a few years ago may no longer apply. Remember there is a time lag in publishing the material so that the most current printed information may be a year or more old.

Accuracy: Read from several sources on each job you explore. Look for consistencies and discrepancies and use this as background for informational interviews.

Stereotyping: Some materials still contain biased information, including pictures showing serious men as engineers and executives, and smiling women as secretaries and nurses. Is the material biased about age or minority status?

Related job possibilities: As you read you may very likely come across names of other jobs you did not previously consider. Mark them down for possible follow-up.

People To Talk To

Printed information is valuable but it is very general compared to talking with persons about the jobs they do and how they feel about them. Printed information is a guided tour through the plant. Information interviewing is the behind-the-scenes view.

Information interviewing is extremely valuable because it provides you with information that is local, up-to-date, and specific. It can give you a sense of the working atmosphere and can answer your unique questions. Although this is not why you're there, information interviews may lead to actual job possibilities.

The caution in talking to people is that the information *is* a very personal view. It is important when talking to persons in a line of work to go to more than one source. The old saying holds—one woman's meat is another woman's poison. It is also important to hear everything they say, and to listen for the "almost said."

Making Contact Many of your contacts will be casual—old friends at a reunion, neighbors, relatives, a conversation at the PTA or a church picnic. You may say to a friend or co-worker, "You've spoken of your sister who is a buyer for Lotsa Clothes. I'd like to talk to her about her work. I'd like to call her one evening this week and arrange to meet her at her office or on lunch break." When you consider all the people you have known, however briefly, and all the people they know, you have a large contact network.

If you are interested in an area of work where you have no connections, it's perfectly acceptable for you to call a company asking who in the company does the kind of work in which you're interested. Say to the telephone receptionist, "I'm interested in talking to someone in your organization who can give me information about the work of a sign painter." The receptionist can put you through to someone. This may or may not be the right person, depending on the size of the company and the job experience of the receptionist. When you reach the one who seems like the appropriate person, state your desire to have about thirty minutes for an interview for the purpose of getting information, and set up a time.

It is important to state clearly that you want *information* about a field or job. You're not after a job. Most persons are interested in talking about what they do. If you get an exception to this and the person says "no," ask for referrals to other workers in that organization or another. If that doesn't work, try another organization.

There are five basic questions to ask in interviewing for information:

- What do you like about this work?
- What don't you like about this work?
- How did you get started (training, entry job, on-the-job training)?
- Who else do you know who does this kind of work or related jobs in other settings?
- What advice would you give to someone who is thinking about getting into this type of work?

Jot down additional specific questions that seem important to you from the list at the beginning of this chapter. In interviewing women who seem similar to you in family responsibilities, see if they are willing to talk to you on a more personal level about how they balance family and work. Ask how they see their being women as positive or problematic influences in that kind of job and job setting.

Asserting Yourself in Information Interviews Many people are reluctant to approach others for an information interview. It's important to remember you are *not* imposing, even on strangers, when you ask. They can say "no"; chances are they'll say "yes." Write down the statement you're going to make over the phone and use that as a prompter. It's certainly permissible to bring a list of questions to the interview as a starter. Once the interview is underway you'll find it flows smoothly and the time goes quickly.

In arranging, conducting, and following up on interviews, it is important that your attitude be positive and your behavior assertive. Assertive behavior is stating your needs, asking for what you want, and giving your viewpoint without putting down or being "pushy" with others. You may find it well worth your time to practice assertive options in an assertiveness training class or workshop in your community.

Here are a few tips on making assertive contacts in information interviewing:

- Think positively. "I have a right to make this request."
- Plan ahead. Jot a few notes to yourself and have them handy.

☐ Practice using the word "I." "I'm interested in the kind of work you do and I'd like to make an appointment to talk to you."

☐ Make the contact as personal as possible. "Betty Jones suggested you as a knowledgeable person."

☐ Respect the person's right to refuse your request. "I'm disappointed although I understand how busy you must be." At this point you may persist: "Could we find a time later—in a few weeks?" Or you may decide to move on: "I'd appreciate the names of other individuals to whom I might speak."

☐ Show up on time. Give the receptionist your name and the name of your contact: "Good morning, I'm Barbara Peterson. I have an appointment with Alice White at 9:30."

☐ Be courteous to everyone. In the interview, express your appreciation, get to the point, and state your objectives. "I appreciate your taking time to talk to me. I'm interested in hearing from you what this job is like on a day by day basis and I'm particularly interested in what you like and don't like about it."

☐ Remember why you're there and keep the interview on its proper course.

☐ Be aware of time. As your time ends, thank the person and ask if she/he can give you the names of others doing this kind of work.

☐ Follow up with a thank-you note.

An additional reminder—remember the importance of non-verbal assertive behavior:

☐ Speak clearly and distinctly.

☐ Be relaxed but alert and poised.

☐ Maintain eye contact.

☐ Be friendly but serious. Some women overdo smiling.

☐ Have a firm handshake.

Things To Do

Earlier in this chapter we mentioned checking to see if professional, industrial, and trade organizations in your interest areas have local or state chapters. If so, they may be able to give you leads to members who would be willing to speak with you, or to experiences that would help you understand the occupation. If you are already a member of such an organization, resume or continue going to their regular meetings and conventions while you are gathering information on jobs. Many "lucky" contacts are made in these meetings, but mainly it's a chance to circulate and get a sense of the issues, new developments, and future of the field.

Other arrangements you may make include visiting a job site to spend a few hours or a day in a design studio, a physical therapy unit, a production line, a television station, a police car, with a telephone repair person. You may volunteer to work in a school, a hospital, a museum, a catering service. Or you may intern for a longer period of time, paid or unpaid, to sharpen and learn the skills of a particular job. You may enroll in a class or two at a college or vocational-technical school as a way to orient yourself or try a few new skills. Later chapters in this section will help you explore options in internships, volunteer work, apprenticeships, and continuing education.

PACE YOUR RESEARCH

The three information sources we've mentioned and the examples we've given are not the only ways to go about your research. Take and make any opportunities you can to fit the pieces of your information-seeking puzzle together. Remind yourself that this research, while time-consuming, represents an investment in your career and therefore deserves your careful attention. Pace yourself to avoid becoming overwhelmed by the sheer quantity of data available.

We suggest that you employ the goal-setting strategies you learned earlier to complete this task. Allot yourself a definite amount of time, decide how much information you want to cover, and then break your research down into manageable, day-size units. It may help you to organize yourself if you fill in a Job Information Sources and Findings sheet for each job you plan to research. Make photocopies of the page we provide, one for each job.

How will you know when you're done with this phase of your research? When you know that you want to investigate further getting volunteer or internship experience, going back to school, working on an alternate schedule, or going into business for yourself—in which cases the chapters ahead will give you more information. Or when you feel ready to pull together information about yourself and the job fields you've researched, in deciding on your job objectives. In this case, go ahead to Chapter 17.

JOB INFORMATION SOURCES AND FINDINGS

for _____ (Job title)

National Organization	State Organization	Local Organization

Name: _____ _____ _____

Address: _____ _____ _____

Phone: _____ _____ _____

Contact:
Person: _____ _____ _____

Things I Can Read: Title: _____ Publication Date: _____

Title: _____ Publication Date: _____

Title: _____ Publication Date: _____

Notes:

People I Can Talk To: Name: _____ Phone # _____

Name: _____ Phone # _____

Name: _____ Phone # _____

Notes:

Things I Can Do: Job Visit (Place) _____

Volunteer/Intern Opportunities _____

Educational Courses _____

Association Meetings _____

Notes:

Related Job Possibilities: _____ , _____ , _____

HIGHLIGHTS

☐ For each of the jobs you chose to research further, gather information about
— content of the job
— preparation for the job
— opportunities for advancement
— prospects of the job

☐ Set goals and develop an information-gathering plan that includes
— things to read, for background
— people to interview, for specific and up-to-date information
— things to do in a job setting or to meet people who work in certain fields

RESOURCES

Arco Career Guidance Series, Arco Publishing Co., 219 Park Ave., New York, NY 10003

50 books, each covering a particular career (e.g., computer programming, banking, small business). $1.95 each. Request book list from Arco.

Career Guide to Professional Associations: A Directory of Organizations by Occupational Field. Cranston, RI: Carroll Press, 1980.

A directory of nearly 2,000 organizations arranged according to the occupational classifications of the Dictionary of Occupational Titles. Entries include information on addresses, career aids, occupational certification, educational/financial assistance, placement assistance, and professional awards.

Catalyst publications (Career Opportunities Series, Career Options Series for Undergraduate Women, Education Opportunities Series) by Catalyst, 14 East 60th Street, New York, NY 10022.

Each of the 27 booklets in the Career Opportunities Series describes a particular field in terms of job duties and specialization, how to prepare for a career in this field, salaries and sample jobs, part-time opportunities, job-hunting strategies. Booklets are $1.50–1.95. Write Catalyst for an order form.

Health Careers Guidebook, fourth edition, 1978. Available from Superintendent of Documents, U.S. Government Printing Office, Washington, DC 20402, Stock Number 029–000–00343–2.

> *Contains overview of the health field, information on career planning, a detailed guide on financial aid for health careers training, calendar showing time to train for particular careers. List of 150 organizations that provide career information.*

Hennig, M. and Jardim, A. *The Managerial Woman.* Garden City, NY: Doubleday, 1977.

> *Discusses rewards and costs to a woman of a management career. Explores the effect of conditioning and traditional beliefs on the attitudes of men and women towards careers, advancement, managerial responsibilities. Contains case studies of women in top management.*

Hricko, A. and Brunt, M. *Working for Your Life: A Woman's Guide to Job Health Hazards.* University of California, Berkeley, CA 94720, 1976.

> *Although many health hazards apply equally to men and women, this guide is to educate women workers about hazards and discrimination they may face in their jobs. It covers hazards in jobs which employ primarily women and those into which women are now moving. It attends to those which may adversely affect offspring of exposed workers, explains laws covering these conditions, and provides references to other materials.*

Kreinberg, N. *I'm Madly in Love with Electricity and Other Comments About Their Work by Women in Science and Engineering.* Lawrence Hall of Science, University of California, Berkeley, CA 94720.

> *This booklet includes quotes of 70 women who work for corporations, government, and colleges describing their work, opportunities, and difficulties for women.*

Kundsin, R. (ed.) *Women and Success: The Anatomy of Achievement.* New York: William Morrow and Co., 1974.

> *Twelve women professionals talk about their individual life experiences in occupations (e.g., architecture, horticulture, consumer advocacy). Other chapters deal with family attitudes, economic factors, problems of professional women.*

Lederer, M. *Blue Collar Jobs for Women: A Complete Guide to Getting Skilled and Getting a High-Paying Job in the Trades.* New York: E.P. Dutton, 1979.

This very good guide tells women what they need to know to choose a trade, get training, get a job. Eighty selected blue-collar jobs— crane operator, carpenter, surveyor, appliance repairer, etc.—are evaluated on working conditions, availability, apprenticeship opportunities, physical requirements, chances of advancement.

Rogalin, W.C. and Pell, A. *Women's Guide to Management Positions.* New York: Simon and Schuster, 1975.

A self-evaluation guide for women considering management careers in business, government, the professions. Addresses currently employed women who seek advancement, re-entry women, and recent college graduates.

Vocational Guidance Horizons Series, VGM Career Horizons, 8259 Niles Center Rd., Skokie, IL 60077.

60 books each describing a field (e.g., environmental careers, free-lance writing, etc.). Request order form from VGM.

Women in Non-traditional Occupations—A Bibliography. U.S. Office of Education, 400 Maryland Avenue S.W., Washington, DC 20202, 1976.

The three sections list overview materials, materials on women in skilled trades, and on women in professional organizations.

Women In Science and Technology, 1976. Available for $1.50 from ACT Publications, P.O. Box 168, Iowa City, IA 52240.

Describes careers in science and technology through case illustrations of employed women. Uncovers myths and realities about women in these fields.

Women's Bureau Publications. Write for brochure of current publications, to U.S. Department of Labor, Women's Bureau, Washington, DC 20210.

Examples include: Job Options for Women in the 80s, A Working Woman's Guide to Her Job Rights, Steps to Opening the Skilled Trades to Women.

13

BRIDGING THE
"EXPERIENCE WANTED"
GAP

How am I ever going to get experience
if everyone tells me that I must have it
before I begin?
Maud Younger, *McClure's Magazine* 1907

*I*F you are a homemaker, a student, or
an employee with considerable time in a particular career, your instant spec-
ulation may be that it's next to impossible to gain experience in a new field—
the "experience wanted" by a prospective employer. Or you may have been
out of your field of work for some time and wonder how to re-enter. You
can gain experience as an intern, volunteer, or apprentice to bridge this gap.

In this chapter we discuss

☐ varieties of field experience available to you

☐ the payoffs you can expect from each

☐ how to employ a goal-oriented approach to building experience

VARIETIES OF FIELD EXPERIENCE

Whatever your interests, you can gain field experience to match. You can
find or create volunteer or internship positions in the arts, communication,
education, business, government, health, religion, or having to do with
environmental issues, public interest and consumer protection, or women's
and minority issues. If you are interested in entering a skilled craft or trade,
apprenticeships are available.

Volunteer Work

Volunteer work is simply work done without pay. This is about the only attribute of volunteerism that has not changed dramatically over the past decade. The stereotype of the altruistic worker, the envelope stuffer, the white-gloved dilettante, has faded, to be replaced with the image of a professionally-oriented, socially aware, activist.

Why Volunteer? There are myriad reasons for volunteering. If you are a homemaker, you can volunteer to investigate career fields, ease back into a field you left years ago, develop contacts, build and polish job skills, and gain on-the-job experience. More and more employers are recognizing the value of this kind of work.

More than one woman has been hired by the organization she volunteered for.

> *Pat Evans had a college degree, fifteen years old, in American Studies. After years at home she was more than ready to get into paid work. What could she do with a liberal arts degree? Pat had always been interested in television production, and thought of one particular local station that developed weekly programs on topics of interest. Pat volunteered to work with one of the producers, helping her get the show put together. She typed, made phone calls, wrote script and started to interview. She began offering ideas of her own as her expertise grew. After several months, as her supervisor moved off into a new responsibility, Pat was on the spot to fill in immediately. She was the best person for the job, and she got it.*

An increasing number of women volunteer to develop a second career theme, a set of competencies for a possible career change. For example, a teacher who thinks she might eventually want to do foundation work could acquire fund-raising skills volunteering with United Way.

And volunteering can provide satisfaction complementary to that you derive in paid work or home life. You might use volunteer work as a way to extend your social relationships and interests, or to express your commitment to issues which you find personally meaningful, such as battered women, or physical fitness programs for the handicapped. For example, a computer programmer might choose to volunteer as a consumer protection advocate at a local hospital.

Some Positions Available   Volunteer positions range from the totally flexible to the totally structured. Here's a sample of the thousands of jobs filled by volunteers:

> public relations worker for a chamber orchestra
> supporting actress in a theater festival
> wildlife conservationist
> production crewperson for a public television station
> teacher of therapeutic horseback riding for the handicapped
> tutor for gifted adolescents
> coordinator for a rural library project
> counselor aide for mentally retarded adults
> environmental education teacher
> occupational health hazards advocate
> issue developer in an urban housing agency
> office manager for a religious ministry
> fund-raiser for a women's resource center
> minority-group school administrative assistant

Thousands of established volunteer programs are advertised by local and national clearinghouses. The leading volunteer agency today is the National Center for Voluntary Action, with 175 Voluntary Action Centers throughout the country. These centers maintain files on many different volunteer programs. If you have trouble locating the center nearest you write to the National Center for Voluntary Action, 1735 I Street, NW, Washington DC 20006.

Internships

Internships are structured positions designed to provide practical experience relative to a career or academic field of interest. An internship can last three months to a year; some are full-time commitments while others require only ten to twenty hours per week. Some require previous training or coursework; many others require only a willingness to work and learn. While a few pay decent salaries, most internships involve no pay or just a small expense stipend.

The Payoff For You   In an internship, you can get training and practice with new methods and equipment, check out a career decision, get current references, expand your contact network, and possibly earn credit through a local college or university. And as with volunteer work, an internship can lead to paid employment.

> *Joyce Clagston was active in student government in high school. In some ways, college was a disappointment to her because she missed "doing." She was intrigued when she heard about a six-month internship at the state legislature. She applied, was accepted, and at the end was hired into a permanent position.*

A Sample of Internships Available   Here are some typical positions that might be offered as internships:

> museum exhibit coordinator
> radio newscaster
> counselor for battered women
> researcher/reporter for a community newspaper
> research assistant for an educational public policy agency
> legislative advocate for higher education interest group
> administrative assistant to leaders in business
> accounting intern
> probation officer
> biological technician in fishery management
> job placement advisor for minority adolescents
> legal research assistant in a public interest agency
> speechwriter for government officials

See the Resources section of this chapter for a list of internship directories.

Apprenticeships

Apprenticeship is a training process in which a person learns a skilled craft or trade through on-the-job supervision and in related classroom experience. After the training the worker is known as a journeyperson. Apprentices are paid while they learn, usually at progressive rates starting at half the journeyperson's rate. Though most apprenticeships are offered in fields not traditionally entered by women, women certainly can become qualified in these jobs.

In fact, the very scarcity of women in these fields at present is a good reason to consider entering them, as we mentioned in Chapter 11. Equal Employment Opportunity in Apprenticeship regulations of the U.S. Department of Labor require sponsors to take on a certain number of women as apprentices. These are therefore excellent training opportunities for women with few marketable skills or looking for higher pay and advancement potential.

Occupations Offering Apprenticeships Following is a list of the leading occupations offering apprenticeships:

aircraft fabricator	platemaker
auto mechanic	pressperson
baker	stripper
barber	leather worker
boilermaker	machinist
bookbinder	meat cutter
brewer	patternmaker
bricklayer	operating engineer
cabinetmaker	painter, decorator, paperhanger
candymaker	photoengraver
carpenter	pipe fitter
carpet, linoleum & tile layer	plasterer
cement mason	plumber
compositor	radio & tv repairperson
cook	refrigeration & air conditioning
dental technician	mechanic
electrician	roofer
electronics technician	sheet metal worker
furrier	stationary engineer
glazier	steamfitter
grading equipment operator	stonemason
ironworker, structural	tile layer
ironworker, ornamental	tool & die maker
jeweler	truck mechanic
lather	upholsterer
lithographic photographer	wood carver

If you are interested in apprenticeship opportunities you should get in touch with your state employment service office (listed in the telephone directory) or the nearest regional office of the Bureau of Apprenticeship and Training. For general information and a list of its publications about apprenticeships, write to the Bureau of Apprenticeship and Training, Department of Labor, Washington, DC 20212.

TAKE A GOAL-ORIENTED APPROACH

No matter which form of field experience you choose, you will benefit from it most if you initiate a goal-oriented, well-organized approach to get what you want. This section will help you define your objectives and locate or create a field experience that meets these objectives.

State Your Objectives

The initial step in planning your field experience is to define your objectives. Do you want to build skills on recently-discovered abilities? Do you want to express some of your interests outside of paid work? Do you want to gain experience in a field you think suits you? At this point you may want to review your Self-Knowledge Synopsis at the end of Chapter 10 and the list of jobs to investigate in the middle of Chapter 11.

Record your field experience objectives in the following checklist.

YOUR OBJECTIVES FOR YOUR FIELD EXPERIENCE

During my field experience, I want to:

_____ Check out my interests (specify: _____
_____)

_____ Build and polish job skills (specify: _____
_____)

_____ Get training and practice with new methods and equipment
(specify: _____
_____)

_____ Get an overview of working conditions in a field (specify: _____
_____)

_____ Check out my career decision (specify: _____
_____)

_____ Expand my contact network (specify: _____
_____)

_____ Gain on-the-job experience in a promising field (specify: _____
_____)

_____ Ease back into my earlier field (specify: _____

_____)

_____ Get current references (specify: _____

_____)

_____ Other (specify: _____

_____)

While you're at it, answer these practical questions:

In what geographical areas will you consider a field experience?

_____

How many hours per week can you work? _____

How long a time commitment are you prepared to make? _____

Find or Create a Position

When you've defined your focus, you're ready to contact organizations which may accept you as an intern, volunteer, or apprentice in the kind of experience you want. You have two choices: you can investigate existing programs you find through directories and clearinghouses, or create your own.

Investigate Existing Programs   The Resources section at the end of this chapter lists some of the most comprehensive of field experiences directories. Many of these contain annotated bibliographies of specialized directories—specialized by content area or geographic region. We've also listed a few moderately specialized directories which may interest you. These directories may be available in your public library or in the career planning and placement office of your local college or university. These directories will also lead you to state, regional, or special interest internship clearinghouses. Examples are the California Advisory Commission on Youth, the Massachusetts Internship Office, the Urban Corps National Association, and the National Conference on State Legislatures.

Remember to use field experience referral resources in local colleges and in womens' resource centers. Most schools have a career planning or placement office which can help you identify a local, national, or international internship and sometimes arrange credit. Go talk with advisors in these offices even if you're not a current student. If you need student status to qualify for a particular program, you may be able to use a part-time special student or extension status.

As you skim field experience directories, make a list of opportunities which spark your enthusiasm. Since many internships have application deadlines, write or phone for information on any experience of this sort you might consider. Some have restrictive prerequisites (e.g., graduate student in public health, animal science background) while others are accessible to a broad range of applicants. Don't be unduly hesitant about checking out qualifications or applying.

Create Your Own   If you decide to create your own field experience, think beyond the directory listings. These directories outline only a part of your working possibilities. Many organizations which have typically not had interns or volunteers could be ready to utilize your help, energy, and fresh perspectives.

For example, if you've read about an exciting placement in a consumer protection agency in California, track down similar local agencies through the yellow pages, your public library, or the Chamber of Commerce. Talk to the organization's management about creating a new internship, utilizing as selling points what you've learned about established field experiences and your own skills and objectives. Likewise, if internships with the American Heart Association or Girl Scouts perk up your interest, contact local branches. An internship may already exist or you can create one.

Initiate Contact   Sending a short letter and following up with a phone call is a good initial strategy in applying for or creating a field experience. In a businesslike, assertive manner, state what you want to get out of the internship and what you can offer in return. Ask for an interview with the person who would act as your supervisor.

Interview for Information   Before your appointment gather background information about the organization, in order to both impress your interviewer and to clarify how you might fit into the organization. If your goal is to create a new internship, you must convince your interviewer that you can make a worthwhile contribution to the organization.

But remember, you are also making a decision about what that organization can do for you. So whether you're creating a new experience or applying for an established one, get answers to these questions:

☐   What will be your everyday tasks and responsibilities? Will you have a job description?

☐ Will you have any training or orientation?

☐ Is this program run by a volunteer/intern coordinator? What are the qualification of the supervisor and staff? How much time can they give you? How much can you expect to learn from them? Will you work on your own or as a member of a team?

☐ Is there a salary or expense stipend?

☐ Is any travel involved? Are there possible work-related hazards?

☐ Will you receive performance appraisals and letters of recommendation upon request?

In summary, before accepting any field placement, understand what will be expected of you and what you can expect from your experience.

Evaluate and Document Your Field Experience

While your field experience is in progress, evaluate it periodically. Are your objectives and the objectives of the organization being met? What additional action steps can you take to reach your goals?

As you complete your experience it's essential to both evaluate and document what you've done. Documentation is a must in using this experience to get a paid job, another field experience, or college credit. Even if you're not sure about your future paths, ask your supervisor for a letter reviewing your performance.

Keep your own brief evaluation of the experience. Jot down the name of the field experience, the organization, your supervisor, dates, and a description of duties. Keep lists of names of possible future contact people. Ask yourself these questions:

☐ What have you accomplished in your field experience? How do your accomplishments compare with your initial objectives?

☐ What new insights do you have about your personal interests, values, strengths, and weaknesses?

☐ What have you learned about this career field? How do your personal interests, values, and skills compare with co-workers you have met?

☐ What have you learned about this particular kind of organization/

community? How are decisions/policies made? What do you like and dislike about working in this kind of environment?

☐ What personal contacts have you developed? List names, addresses, phones.

☐ In light of your field experience, is this career field a possible option for you? What further information do you need about yourself or the field to make a decision? What is your first step in obtaining this information?

HIGHLIGHTS

☐ If you face a time or experience gap in a possible career field—an internship, apprenticeship, or volunteer position could be the way to bridge it.

☐ Defining your objectives and how they relate to your short- and long-range life plans will help you

— locate a suitable field experience position, or

— create one of your own.

☐ It is essential for you to evaluate and document your field experience.

RESOURCES

Apprenticeship and Other Blue Collar Job Opportunities for Women. Educational Equity Communications Network, 1855 Folsom St., San Francisco, CA 94103, 1978.

Offers a guide to the apprenticeship process and general information on blue collar jobs. Includes resource list and bibliography.

A Woman's Guide to Apprenticeship. The Women's Bureau, Department of Labor, Washington, DC 20213.

This guide informs about the apprenticeship system and how it operates, some background on problems women sometimes encounter, the laws governing apprenticeship, and the application process.

Comprehensive Directories

Directory of Internships—1978 Edition. Available at college bookstores or write: Career Planning Office, Haverford College, Haverford, PA 19041, Attn: NSDI.

Lists nationwide internships.

Invest Yourself, annual edition. Available from: Commission on Voluntary Service Action, 475 Riverside Dr., Rm 1700 A, New York, NY 10027.

Lists many volunteer positions around the world according to skills and type of service.

Mitchell, J. S. *STOPOUT! Working Ways to Learn.* Garrett Park, MD: Garrett Park Press, 1978.

137 ongoing internship or volunteer programs within these clusters: arts, communication, education, environment, government, health, public interest and consumer protection, religion, women and minorities.

Renetzky, A. and Schlachter, G. (eds.) *Directory of Internships, Work Experience Programs, and On-the-job Training Opportunities.* Thousand Oaks, CA: Ready Reference, 1976.

Outlines programs sponsored by government agencies, business and industry, professional associations, foundations, social and community agencies. A first supplement to this directory was published in 1978 and covers additional programs.

The Directory of Undergraduate Internship Programs, 1980. Available from National Society for Internships and Experiential Education, 1735 I St. N.W., Suite 601, Washington, DC 20006.

A comprehensive listing of specific internships throughout the US within these categories: arts, humanities, government service, journalism, natural science, social development and welfare. Each listing explains: internship objectives and duties, application procedures, and remuneration. An excellent bibliography of related directories, clearinghouses, provides access to additional internships.

The Directory of Public Service Internships: Opportunities for the Graduate, Post Graduate and Mid Career Professional, 1976.

Listing of post-college internships and fellowship opportunities throughout the United States. Available from the address above. Contains some excellent bibliographies.

Specialized Directories

Fellowships and Internship Opportunities for Federal Employees, 1976. Available from: Program Specialist, US Office of Education, Room 2117, FOB 6, Washington, DC 20202.

Lists 25 programs for federal employees who desire to develop their leadership potential.

International Directory of Youth Internships, 1977–8. Available from: United States Committee for UNICEF, 331 38th St., New York, NY 10016.

Internship/volunteer opportunities through United Nations, its agencies, and related non-governmental organizations. Most options available primarily to graduate students; some are open to undergraduates or high school students.

Murphy, T. P. *Government Management Internships and Executive Development,* 1973. Available from: Lexington Books, 125 Spring St., Lexington, MA 02173.

Details several internship programs at federal level plus more specialized programs. Includes city manager, urban internships.

The Directory of Washington Internships, annual edition. Available from: National Society for Internships and Experiential Education, 1735 I St. N.W., Suite 601, Washington, DC 20006.

Details opportunities in the Metropolitan area, primarily for undergraduate and graduate students but also includes information for high school students and mid-career professionals.

14

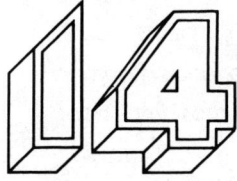

RETURNING TO SCHOOL

*I wanted to go to college
to make more money. Although I'm now eligible
for better paying jobs, what I really found
was a better understanding
of the world and other people—and most important,
myself.*

One woman who did return

*C*AN a return to school help you define or carry out your goals? An increasing number of adults, particularly adult women, are answering "yes" to this question. We will help you discover your own answer in this chapter, as we discuss

- □ reasons for returning to school
- □ how to choose an appropriate school
- □ how to find financial aid and revitalize your study skills

WHY RETURN?

As adults, we know that learning and going to school are not necessarily synonymous. There are many ways to learn: going to school is one of those ways. Perhaps school can offer you the structure and motivation you need in order to learn. Beyond that, it's important for you to be clear about what you hope to gain by returning.

Some Good Reasons

See if you can identify with any of the following possible reasons for returning to school.

To Clarify Interests Completing coursework can help you evaluate the strength of your interests. Is a particular interest really strong enough to turn into full or part-time work? Would you prefer to channel this enthusiasm into a leisure activity? On the other hand, you may discover that an option that feels right in fantasy, whether it's creative writing, counseling, or computer programming, fizzles out when you try it through an actual course or two.

Would it make sense to try out one or some of the interests you listed in Chapter 8 this way?

To Learn Skills One of the most exciting aspects of today's educational smorgasbord is the diversity of practical, skills-based courses available. Taking a few of these courses can be a way for you to learn, polish, or revitalize skills you can use in future work. You can gain hands-on experience in subjects like accounting, piano, commercial illustrating, interviewing, cooking, or technical writing, through classroom activities, homework assignments, and related field experiences.

Consider your abilities and the skill requirements in work fields that interest you. Are there new skills you would like to learn?

To Earn Credentials There are some jobs in which a credential or license is necessary: public school teacher, registered nurse, licensed psychologist, beautician, chiropractor. In other jobs, a credential is not absolutely necessary, and you can sometimes substitute experience for credentials. On the other hand, even though a credential may not be strictly required, it may be extremely helpful to have in certain jobs.

The trick is to find out how helpful or necessary a credential is in getting the kind of employment you want. Talking to people currently working in these kinds of jobs is one way to find this out. You can also check with professional organizations and employers in your field of interest for this kind of information.

To Enable Personal Growth Channeling all of your energies and intellect into motherhood, homemaking, or specialized job functions can easily narrow your horizons and even lead to boredom. Involvement in a new course and with new contacts can be a way to counteract this while building your confidence and renewing your sense of identity.

A desire to redefine yourself through learning can surface at any point in your adult life, from your twenties through your senior years. Intelligence does not decline through adulthood and people don't ever lose their capacity to learn. Sending your last child to first grade or to college, experiencing divorce or widowhood, anticipating career burnout or retirement, or having empty time on your hands—any of these can propel you back to school.

Do you feel a need to redefine yourself, to strengthen your confidence or competence? Is there anything you've always wanted to study or learn about? Listen to these two women:

> *I started working on my degree shortly after our third child was born. It took twelve years to do two years of work! I said it was because I told my parents I would finish school, but I really did it because it created space for myself. Going to school helped me say, 'I count; I have important things to do.'*

> *I hadn't talked much about returning to school. Everyone thought I was only taking a course. I knew I was more serious, that I was proving something to myself. Could this old brain compete?*

To Use Student Services Many schools make a variety of career exploration services available to their students. For example, some schools organize career days and career panels to introduce students to workers in numerous fields; many offer orientation courses about particular job or career fields; a good number offer vocational counseling and career planning workshops. Many arrange for students to participate in internships, cooperative education, and work-study programs which combine paid work experience with credit classes. And institutions often provide placement services to assist students in finding jobs upon program completion.

You may be able to take advantage of these services by registering for just one course. It all depends on the school. Programs geared to adults returning to school are often more flexible and involve less red tape than those for regular students.

Know Your Own Objective

What are your objectives in returning to school? Use this checklist to clarify them.

YOUR OBJECTIVES FOR YOUR RETURN TO SCHOOL

I want to return to school in order to:

_____ Clarify my interests (specify: _____)

_____

_____ Learn skills (specify: _____

_____)

_____ Earn credentials (specify: _____

_____)

_____ Enable personal growth (specify: _____

_____)

_____ Use student services (specify: _____

_____)

_____ Other (specify: _____

_____)

CHOOSING A SCHOOL

You are likely to have a wide variety of educational settings and offerings to choose from, even if you decide to consider only alternatives in your present community. You can further your formal education in the following settings:

> adult education courses, YWCAs, community centers
> two-year community or junior colleges
> public and private technical institutes
> state colleges and universities
> private educational institutions
> professional schools

You can enroll in part-time or full-time study, in day, evening, or weekend classes. You can enroll in non-credit workshops and seminars, credit courses, certificate programs, degree programs, extension programs, continuing education for women programs. You can pursue nontraditional studies via correspondence courses, t.v., radio, or cassette courses, or directed study courses. You can get credit via examination for knowledge you already have, or for life experiences.

With all these options from which to choose, it's essential that you plan an organized approach to gathering information. Break your goal of finding a school or program into manageable units (see Chapter 5 to refresh your memory). In the same way that you researched occupational options, you will want to work back and forth between reading printed material and talking with key people. Get yourself a notebook and file folder and set aside calendar time for library trips and information interviews.

Search the Literature

First you will want to consult a general directory to compare programs, costs, degrees offered, prerequisites, especially if you're considering education outside your present community. In the Resources section at the end of this chapter we list a number of directories that you may find useful. Look for these in the same libraries where you found occupational literature. If you plan to stay where you now live, consult the yellow pages under "Schools."

Once you've identified schools or programs which could meet your objectives, you'll need to obtain a bulletin or program description for each. Again, libraries are an excellent source for local bulletins, and college libraries often have bulletin collections arranged by state or type of school. Of course, you can call or write for your own. Many college departments have their own printed information which expands on general bulletin information. Skim appropriate bulletins, taking notes about program content, admission procedures, costs. Jot down questions you have.

Interview for Information

Your next step is to have an information interview with one or more educational advisors in each possible program. You can find out who the appropriate advisor/admissions officer is from the admissions office, women's center, continuing education program, or from present students. Call and make appointments for your interviews.

As you would do in a job information interview, make a list of questions to ask the counselor. Examples include:

- ☐ What courses, curriculums, innovative programs are available in my interest area?

- ☐ Are these courses offered days, evenings, through correspondence?

- ☐ Can I transfer credits from previous education and volunteer/life experiences?

- ☐ Can I get credit by examination?

- ☐ Can I take courses without being formally admitted?

- ☐ How do I get admitted, registered, find financial aid and child care?

- ☐ Are any admissions tests required?

Ask anything you want to know. It's normal to feel apprehensive and awkward when confronting any unknown bureaucracy. They're there to serve you, so ask questions and discuss your doubts and apprehensions.

Sara McCafferty arranged an appointment with an advisor at Syca-more Grove Community College. The advisor seemed friendly, but Sara wondered if she would understand. She talked about her life situation, asked questions, explained what she saw as her needs for information, financial aid, child care, etc. The advisor not only answered her questions but anticipated other information Sara would need. She referred Sara to other sources as well. Sara left feeling she had taken an important step on her return-to-school path.

Make Application

Carefully decide on the programs that will best meet your objectives, weighing anticipated risks and gains, and then make application. Depending on the program to which you are applying, this may be a time-consuming, expensive, and difficult process requiring lots of thought and planning ahead to meet deadlines, or it may be a quick and painless process. Whatever the case, remember to congratulate and reward yourself when you've completed this big step.

FINANCING YOUR EDUCATION

If returning to school is truly important to you, cost need not be the imposing barrier it may at first appear to be. Financial aid is available from a number of sources, and you could not make a more worthwhile investment than in your own education.

Calculate Your Need

Before starting your financial aid search, estimate the expenses you're likely to incur in a return to the classroom. You'll probably need money for tuition and other student fees, books and course supplies, child care, transportation, and increased expenses for food, clothes, and maintenance due to less time at home. If you plan to quit a paid job, you'll have to replace your basic living allowance. You should be able to make rough expense calculations for each school you've researched. Financial aid staff at schools are there to help you with such budgets and may have worksheets available with expense listings.

Check Many Sources

The key to a successful financial aid search is checking many sources through a well-organized, detail-minded approach. Since many types of aid have strict deadlines or applications take several weeks to months to process, you must plan far in advance. As in researching schools, set goals for yourself and break them into manageable action steps.

Financial Aid Offices   The best place to start your search is at the financial aid office of the school you wish to attend. They will have information about a variety of sources of funding, and the counselors there can provide you with the applications you need and help you plan a package to meet your expenses. The package may include:

- ☐ Grants and scholarships: These are direct monetary payments that do not have to be repaid; both are given for financial need. Scholarships are often awarded on a competitive basis to recognize academic achievement or intent to study in a particular major area.

- ☐ Loans: Most loan programs permit students to borrow at a low interest rate (9 percent and up) and repay the loan after completing studies. Financial aid offices often administer loan programs for second parties (e.g., federal or state government and foundations).

- ☐ Work-Study: This is a federal government program which makes available part-time jobs for students on or off campus.

In addition, check with the department in which you intend to study. They may offer special departmental scholarships, fellowships, or assistantships.

Organizations and Associations   A good number of organizations and associations offer financial aid to students in certain circumstances. Special funds earmarked just for returning women students are on the increase. Some of these scholarships and loans are for any continuing education after high school. Others are for those with particular career goals, such as engineering, business, nursing, college teaching, international affairs. In the Resources section at the end of the chapter we list a couple of directories of financial aid sources for women only, and some examples of financial aid of this type.

Organizations and associations in your community may also have financial aid funds for which you might qualify. Check with your local chapter of professional societies related to your career interests, trade unions, service organizations, women's resource centers and action groups. You may qualify for aid from the federal government's Division of Vocational Rehabilitation (aid to the physically and mentally handicapped), Veterans Administration (aid to wives and children of disabled veterans, plus assistance to veterans themselves), or the Aid to Families with Dependent Children program (often covers tuition, books, and child care expenses).

Your Employer   If you are presently employed and plan to continue your job while you return to school, check to see if your employer offers an employee tuition reimbursement plan. Many companies do reimburse their employees for learning new skills directly or indirectly applicable to their job duties.

Your Family   You may be able to use family income or savings to finance part of your education. Money put away for a rainy day or for your children's education may be more wisely invested in your education and future. Contemplate loans from family members or friends, or personal bank loans.

In summary, then, finding enough financial aid to cover expenses *is* possible but you will probably have to put it together from a variety of sources. Your motto should be, "Leave no stone unturned." And always believe in the worthiness of your cause.

REVITALIZING YOUR STUDY HABITS

Chances are that if you've been away from the classroom for long, you'll feel anxious about tests, performance, and your ability to learn how to study all over again. Take heart, because these skills *can* be relearned, and your motivation to learn, maturity, and diverse life experiences since you were last in school will be real assets to you in the classroom.

Mature women students earn slightly better grade point averages than younger undergraduates, according to studies done independently at the Universities of Michigan and Wisconsin. Both of these 1976 studies also show that re-entry students' grades improve in direct proportion to their period of interrruption—the longer away, the higher the grades.

Study Skills Strategies

There are a number of things you can do to help yourself brush up or learn new study skills. We suggest that you:

- ☐ start school gradually
- ☐ enroll in a study skills workshop or course
- ☐ read one of a number of self-help study skills books
- ☐ apply time management techniques
- ☐ maintain a sense of humor

Start School Gradually   Limit yourself to one or two courses for the first term at least, if you feel unsure of your abilities. This will give you time to re-establish study habits and build these into a daily routine. If you instead jump into a full course load, you may end up overstressed and frustrated.

Many schools allow new students to register for part-time course-work without being formally admitted. This way you can try school slowly with fewer red-tape hassles.

Enroll in a Study Skills Workshop   Taking such a course is a way to schedule study skills building into your weekly routine. You will cover such topics as taking lecture notes, recognizing essential points in textbooks, preparing for exams, writing papers, and budgeting your study time. You will have numerous opportunities to practice new techniques and receive feedback on your progress. In addition, sharing your fears and doubts with other re-entry classmates will often lead to concrete solutions and a renewed sense of belief in yourself. For a referral to such a class, call a community college, extension division of a college/university, or a continuing education for women program.

> *Carol Lambert married and raised six children before she went to college. She was fairly sure of her interests and wanted to jump right in, but, unsure of her ability and study skills, planned to take only one course. She went to a continuing education for women "orientation to study" workshop. She found this encouraging and sought out the study skills service recommended by the workshop leader. To her delight she found her ability tested in the upper ten percent of college students and her reading comprehension scores were equally*

high. She signed up for a study skills program and began her college work with one course. By her fourth term she had eased into a full program.

Read a Study Skills Book   We list two highly recommended manuals in the Resources section at the end of the chapter. Reading either of these can help you if you set small, tangible study skills goals after reading each chapter.

Apply Time Management Techniques   Effective time management is one of the crucial keys to academic success. Most returning students are juggling many roles—worker, wife, mother, ETC. (Every Terrible Crisis). Schedule your studying as a top priority, but allow time for yourself and for your other roles. Revise your schedule again and again until you find what works best for you. A good time schedule will free you and help you keep your life in balance.

Maintain Your Sense of Humor   Finally, keep perspective on the relative importance of school in your life. Looking for the humor in your return to the classroom can be therapeutic. The best way to keep perspective is to review the purpose(s) behind your returning. Are you getting what you want out of school?

> *'You are really here,' I half sang to myself as I walked across campus. The dream of twenty years was about to begin and I was excited. I knew it would not be easy, but neither had managing a house and five children always been a lark—I was ready.*

HIGHLIGHTS

- ☐ The most important step in returning to school is defining your own objectives.

- ☐ Choose the school or program that's appropriate for you by considering both printed literature and information gleaned in interviews.

- ☐ Financial aid is available from a variety of sources, but you will have to track it down.

☐ Once you've conquered initial apprehensions about tests and performance, you can expect to do quite well compared to younger students and your own prior academic record.

RESOURCES

General Back-to-School

Bolles, R. N. "Toward a Balanced Life: Life Long Learning," in *The Three Boxes of Life*. Berkeley, CA: Ten Speed Press, 1978.

Ekstrom, R. B., Harris, A. M. and Lockheed, M. *How to Get College Credit for What You Have Learned As a Homemaker and Volunteer*. Princeton, NJ: Educational Testing Service, 1977.

General Information for the Returning Student. Educational Opportunities Series. New York: Catalyst, 1975.

Gray, E. *Everywoman's Guide to College*. Millbrae, CA: Les Femmes, 1974.

Lenz, E. and Shaevitz, M. H. *So You Want to Go Back to School: Facing the Realities of Re-entry*. New York: McGraw-Hill, 1977.

Mendelsonn, Pam. *Happier By Degrees: A College Re-entry Guide for Women*. New York: E. P. Dutton, 1980.

School Directories

Junior Colleges

Barron's Guide to Two-Year Colleges. Vol. I (college descriptions), 6th ed., 1978.

Cass, J. and Birnbaum, M. *Comparative Guide to Two-Year Colleges and Career Programs*. New York: Harper and Row, 1976.

Colleges and Universities

Berman, S. *Underground Guide to the College of Your Choice*. New York: New American Library, 1971.

The College Blue Books: Occupational Education. New York: MacMillan Publishing Co., 16th ed., 1977.

The College Handbook, 1979–80 and *Index of Majors, 1979–80.* 17th ed., Princeton, NJ: College Board Publications, 1979.

Lovejoy's College Guide. New York: Simon and Schuster, 1979.

Peterson's Annual Guide to Undergraduate Study. Princeton, NJ: Peterson's Guides, Inc.

Graduate Schools

Graduate Programs Admissions Manual 1979–81. Graduate Record Examination Board.

Innovative Graduate Programs Directory. Empire State College, SUNY, Saratoga Springs, NY: Learning Resource Center, 1976.

Peterson's Annual Guide to Graduate Study. Princeton, NJ: Peterson's Guides, Inc.

Nontraditional Studies

Blaze, W. et al. *Guide to Alternative Colleges and Universities: A Comprehensive Listing of Over 250 Innovative Programs.* Boston: Beacon Press, 1974.

Guide to Independent Study through Correspondence Instruction. Available from National University Extension Association, Book Order Department, P.O. Box 2123, Princeton, NJ 08540.

Splaver, S. *Nontraditional College Routes to Careers.* New York: Simon and Schuster, 1975.

Continuing Education Programs

Continuing Education Programs and Services for Women. Available from Women's Bureau, Employment Standards Administration, U.S. Department of Labor, Washington DC, 20210, free.
> *Lists 450 continuing education for women programs, state by state.*
> *Explains courses, admissions policies.*

A Guide to Women's Educational Opportunities in Western Colleges and Universities. Available from Western Interstate Commission for Higher Education, P.O. Drawer P, Boulder CO 80302, free.
> *Lists special programs on 178 western campuses.*

Thompson, F. (ed.). *The New York Times Guide to Continuing Education in America.* Chicago: Quadrangle Books, 1972.

For information on education brokers of continuing education near your community (i.e., they provide referrals to educational resources) write: National Center for Educational Brokering, 405 Oak Street, Syracuse NY 13203.

Vocational-Technical Institutes

The Handbook of Trade and Technical Careers and Training. National Association of Trade and Technical Schools, 2021 K St. NW, Washington DC 20006, free.

Lovejoy's Career and Vocational School Guide. New York: Simon and Schuster, 1973.

Financial Aid: General Resources

Guide to Graduate and Professional Majors: Financing Graduate Study. Moravia, NY: Chronicle Guidance Publications, 1977–78.

> *Discusses all types of financial aid for graduate study.*

A Guide to Student Assistance. Committee on Education and Labor, U.S. House of Representatives, House Document 91–221, available from the Superintendent of Documents, U.S. Government Printing Office, Washington DC 20402.

> *Lists federal scholarships, fellowships, and loans for undergraduate and graduate study.*

Meeting College Costs. College Board Publications Orders, Box 2815, Princeton, NJ 08541, free.

> *Discusses college costs, how to determine one's financial need, and how to apply for aid.*

Paying for Your Education: A Guide for Adult Learners. College Board Publications Orders, Department C-88, Box 2815, Princeton, NJ 08541.

> *Lists many resources for the part-time and full-time adult learner at two- and four-year colleges. Outlines how to organize a financial aid campaign.*

A Selected List of Major Fellowship Opportunities and Aids to Advanced Education for United States Citizens. National Academy of Sciences, 2101 Constitution Avenue NW, Washington DC 20036, free.

> *Fellowships for undergraduate and graduate study.*

Financial Aid: For Women Only

Directories

Financial Aid: A Partial List of Resources for Women. Project on the Status and Education of Women, Association of American Colleges, 1818 R Street NW, Washington DC 20009, free.

Selected list of financial aid for women undergraduate and graduate students, many geared toward older women, returning students, minority women, and those in professional and technical training programs.

Schlachter, G. A. *The Directory of Financial Aids for Women.* Los Angeles: Reference Press Service, 1978.

Describes scholarships, fellowships, loans, grants, internships, awards, and prizes designed primarily or exclusively for women, including an annotated bibliography of general financial aid directories.

A Sample of Funds Available

Altrusa International Foundation—Provides awards to women for training or retraining to qualify for employment. Emphasis on vocational education, such as nursing, x-ray technology and bookkeeping, rather than a college degree. Stipends usually average $350 per year. Contact: Chairman, Founders Fund Vocation Aid Committee, Altrusa International Foundation, Inc., 332 South Michigan Avenue, Chicago IL 60604.

American Association of University Women—Awards dissertation fellowships to women who have completed all course work and qualifying examinations in a doctoral program. Also offers graduate fellowships to women in their final year of study in law, medicine, dentistry, veterinary medicine and architecture; and to foreign women planning to return to their native country to pursue a career. Contact: Director, AAUW Education Foundation Programs, 2401 Virginia Avenue NW, Washington DC 20037.

Business and Professional Women's Foundation—Awards Career Advancement Scholarships to adult women who need further training or education to begin a career or to improve professional opportunities. Scholarships are offered based on financial need to women twenty-five and over who are returning for vocational training, undergraduate, or graduate work after a break in their education. Scholarships usually average $400. Contact: Business and Professional Women's Foundation, 2012 Massachusetts Avenue NW, Washington DC 22036.

The Business and Professional Women's Foundation Loan Fund for Women in Engineering Studies—Beginning in January, 1976, this organization made over $100,000 available in loan funds to women who had been accepted for undergraduate and graduate level courses at schools accredited by the Engineers' Council for Professional Development. Women may qualify for individual loans up to $10,000. Repayment of loans is scheduled over a five-year period at five percent interest beginning one year after graduation. The program is administered by the Business and Professional Women's Foundation.

Clairol Loving Care Scholarship Program—The $50,000 Clairol Program is the only nationwide company-sponsored fund for women thirty and older who are continuing post-secondary educations to achieve career goals. Scholarships up to $1,000 are available for full- or part-time study in vocational schools, undergraduate college degree programs or graduate work at the Master's or professional level. Applicants must be admitted and be within two years of completing program. An application form which covers application for both the Loving Care and BPW Career Advancement Scholarships may be obtained from the Business and Professional Women's Foundation.

Study Skills Manuals

Pauk, W. *How to Study in College.* Boston: Houghton Mifflin, 1974.

Raygor, A. L. and Wark, D. M. *Systems of Study.* New York: McGraw-Hill, 1970.

15

INVESTIGATING ALTERNATE WORK SCHEDULES

*The economy of the future will be
based on individuals who are growing and changing
on timetables that have nothing to do
with their sex. There won't be
many more people than there were in 1979,
but they will be better and happier people.
More of them will be adults. More of
the adults will be earners. And more
of the earners will be working at jobs
and schedules of their own choosing.*
Caroline Bird, *The Two-Paycheck Marriage*

*P*ROGRESS! The standard eight-hour day, forty-hour week and the low pay, low status part-time job are no longer the only options for when and how much you work. During the 70s several work schedule alternatives emerged, offering the employed woman more flexibility. If you are juggling paid work with home and family or a return to school, you may find these alternatives especially attractive.

In this chapter we

☐ describe the new options available

☐ give you an idea of the advantages and disadvantages of each, and where to look for employers who offer them

GOODBYE NINE TO FIVE

About fifteen percent of the year-round work force are now on schedules different from the traditional eight-hour day, five-day week routine, according to the Bureau of Labor Statistics. New options are available in both full-time and part-time work. They include:

flexitime
compressed work week

permanent part-time jobs
job sharing
temporary work
consulting

Flexitime

Under a flexitime program, an employee chooses, within guidelines, her own working schedule, based on a specified number of hours which everyone must work. A typical flexitime schedule permits workers to come in anytime between 7:00 A.M. and 9:30 A.M. and go home anytime between 4:00 P.M. and 6:30 P.M., so long as they put in eight hours a day and forty hours a week. In addition, all workers must be present during a core time period each day, perhaps 9:30 A.M. to 2:30 P.M.

Variations on this flexitime schedule are many. For example, flexitime by the week and flexitime by the month permits workers to carry debit and credit hours into a weekly or monthly time bank. Seven percent of all American employees were on flexitime schedules in 1977, according to a nationwide survey conducted by the American Management Association. Ninety-seven percent of the responding organizations reported flexitime improved employee morale.

Advantages   Here are some typical employee reactions to flexitime:

I feel less frazzled—no more beat the clock rush.

I see my children off to school and still put in a full day's work.

I'm able to schedule a 4:15 P.M. class at the University.

I feel more in control of my workday, more personally accountable, less watched.

Rush hour stress is reduced for flexitime workers as they avoid peak periods on freeways and public transportation, in parking lots and elevators. "Morning people" and "night people" can work when they're most energetic, with more enthusiasm and concentration. Continuing education classes are easier to work into a flexitime schedule. And personal affairs such as medical appointments, recreation, and shopping are easier to arrange.

Where To Look   Consult the Resources section at the end of this chapter for sources of more information about flexible work patterns and the companies that use them. You will need to implement a well-organized, thorough campaign to locate a company offering flexible work patterns—or to persuade your present employer to experiment with flexitime.

Compressed Work Week

Under a compressed work week program, full-time work hours are compressed into four ten-hour days or three twelve-hour days. The most common compressed schedule is the four-day forty-hour work week, known as the 4-40.

Over a million full-time employees work only three or four days a week. About 700 companies use the four-day week, in an attempt to increase plant utilization, profits, and the supply of skilled workers. Most of these companies are small non-union manufacturing shops, but retail, publishing, and banking institutions have also used this approach. The computer industry has been the chief proponent of the three-day week.

Trade-offs   The initial enthusiasm that greeted compressed schedules when they were introduced in the early 70s has diminished somewhat: twenty-eight percent of the organizations that initially tried the compressed work week have discontinued it, according to an American Management Association survey. While some workers like this arrangement, others experience fatigue from the long hours of sustained concentration.

For the employee, the chief advantage of the compressed work week is a longer weekend for family, schooling, or leisure. On the other hand, there is little time to do anything except work during the work week. Thus, if you are considering a compressed work week, make sure to examine all the trade-off factors.

Permanent Part-Time Jobs

The number of part-time workers grew three times as fast as the number of full-time workers in the 70s, and the stereotype of the part-time worker as less dependable and less committed began to fade. More than half of the over seventeen million who worked less than thirty-five hours per week were working mothers.

A promising impetus to the growth of higher-status part-time jobs was a 1978 law requiring federal agencies to set goals and timetables for creating more part-time jobs in government. Within months after enactment of this law, six thousand permanent part-time jobs had been established, with a large percentage in the higher grade levels. In addition, eight states began programs to create more part-time jobs at every level of state government.

Is Part-Time Work For You?   Your gains over a full-time position would probably include greater flexibility and more time for other responsibilities and interests. On the loss side, you would certainly face a smaller paycheck and you might lose important fringe benefits.

If you haven't worked for pay for several years, consider why you're returning to work and how you'll manage a part-time versus a full-time job. Part-time workers sometimes try to do everything—be superworkers, supermoms, superstudents. Recognize that your activities will have to change somewhat, even if you work only a few hours a week.

If you're thinking of changing your full-time job to a part-time one, examine your motivation. Dissatisfaction with current work might be more effectively alleviated by switching jobs entirely, rather than cutting down your hours. In addition, plot out how you'll actually reduce your work load to part-time. No sense getting paid part-salary to do full-time work, and this happens to some part-time workers.

Finding a challenging part-time job requires a thoroughly organized, assertive approach. Try breaking into the part-time job market by doing volunteer work for a nonprofit organization. Many women have found satisfying paid positions this way, after conceptualizing a new project or proving their indispensability. Or consider job-sharing, as described next.

Job Sharing

The concept of job sharing is gradually spreading nationwide as pairs of workers split the duties, salaries, and benefits of permanent full-time positions. Two women alternate weeks as a women's page reporter on a major metropolitan newspaper. Another pair share the position of project resource coordinator at a community design center. Others split the position of teacher, facilities engineer, office manager, library aide, lawyer, employment counselor, organizational development specialist, receptionist.

Job sharers divide their labor in varied ways. The project resource coordinators each work the same four hours each day. They tried splitting mornings and afternoons between them when they first took the position, but soon found too much duplication of effort. Others split their weeks into two- and three-day work modules or 2½–2½, overlapping a few hours or none at all. Job teams can create schedules to match personal and organizational needs.

The amount of overlapping of responsibilities determines whether a job is *shared* or *split*. For example, two case workers, with their individual clients, would probably split their position. The amount of necessary communication between them could be quite minimal. On the other hand, co-administrators of an early childhood education center would communicate extensively on major decisions in a shared position. Most positions would be between these two extremes.

Job-sharing studies have shown no significant increase or decrease in the cost of two workers sharing one position. Increased performance has been noted both by supervisors and job sharers and overall productivity has been found to be higher than that of comparable full-time employees. Job satisfaction has also been found higher for job sharers and turnover lower compared to full-time counterparts.

Risks and Benefits   "You have to be willing to risk a little and be creative with job sharing" says Shirley Reinertson, a job sharer at the Minnesota Early Learning Design Center in Minneapolis. While job sharing is certainly not for everyone, the benefits can be well worth the risks.

Job sharing began as a way women with child-rearing responsibilities could work part-time in challenging, established positions. Others soon took advantage of this new work option—individuals combining work with schooling, leisure activities, second careers. Persons who were handicapped or easing into retirement also saw job sharing as a manageable option. Part-time jobs—typically scarce—were often low-pay, no-benefit positions. Job sharing meant pro-rated salaries and benefits and a more committed, responsible worker image.

The advantages of job sharing include:

- [ ] increased flexibility and free time for other personal pursuits

- [ ] another worker to cover duties during illnesses and crises

- [ ] pro-rated pay and benefits

- [ ] opportunities for administrative, decision-making responsibilities not often included in traditional part-time jobs

- [ ] more productive creative work as partners combine their skills and insights

Of course there are disadvantages, too—a smaller paycheck and pro-rated benefits. In addition, highly competitive individuals who dislike teamwork would not find job sharing amenable. Job sharing requires cooperative personalities who function well as a team.

How to Get Started   Does job sharing sound like a possible option for you? If so, you need to accomplish these three tasks:

- ☐   Locate a compatible work partner.

- ☐   Outline a work plan, including division of duties, working hours, and a communication scheme.

- ☐   Sell your team and work plan to an employer, negotiating duties and benefits.

Successful job sharers emphasize the importance of a cooperative, compatible relationship with their work partner. You have to get along philosophically with the person you're working with. "You have to have similar work styles," said one job sharer. Some have met their work match at one of the excellent job sharing advocacy centers listed at the end of this chapter. Others have found partners while doing volunteer work. Co-workers, friends, spouses are sometimes feasible choices.

Temporary Work

Do you want to work but not at a year-round job? Would you like to explore different kinds of businesses first-hand? Have you just moved and don't know where to get a job? Do you need an income immediately while you explore long-term options? If so, you might opt to work for a temporary help contractor.

Temporary help companies hire individuals and contract them out to companies needing extra help. A particular work assignment may last a few hours to several months. If you become a "temp," your employer—the temporary help company—will pay you an hourly rate, withhold your taxes, and provide statutory benefits.

Typically, temps fill in for absent or vacationing employees. Yet in the past decade, temporary workers have become an increasingly integral part of everyday business operations. Temps solve scheduling problems during peak periods, work on special projects such as computer installations, advertising campaigns, conventions. They smooth the transition between one employee's leaving and the replacement's hiring. When valuable employees reach mandatory retirement, they may continue to work through a temporary contractor.

About two-thirds of all temporary workers are in clerical occupations as secretaries, data processors, bookkeepers, but temporary contractors are rapidly expanding into other fields. Many health care personnel, especially nurses, see temporary work as an attractive alternative to the rigid, rotating schedules of permanent hospital jobs. In addition, some temporary services have industrial service divisions for machinists, welders, truckdrivers. Marketing divisions contract product demonstrators, survey interviewers, Santas, while technical divisions hire engineers, computer programmers, and technical writers.

Why Choose Temporary Work?   Flexibility is the key reason that most workers chose the temporary route. Temps can control how much or how little they work, opting for a free summer or a busy one. Of course this flexibility is a trade-off. Temps may not be able to work full-time during a particular period. Their pay is sometimes lower than that of permanent employees doing similar work, fringe benefits are minimal to nonexistent, as are opportunities for on-the-job training. Child care may be difficult to arrange without a reliable schedule.

Many see temporary work as a way to brush up skills, learn new procedures, and evaluate their interests and abilities in a realistic setting. While some are dissatisifed with the salaries and types of jobs offered by temporary companies, others accept permanent jobs with organizations with whom they had been placed as temps.

Temporary work is not for everyone. While some enjoy the unpredictability of their next assignment, many dislike a constantly changing work environment. There is little time to get to know co-workers, to feel personally at home on the job. Temps are expected to learn new procedures quickly, to perform at top level every day. Many aspects of temporary work may be either pluses or minuses for you, depending upon what you want from work.

Consulting

A consultant is a paid problem solver, an expert who completes short-term projects for a variety of organizations. The expertise of a consultant can be in one of hundreds of marketable fields—including public relations, accounting, teaching secretarial services, interior design, health care administration, employee benefits, evaluation research, management, and many more. Think about it. Do you have any expertise you could sell?

Rewards and Costs   Consulting offers opportunities for creative, challenging work—the kind of work often not accessible to women in the nine-to-five work world. Successful consultants thrive on independence and flexibility, setting their own hours, pacing their work loads, working out of their homes or in downtown offices, alone or with partners. The variety of projects and clients provides excitement, challenge, growth opportunities.

But like all other options mentioned here, the rewards of consulting bear a price tag. Consulting requires *at least* one-hundred percent professional commitment—a willingness to go many extra miles to develop clientele, meet project deadlines, handle legal and financial matters, deliver a quality service or product. As you finish one job you may not know where or when your next job will be.

Could You Do It? To succeed as a consultant you need solid professional skills, skills recognized as credible in your professional area. You also need to use all your previous contacts to establish a client base.

If you're considering the consulting route, confront these three critical questions, outlined by Maggie Riechers in "Is Consulting for You?" (*Women's Work,* September/October, 1977):

- ☐ Are you willing to exert the time and energy necessary to attract clients?

- ☐ Can you afford to live for at least a year without a steady income?

- ☐ Is your service in sufficient demand to sustain you financially?

Affirmative answers to these questions means you're ready to consider some starting-up issues. Be sure to contact the Small Business Administration about helpful seminars and special publications about consulting. As a consultant you face the advantages and disadvantages of all small business owners. Give special attention to the next chapter, "Going into Business for Yourself."

IS AN ALTERNATIVE SCHEDULE FOR YOU?

You will want to weigh the advantages and disadvantages of these scheduling options in relation to your own situation. Since these work patterns have just recently emerged, openings rarely will appear in newspapers or quickly be offered in job interviews. You'll need to talk to receptive employers and do your share of persuading. Even if these alternatives are not feasible in your career right now, keep them in mind for later.

HIGHLIGHTS

☐ You need not work in a nine-to-five job. Alternatives available are:

— flexitime, where you choose *which* eight hours you'll work in a day

— compressed work week, where you work more hours per day for fewer days

— permanent part-time jobs, where you work less than thirty-five hours per week on a permanent basis

— job sharing, where you split a full-time position with another worker

— temporary work, where you choose when and how long you'll work

— consulting, where you offer your expertise as an independent contractor.

☐ Each alternative has costs and benefits; these jobs may take more initiative to find than traditional ones.

RESOURCES

Flexitime

Catalyst Report on Flexitime, 1974.
Companies and Institutions Using Flexitime, a nationwide list.
Alternate Work Patterns: General Bibliography PIA, 1977.
Order from: Catalyst, 14 East 60th Street, New York NY 10022.

Flexitime—A Guide, 1974. Order from Superintendent of Documents, U.S. Government Printing Office, Washington DC 20402, number 006–000–00809–7.

Assists organizations in determining the feasibility of flexitime and offers guidance in planning and implementing flexitime.

Lipman, V. "There may be a better way," *Glamour,* March 1979, 235–301.

Summarizes AMA survey on flexitime.

Part-time Jobs

Dupont, H. "Playing the Part-time Game," *Women's Work,* November/December, 1976.

Levine, J. "Part Time Work . . . Full Time Parents," *Working Woman,* March, 1977.

Job Sharing

Working Less But Enjoying It More: A Guide to Splitting or Sharing Your Job. Available from New Ways to Work, 149 Ninth St., San Francisco CA 94301.

Includes suggestions for finding partners, describes the process involved in negotiating a shared job, and gives a sample proposal.

The following organizations offer counseling for anyone interested in job sharing, and sometimes match up teams. They also provide excellent general information.

Flexible Careers
37 South Wabash
Chicago, IL 60603

Focus on Part-time Careers
509 – 10th Avenue East
Seattle, WA 98102

Job Sharers, Inc.
8101 Wolf Trap Road
Vienna, VA 22180

New Ways to Work
149 Ninth Street
San Francisco, CA 94301
(excellent publications and bibliographies)

Options for Women
8419 Germantown Avenue
Philadelphia, PA 19118

Temporary Work

Both these articles include tips on selecting a temporary help company.

Rivchum, S. "Temping: R$_x$ for an Ailing Career," *Women's Work,* September/October, 1977.

Rudney, S. "Is Temporary Work for You?" *Occupational Outlook Quarterly,* Winter, 1978.

Consulting

Riechers, M. "Is Consulting for You?" *Women's Work,* September/October, 1977.

16

GOING INTO BUSINESS FOR YOURSELF

If you don't have a good idea — don't.

If you don't have enough capital — don't.

And if you think you're going to work at it

part-time, for heaven's sake, don't.

Because there is no more demanding job

known to man or woman than working for oneself.

Guin Hall, former director of the Women's
Bureau, New York State Department of Commerce

*H*AVE you ever dreamed of starting your own business? It's an important option to consider. When we think of business, we tend to think of the corporate giants—the Fortune 500—yet seventy-five percent of all businesses have less than five employees and eighty-seven percent of new employment in the economy since 1969 has been created by small business. Women have not been well-represented as business owners—they own just four and a half percent of American businesses.

This chapter is designed to stimulate your thinking about how possible or desirable starting a business might be for you.

- ☐ Do you have what it takes to succeed in your own business?

- ☐ What type of business could you start?

- ☐ What are the practical considerations you would need to address?

COULD YOU DO IT?

In your own business, you can put *your* skills and *your* ideas to work for *you*. But not everyone is cut out to be an entrepreneur. Do you have the characteristics that would enable you to succeed in a business of your own? Taking the following quiz, adapted from the Small Business Administration booklet "Checklist for Going Into Business," will give you some clues about your potential.

THE "COULD YOU DO IT?" QUIZ

Are you a self-starter?

☐ I do things on my own. Nobody has to tell me to get going.

☐ If someone gets me started, I keep going all right.

☐ Easy does it. I don't put myself out until I have to.

How do you feel about other people?

☐ I like people. I can get along with just about anybody.

☐ I have plenty of friends—I don't need anyone else.

☐ Most people bug me.

Can you lead others?

☐ I can get most people to go along when I start something.

☐ I can give the orders if someone tells me what we should do.

☐ I let someone else get things moving. Then I go along if I feel like it.

Can you take responsibility?

☐ I like to take charge of things and see them through.

☐ I'll take over if I have to, but I'd rather let someone else be responsible.

☐ There's always some eager beaver around wanting to show how smart she is. I say let her.

How good an organizer are you?

☐ I like to have a plan before I start. I'm usually the one to get things lined up when the gang wants to do something.

☐ I do all right unless things get too goofed up. Then I cop out.

☐ You get all set and then something comes along and blows the whole bag. So I just take things as they come.

How good a worker are you?

☐ I can keep going as long as I need to. I don't mind working hard for something I want.

☐ I'll work hard for a while, but when I've had enough, that's it!

☐ I can't see that hard work gets you anywhere.

Can you make decisions?

☐ I can make up my mind in a hurry if I have to. It usually turns out okay, too.

☐ I can if I have plenty of time. If I have to make up my mind fast, I think later I should have decided the other way.

☐ I don't like to be the one who has to decide things. I'd probably blow it.

Can people trust what you say?

☐ You bet they can. I don't say things I don't mean.

☐ I try to be on the level most of the time, but sometimes I just say what's easiest.

☐ What's the sweat if the other person doesn't know the difference?

Can you stick with it?

☐ If I make up my mind to do something, I don't let anything stop me.

☐ I usually finish what I start—if it doesn't get fouled up.

☐ If it doesn't go right away, I turn off. Why beat your brains out?

How good is your health?

☐ I never run down!

☐ I have enough energy for most things I want to do.

☐ I run out of juice sooner than most of my friends seem to.

Now count the checks you made.

How many checks are there beside the first answer
to each question? _____

How many checks are there beside the second answer
to each question? _____

How many checks are there beside the third answer
to each question? _____

If most of your checks are beside the first answers, you probably have what it takes to run a business. If not, you're likely to have more trouble than you can handle by yourself. Better find a partner who is strong on the points you're weak on. If many checks are beside the third answer, not even a good partner will be able to shore you up.

WHAT KIND OF BUSINESS?

Having decided you do have the traits necessary to run your own business, you must next consider what kind of business you want to start. There are three major types of businesses: service, production, and merchandising. We'll give you some examples of each type; jot down those that interest you, and brainstorm all the possibilities you can.

Service

In this type of business, you provide a service to others. In Minneapolis, Broom Service, started by two women, vacuumed up more business than they could handle. They now have fourteen employees involved in their team cleaning approach. In 1973, two young women invested $200 in a plant sitting business and now gross about $100,000 yearly offering plant-care services to business and residential clients.

Another young woman with several years experience working for a temporary help agency spent weekends, evenings, and lunch hours doing research before opening her own agency. She scouted the competition, studied laws that would affect her, checked locations, and worked out a balance sheet, proposed budget, and a loan repayment plan with an accountant.

These are just a few of the diverse and innumerable services that are offered by businesses. Can you see yourself offering any of the following services? Child care; grounds maintenance; pet grooming; telephone answering; catering; bookkeeping and accounting; party planning; window displaying; personal shopping; dog training; pet boarding; modeling; entertaining; event announcing; travel advising; tailoring; promoting; writing; floral arranging; raising a specialty—mushrooms, violets; photographing; plant sitting; renting; delivering; hair and beauty styling; translating; designing games; refinishing furniture; repairing; soil testing; speech writing; typing.

Production

In this type of business you sell the products of your work. Jennifer Fredricks had always loved to sketch clothing designs, and when she became a mother she designed and made clothing for her children. When people began commenting on the well-made and cute items, she began making garments for a few friends. When she couldn't handle the number of requests anymore she began to hire others to cut, sew, and put on the finishing touches. The result was a small clothing manufacturing business. A midwestern woman turned to cheesemaking as a way to have a career and stay at home. She works ten hours a day at it but says, "It's worth it." Another woman, tired of non-nutritious snacks, wrote a book of nutritious recipes for children.

Again, innumerable products can be sold based on your skills, interests, and opportunities. You can produce a product to sell by gardening; animal breeding; all sorts of handycrafting; cooking and baking; printing (including calligraphy); candy making; making toys and play equipment; fabric designing; painting; inventing; making beauty products; making products of wood; jewelry-making. When you have produced a product, it is then necessary for you, a sales representative, or a retailer to sell your product.

Merchandising

This is selling a product manufactured by someone else. You can open an outlet in your home, go on a selling route, publish a mail catalog, sell the product on a store rack or in a vending machine. Some national businesses sell franchise permits. Some of these call for a considerable outlay of money and a financial risk as well.

PRACTICAL CONSIDERATIONS

Once you have determined that you have the right personal traits, and have some idea of the kind of business you might start, you must face a myriad of practical concerns and considerations. The following checklist will help you to see where you are right now in your planning. It will probably point up several or many areas where you need to get more information, get organized, and get down to business. Again, this is from the booklet "Checklist for Going Into Business."

CHECKLIST FOR GOING INTO BUSINESS
Before You Start

How about you?

Are you the kind of person who can get a business started and make it go? (See the "Could You Do It?" quiz) _____

Think about why you want to own your own business. Do you want it badly enough to work long hours without knowing how much money you'll get in the end? _____

Have you worked in a business like the one you want to start? _____

Have you worked as a manager or supervisor for someone else? _____

Have you had any business training? _____

Have you saved any money? _____

How about the money?

Do you know how much money you will need to get your business started? _____

Have you counted up how much money of your own you can put into the business? _____

Do you know how much credit you can get from your suppliers—the people you will buy from? _____

Do you know where you can borrow the rest of the money you need to start your business? _____

Have you figured out what net income per year you expect to get from the business? _____

Can you live on less than this so that you can use some of it to help your business grow? _____

Have you talked to a banker about your plans? _____

How about a partner?

If you need a partner with money or know-how that you don't have, do you know someone who will fit—someone you find agreeable? _____

Do you know the good and bad points about going it
alone, having a partner, or incorporating your business? _____

Have you talked to a lawyer about these matters? _____

How about your customers?

Have you tried to find out whether businesses like the one
you want to open are doing well in your community and
in the rest of the country? _____

Do you know what kind of people will want to buy what
you plan to sell? _____

Do people like that live in the area where you want to
open your business? _____

Do they need a business like yours? _____

If not, have you thought about starting a different kind
of business or going to another neighborhood? _____

Getting Started

Your location

Have you found a good location for your business? _____

Will you have enough room when your business gets bigger? _____

Can you fix the space the way you want it without spending too much money? _____

If necessary, can people get to it easily from parking
spaces, bus stops, or their homes? _____

Have you had a lawyer check the lease and zoning? _____

Equipment and supplies

Do you know just what equipment and supplies you need
and how much they will cost? _____

Can you save some money by buying secondhand equipment? _____

Your merchandise

Have you decided what product or service you will sell? _____

If a product, do you know what size inventory you will need to open your business?   _____

Have you found suppliers who will sell you what you need at a good price?   _____

Have you compared the prices and credit terms of different suppliers?   _____

Your records

Have you planned a system of records that will keep track of your income and expenses, what you owe other people, and what other people owe you?   _____

If you sell a product, have you worked out a way to keep track of your inventory so that you will always have enough on hand for your customers but not more than you can sell?   _____

Have you figured out how to keep your payroll records and take care of tax reports and payments?   _____

Do you know what financial statements you should prepare?   _____

Do you know how to use these financial statements?   _____

Do you know an accountant who will help you with your records and financial statements?   _____

Your business and the law

Do you know what licenses and permits you need?   _____

Do you know what business laws you have to obey?   _____

Do you know a lawyer you can go to for advice and for help with legal papers?   _____

Protecting your business

Have you made plans for protecting your business against thefts or losses of all kinds?   _____

Have you talked with an insurance agent about what kinds of insurance you need?   _____

Buying a business someone else has started

Have you made a list of what you like and don't like about buying a business someone else has started?   _____

Are you sure you know the real reason why the owner wants to sell her/his business? _____

Have you compared the cost of buying the business with the cost of starting a new business? _____

If there is stock, is the stock up to date and in good condition? _____

Will the owner of the site transfer the lease to you? _____

Have you talked with other business persons in the area to see what they think of the business? _____

If there is a product, have you talked with the company's suppliers? _____

Have you talked with a lawyer about it? _____

Making It Go

Advertising

Have you decided how you will advertise (newspapers—posters—handbills—radio—by mail)? _____

Do you know where to get help with your ads? _____

Have you watched what other businesses do to get people to buy? _____

The prices you charge

Do you know how to figure what you should charge for your service or product? _____

Do you know what other businesses like yours charge? _____

Buying

Do you have a plan for finding out what your customers want? _____

If you have a product, will your plan for keeping track of your inventory tell you when it is time to order more and how much to order? _____

Do you plan to buy most of your stock from a few suppliers rather than a little from many, so that those you buy from will want to help you succeed? _____

Selling

Have you decided whether you will have salespersons?   _____

Do you know how to get customers to buy your product or service?   _____

Have you thought about why you like to buy from some salespersons while others turn you off?   _____

Your employees

If you need to hire someone to help you, do you know where to look?   _____

Do you know what kind of employees you need?   _____

Do you know how much to pay?   _____

Do you have a plan for training your employees?   _____

Credit for your customers

Have you decided whether to let your customers buy on credit?   _____

Do you know the good and bad points about joining a credit-card plan?   _____

Can you tell a deadbeat from a good credit customer?   _____

A Few Extra Questions

Have you figured out whether you could make more money working for someone else?   _____

Does your family go along with your plan to start a business of your own?   _____

Do you know where to find out about new ideas and new products?   _____

Where to Go For Answers

The first place to turn to for help in filling in the blanks is the Small Business Administration (SBA) of the U.S. government. The main office is in Washington, but there are nearly 100 field offices around the country. These offices offer hundreds of free publications, introductory workshops on going into business, and free counseling sessions with active or retired executives. The SBA recently launched a National Women's Business Ownership campaign.

The SBA also guarantees business loans and monitors government transactions to ensure that small businesses receive a share of government contracts.

Look into courses on starting a business, on management, and on bookkeeping offered at local vocational schools and colleges. Join an association representing the industry you want to enter. Attend their meetings and talk with people you meet through these contacts. Talk to your banker and to an accountant about your plans. They can provide invaluable advice.

Think about working for a business of the kind you are planning to start. By getting this experience you can increase your chances for success. There is nothing like the nitty-gritty of this daily contact to acquaint you with the problems and opportunities of a particular type of business.

Contact the National Association of Women Business Owners to see if they have members in your line of work, and go talk to these women. Your state may have its own chapter of this association. Your local Chamber of Commerce can also be a source of information about the number of existing businesses like the one you want to start, where they're located, and so on.

In the Resources section we list a number of other associations you can write to for information and assistance, or join to meet others with information to share. If this chapter has whet your interest, dig in—a great adventure awaits you.

HIGHLIGHTS

- ☐ Running your own business is hard work, and not everyone is cut out for it.

- ☐ There are basically three types of business: service, production, and merchandising.

- ☐ There are a myriad of details to attend to in starting a business venture. Be sure you are well-prepared by reading, attending meetings and courses, talking to people.

RESOURCES

Organizations

Small Business Administration
1441 L Street NW
Washington, DC 20416

Call this toll-free number to order any of their booklets: 800-433-7212. Initially, from about 150 free publications you might order:

MA-5 "Women's Handbook—How SBA Can Help You Go Into Business"
MA-4 "Management Assistance"
OPI-18 "Small Business Loans"
OPI-6 "SBA—What it Does"
115-A "Free Management Assistance Publications"
The SBA also has about 50 booklets for sale which are more extensive than the free ones.

The National Federation of Independent Business
150 W. 20th Avenue
San Mateo, CA 94403

National Association of Women Business Owners
2920 M Street NW
Washington, DC 20007

Business & Professional Women's Foundation
2012 Massachusetts Avenue NW
Washington, DC 20036

Institute for Independent Businesswomen, Inc.
4101 Nebraska Avenue NW
Washington, DC 20016

Periodicals

Enterprising Woman, subscriptions available by writing to 217 E. 28th St., New York, NY 10017.

Small Business Reporter Publication Index, available from Bank of America, Department 3120, P.O. Box 2700, San Francisco, CA 94137.

Briarpatch Review, subscriptions available by writing to 330 Ellis Street, San Francisco, CA 94102.

Women's Work, published by Washington Opportunities for Women, Suite 101, Vanguard Building, 1111 20th Street NW, Washington, DC 20036.

The Spokeswoman, subscriptions available by writing to 5464 South Shore Drive, Chicago, IL 60615.

Books

Dible, D. M. *Up Your Own Organization.* Vacaville, CA: Entrepreneur Press, 1971.

Jessup, C. and Chipps, G. *The Woman's Guide to Starting a Business.* New York: Holt, Rinehart & Winston, 1976.

The first section of this book tells how to calculate costs, pick a location, raise money, gives advice (finding a lawyer, talking to bankers, advertising), and clarification (taxes, pension plans, franchising). The second section provides examples and tips from successful businesswomen.

Kahn, H. S. *101 Businesses You Can Start and Run With Less Than $1,000.* New York: Doubleday, 1973.

Lembeck, R. *Job Ideas for Today's Woman.* Englewood Cliffs, NJ: Prentice-Hall, 1974.

While not primarily a book on starting your own business, this book provides many job ideas which could be done at home, as a free lance, or turned into businesses.

Postyn, S. and Postyn, J. K. *Raising Cash: A Guide to Financing and Controlling Your Business.* Belmont, CA: Lifetime Learning Publications, 1981.

Winston, S. *Entrepreneurial Woman.* New York: Newsweek Books, 1979.

Informal style and examples of women through all phases of having a business. Starts with basic self-assessment—"Is it for you?"—to what kind of business, being assertive, handling stress, managing home responsibilities, and running the business.

SECTION V

GOING ABOUT YOUR JOB SEARCH

17

STALKING
THE JOB MARKET

A job hunt, like a good wine,
should improve as it ages. False starts
and a few trials and errors should allow you
to work better, not harder, at the job
of finding a job.
Phoebe Taylor, *Women's Work* September/October 1978

CREATIVE job-seeking is a natural outgrowth of the self-assessment and exploration of work options you have done so far. The knowledge you have accumulated will enable you to tap into an incredible storehouse of employment opportunities, once you know the key. In this section we teach you that key—a creative job search strategy that will give you a major competitive edge for the rest of your working life.

In this chapter you will

□ preview the creative job search strategy

□ decide on your career and job objectives

□ set goals and develop an action plan

STRATEGY: YOUR KEY TO TAPPING THE HIDDEN JOB MARKET

Until Richard Bolles and others published their nontraditional job search ideas, most advice recommended some variation on the "Numbers Game." "Doing it by the numbers" has meant answering advertisements, visiting employment agencies, and dumping a lot of letters and resumes into the mail with the hope that someone on the other end will pick you out of the crowd, give you a call, and offer you a job. For the majority of job seekers, this method *does not work at all*. Many millions of job seekers are still using this method and winding up underemployed or unemployed. Fortunately, you do not have to repeat their mistakes.

The fact is that the best bet for job seekers, and particularly re-entry women or those making a change in career direction, is to tap into the *hidden job market*. These are jobs that are not listed in the classified ads or with placement agencies. In fact, about half of these jobs are potential, not current, jobs, which depend on the job seeker's initiative and creativity to discover and develop. Estimates are that on any given day more than three-quarters of all available jobs exist in the hidden job market.

The secret to tapping into this hidden job market is in having a creative and systematic job search strategy. If you have a strategy, you are *not* at the mercy of the job market; *you* retain control. You cultivate luck by creating a situation in which fortuitous events are likely to occur. As counselors, we have seen which strategies have worked well, and which have subjected women to more than their share of frustration and disappointment. The strategy we recommend involves knowing *what* you want, *where* you can do it, and *how* to get hired. Its steps are as follows:

KNOW *WHAT* YOU WANT

Step 1:   Decide on your primary job objective

Step 2:   Set goals and develop an action plan

KNOW *WHERE* YOU CAN DO IT

Step 3:   Identify potential employers

Step 4:   Research your best prospects in depth

KNOW *HOW* TO GET HIRED

Step 5:   Develop your resume

Step 6:   Promote yourself to the person who can hire you

Step 7:   Follow through

Since you've come this far in the book, you have a solid foundation in knowing what you want, and some idea of where you can do it. In this chapter we'll help you focus even more sharply on what you want; in the next chapter we'll help you gather more, very specific, information about where you can do it. In the last two chapters of this section we'll show you how to get hired.

DECIDE ON YOUR OBJECTIVE

As a result of your work in Chapter 12, you have in-depth knowledge of a few job fields where jobs are likely to be available and where jobs are likely to fit you. The more focused and specific you can be about what you are looking for, the more effective your job search is likely to be. So now you are ready to decide on your primary job objective by using the planning approach to decision making that you learned in Chapter 4.

Let's review the steps.

- ☐ State your decision to be made
- ☐ List and rank your criteria
- ☐ Generate and explore alternatives
- ☐ Evaluate risks
- ☐ Make a tentative decision
- ☐ Set goals and take action

Your decision to be made at this point is: What is your primary job objective?

List and Rank your Criteria

In Section III you gathered the necessary information about yourself so that you could list and prioritize your job objective criteria. Take a moment now to fill in your criteria in the following chart. Refer to your Self-Knowledge Synopsis on page 115 and your Values Synopsis on page 71 to refresh your memory.

YOUR WORK CRITERIA

What skills and abilities do I want to use?

_____

_____

_____

What values and interests do I want to express?

_____

_____

_____

What type of work setting do I want or need?

_____

How do I want to balance my work and personal life?

_____

What type and amount of contact do I want to have with people?

_____

_____

What salary and benefits do I need?

_____

How close to home do I want or need to work?

_____

What kind of opportunities for advancement or on-the-job training do I want?

_____

Do I want to work in a field where there will be plenty of job openings, even though the job may be a little less desirable?

_____

What else is important to me in a job?

_____

_____

Jot down in your own words some abbreviation of each of these factors in the space provided on the following Alternative Comparison Chart. Then indicate how important each factor is to you on a scale of zero to four, with zero being unimportant and four being very important. Avoid giving all job factors the same ratings. This exercise will be more meaningful if you differentiate the *relative* importance of various factors.

For example, one woman decided that she wanted a job that emphasized her public relations and writing skills, involved part-time work, and fit well with her family life. All other factors were less important to her.

Shirley Zimmerman, a junior high school English teacher who had begun to feel burned out teaching adolescents, decided the most important factors for her had to do with salary and advancement. She wanted to be earning $5,000 more than her current salary within two years, to have the opportunity to learn on the job, and to be given increasing pay and responsibilities. Least important to her was finding work related to her education or conveniently located.

Generate and Explore Alternatives

You began this step of your decision-making in Chapters 11 and 12. Now jot the alternatives you researched in depth that you are still willing to consider in the space provided on the Alternative Comparison Chart. If there's even a slight chance that you might choose the option you're currently pursuing, be sure to list this as an alternative, too. For example, if you would consider staying in your present work as a full-time underwriter or traffic controller, write this down. Many times staying where you are *is* a valid choice. You'll be more satisfied with an eventual decision if you've weighed currently-pursued options with new ones.

Despite feeling quite burned out, Shirley Zimmerman listed her current job as an alternative she might pursue. Her other job objective alternatives were public relations director for a nonprofit organization, technical writer, pension planner for an insurance company, and real estate sales.

Compare Alternatives   Now you will want to determine which alternative meets the largest number of important criteria. To do this, rate on the chart

ALTERNATIVE COMPARISON CHART

FIRST, list your criteria for your current decision, under "Factor."

For each factor circle the number that best describes how important it is.

      0 = unimportant
      1 = slightly important
      2 = moderately important
      3 = important
      4 = very important

THEN, write your alternatives in the slots provided below.

Rate each alternative on how well it fits each of the factors listed on the left.

      0 = poor fit
      1 = some fit
      2 = good fit

FINALLY, multiply the importance rating times the fitness rating for each alternative and insert the product in the appropriate small box. Total the numbers in the small boxes for each column or alternative.

Factor	Importance Rating	Alt. 1:	Alt. 2:	Alt. 3:	Alt. 4:	Alt. 5:
	0 1 2 3 4					
	0 1 2 3 4					
	0 1 2 3 4					
	0 1 2 3 4					
	0 1 2 3 4					
	0 1 2 3 4					
	0 1 2 3 4					
	0 1 2 3 4					
	0 1 2 3 4					
	0 1 2 3 4					
	0 1 2 3 4					
	0 1 2 3 4					
	0 1 2 3 4					
	0 1 2 3 4					
	0 1 2 3 4					
TOTALS						

ALTERNATIVE COMPARISON CHART

Factor	Importance Rating		Job 1: Public Relations, nonprofit		Job 2: Technical Writer		Job 3: Pension Planner, insurance		Job 4: Real Estate Sales		Job 5: Current Job, Teacher	
Must use problem solving, exchanging information with others, writing skills	0 1 2 ③ 4		2	6	1	3	2	6	1	3	1	3
uses my education	0 ① 2 3 4		1	1	1	1	1	1	0	0	2	2
fits my values: social contribution, honest, direct interaction	0 1 2 ③ 4		2	6	1	3	2	6	1	3	1	3
fits my interests	0 1 ② 3 4		2	4	1	2	1	2	2	4	1	2
uses my abilities	0 1 ② 3 4		1	2	1	2	1	2	2	4	1	2
fits my family life: time evenings and weekends	0 1 2 ③ 4		2	6	2	6	2	6	0	0	1	3
has desirable type/amount people contacts	0 1 2 ③ 4		2	6	0	0	2	6	2	6	0	0
pays $20,000 within 2 years	0 1 2 3 ④		0	0	1	4	2	8	2	8	0	0
has desired working hours	0 1 2 ③ 4		2	6	2	6	2	6	0	0	1	3
has convenient location	0 ① 2 3 4		0	0	2	2	1	1	1	1	2	2
want salary & responsibilities to increase	0 1 2 3 ④		0	0	1	4	2	8	2	8	0	0
want to learn on job	0 1 2 3 ④		1	4	1	4	2	8	1	4	0	0
has number of job openings	0 1 ② 3 4		1	2	2	4	1	2	1	2	0	0
	0 1 2 3 4											
	0 1 2 3 4											
TOTALS				43		41		62		43		20

how well each alternative satisfies each factor you have listed. Then rank order your alternatives by how well they generally fit your most important factors.

You may just be able to look at the chart, focusing on which factors received the highest importance ratings and which jobs got the highest fitness ratings for these particular factors, to pick out your first, second, and third alternatives. However, you'll probably find it easier to go strictly by the totals at the bottom of the right-hand part of the chart. The job alternative with the largest total gets the first rank, and so on.

Shirley Zimmerman noticed that her current job offered very little in terms of her most important factors. This confirmed her feelings in black and white: she needed a more satisfying career. Shirley could also tell that the pension planning job offered the best fit on her most important factors.

Thinking through the positive aspects of this kind of insurance position, it made sense to her in ways that she hadn't previously noticed. Pension planning combined opportunities for advancement and salary increase with on-the-job training programs. It fit well with family responsibilities. Finally, she could see that the other three options offered some but not all of what she wanted.

At this point, then, Shirley ranked her alternatives as follows:

RANK	JOB OBJECTIVE	RANK	JOB OBJECTIVE
1	pension planner		
2	public relations		
3	real estate sales		
4	technical writer		
5	current teaching job		

Now fill in the blanks next to Shirley's list with your own ranked job objectives.

Evaluate Risks

As we mentioned in Chapter 4, encountering possible risks, losses, or obstacles is part of all major personal decisions. Writing down specific risks can help you clearly see what you're anticipating and plan stand-by action steps. Then you can decide how willing you are to accept these risks. We provide a Risk Comparison Chart on the next page for you to do this. When you are ready to fill it out, list all alternatives you are still considering after doing the Alternative Comparison Chart.

Next, list risks, losses, obstacles anticipated for each alternative. Be as specific as you can. Risks might include "Opportunities for advancement beyond entry level job might not pan out," "Might find co-workers difficult to work with," or "Might not like fast pace of job as much as I thought." Losses refer to positive things you're experiencing now that you might lose— for example, "Less time to spend with my children," "Little use of my counseling skills," "Less time for professional development activities."

After listing possible risks, losses, and obstacles, take a minute to read your entire list. These events *might* occur. Some are much more probable than others. At this point you may want to determine how realistic your estimations are. What can you read, to whom can you talk, and what can

Alternatives	RISK COMPARISON CHART		
	Possible Risks, Losses, Obstacles	Contingency Action Steps	Acceptability Rating
Pension Planner	1) Opportunities for advancement might not materialize. 2) Might find deadline pressures too stressful. 3) Might find co-workers or clients difficult to relate to.	1) Talk with boss about concrete steps I can make to advance, cultivate mentor relationships. Join professional women's network. 2) Take time management course. 3) Learn about their interests and goals. Examine my competitive tendencies.	3
Public Relations, Nonprofit Organization	1) New position might not get re-funded. 2) Might be dead-end job, no place to advance. 3) Might require evening, weekend work on special events.	1) Track progress, impact of position so re-funding more likely; talk with boss to encourage re-funding. 2) Involvement in Women in Communications to meet other public relations workers in other settings 3) Talk with family. Clarify expectations	3
Real Estate Sales	1) With tight market, may not make decent income. 2) May not be able to compete with highly aggressive salespeople. 3) Evening, weekend work will strain my family life.	1 & 2) Take a sales seminar. Polish my sales approach in ways consistent with my values. 3) Talk with family. Experiment with different working hours.	1

you do to check out the accuracy of your estimations? Yet keep in mind that no matter how much information you obtain, you'll still be estimating. You can't know *for sure* till you try the alternative.

Having in mind some stand-by action steps is an excellent way to handle risks and obstacles. On the Risk Comparison Chart, list specific action steps you can take if the event comes about or to prevent the event from happening in the first place.

Finally, think about your willingness to accept the risks, losses, and obstacles listed for each job objective alternative. This is the scale by which to rate each alternative:

0 = totally unacceptable
1 = mostly unacceptable, very uncomfortable with it
2 = somewhat unacceptable, some reservations
3 = mainly acceptable, a few reservations
4 = acceptable

You have a right to choose the kinds of risks, losses, obstacles you will and will not accept. You also have the responsibility to live with the consequences of your decision, whether satisfying or difficult.

We provide Shirley Zimmerman's filled out chart on the next page as an example.

Make a Tentative Decision

Now it's time to integrate insights from previous steps to make a tentative decision. You want to choose an alternative that fits what's important to you *and* that has acceptable risks. If the alternative that best fits your important criteria has acceptable risks, choose this one. However, if these risks are not acceptable to you, consider options with acceptable risks and a more moderate fit with important factors.

Shirley Zimmerman decided to begin job hunting in the pension planning area, believing that this career could give her what she wanted and still have acceptable risks. While she believed real estate sales might involve bigger risks that she chose to take at the time, she saw that option as somewhat more possible once her children were independent. She figured if she were not able to land a pension planning position, she would investigate public relations further, broadening her investigation to profit-making corporations. She felt good about her decision-making.

Now write your primary job objective here:

_____

Alternatives	RISK COMPARISON CHART		
	Possible Risks, Losses, Obstacles	Contingency Action Steps	Acceptability Rating

Remember that no decision is perfect or irreversible. When you begin your job hunt you may find fewer positions available in your area than you expected, you may discover certain aspects to the jobs available that you don't like, or any of a number of new items of information may cause you to want to adjust your objective. That will be perfectly appropriate; the point is to begin your search with one objective clearly and firmly in mind.

The last step in the decision-making model is also the next step in your creative job search strategy: setting goals and developing an action plan.

SET GOALS AND DEVELOP AN ACTION PLAN

Now that you have your job objective in mind, you are ready to set goals and develop a plan of action. First, ask yourself how soon you want to or have to be employed, and how much time per week you want to spend on your job search. Tom Jackson and Davidyne Mayleas, authors of *The Hidden Job Market,* find that the average job search campaign requires 100 to 200 hours, although some reach their objectives in very little time while others spend far more than 200 hours.

You should plan to commit yourself to 60 to 75 hours of job prospect research, and time for developing your resume, phone calls, interviews. Set weekly goals for yourself and plan your week for the most efficient use of time. Use weekends to plan the week ahead and sort and read information. Use weekdays to make people contact. Make phone calls early in the day so that you have time to return calls or follow up leads. Do anything that you dread doing early so that it doesn't drag on and stall your campaign.

Write it Down

You may find it helpful to write down a weekly job search plan. We have provided a sample form on the next page; you may want to photocopy it and keep a number in a looseleaf job search notebook. At this point you may want to quickly review Chapter 5 to refresh your memory about how to turn long-term goals into action.

Plan for Success

Also, it's especially important for you to plan for success, as discussed in Chapter 5, by deciding on rewards to motivate yourself, taking stock of support, anticipating obstacles, and making time to periodically review your

WEEKLY JOB SEARCH PLAN

Week # _____   Date _____

Job objective: _____

Major goals for this week: _____

_____

What	**When**
Things to read:	
_____	_____
_____	_____
_____	_____
_____	_____
_____	_____
_____	_____
People to talk to:	
_____	_____
_____	_____
_____	_____
_____	_____
_____	_____
_____	_____
Things to do:	
_____	_____
_____	_____
_____	_____
_____	_____
_____	_____

plan. You can expect that looking for a job will be emotionally and intellectually demanding. Take care of yourself by planning enjoyable, non-jobhunt activities. Try to limit yourself to no more than five hours per day of creative job search work, but keep your momentum going by requiring a minimum number of hours per week, probably not less than five.

With the momentum of a job objective and a written plan behind you, you're now ready to go on to Step 3 in your creative job search strategy.

HIGHLIGHTS

☐ Don't put yourself at the mercy of the job market by playing the "Numbers Game."

☐ Tap the hidden job market with a creative job search strategy:
— know *what* you want
— know *where* you can do it
— know *how* to get hired.

☐ The first two steps are clearly defining your primary job objective and setting goals for action.

RESOURCES

Bolles, R. *What Color is Your Parachute?* Berkeley, CA: Ten Speed Press, 1979.

This is probably the best known book in the job-hunting field. The 1979 edition attempts to address women's issues more specifically with appendices on job-hunting publications for women and a state-by-state list of women's resource centers. Chapter 4 on how to evaluate professional help is especially useful.

Djeddah, E. *Moving Up*. Berkeley, CA: Ten Speed Press, 1978.

Djeddah outlines a "hidden job market" approach for job relocation and advancement, and provides an excellent review of all job hunt methods. His strategies for salary negotiation and handling tough questions about your weaknesses are useful.

Figler, H. *The Complete Job Search Handbook*. New York: Holt, Rinehart and Winston, 1979.

Figler places special emphasis on communication skills, personal insights, and feelings as opposed to purely rational models of career choice. He expands the ideas proposed by Bolles and others into a comprehensive model of career skills. These are the specific self-assessment, communication, and research skills that are essential pre-requisites for successfully implementing career search strategies. Sensible, empathic advice by a counselor with many years experience in his field.

Jackson, T. and Mayleas, D. *The Hidden Job Market*. New York: New York Times Book Co., 1976.

A good step-by-step guide to creative job search techniques which target the hidden job market. Not much of a departure from Bolles' views but this book is set up as a workbook which is systematic and detailed.

Miller, A. *Finding Career Alternatives for Teachers*. New York: Apple Publishing Company, 1979.

Excellent guidelines on doing field research, informational interviews, identifying contacts, preparing resumes, and preparing for job interviews.

18

LOCATING JOB PROSPECTS

Never turn down a job

because you think it's too small;

you don't know where it can lead.

Julia Morgan, architect,
who designed San Simeon for William Randolph Hearst,
quoted in *Architect and Engineer*, 1918.

W*ITH* your job objective clearly in mind, you're now ready to move out and look for employers who can use your skills and for whom you are interested in working. Basically, you have a matching problem: you don't know who needs you and the people with the jobs don't know that you are looking. In this chapter we show you how you can become highly visible and develop access to potential employers, by

□ cultivating a network of contacts

□ using traditional job information sources to your advantage

□ researching potential employers in depth

IDENTIFY POTENTIAL EMPLOYERS

In this third step of your creative job search strategy, it's especially important for you to remember you're in control here. Avoid lapsing into a wallflower-at-the-school-dance mentality, wistfully hoping you'll be offered a job by a good employer. Remember, you have valuable skills and energy to offer, and the employer for whom you decide to work will be fortunate indeed. And you *do* have a large amount of control over the situation, if you will proceed as we describe and stay firmly grounded at all times in your self-knowledge.

Cultivate a Network of Contacts

Because three quarters of all available jobs are not listed anywhere, it stands to reason that you can only find out about them through word of mouth. Indeed, the most effective way for you to tap into the hidden job market is by cultivating a network of contacts who can tell you about job openings they become aware of from their vantage points. And "contacts" don't necessarily have to be those in positions of power.

Everyone you meet is a potential contact. The woman at your bus stop might have an uncle who is looking for a medical illustration trainee when you are trying to figure out what to do with a degree in biology and a hobby in art. Let everyone you talk to know that you are looking for a job. This includes both people you would normally talk to in the course of a day, and those you specifically seek out for job information.

Mention your job search to:

☐ your friends, relatives, neighbors, co-workers—and their spouses, families, friends . . .

☐ people you meet at social functions

☐ classmates, instructors, professors, deans

☐ your former boss

☐ people who see a lot of other people—your doctor, your checker at the supermarket, politicians, real estate agents, insurance agents, religious leaders

☐ people you have done volunteer work for or with

☐ other job seekers

You may find it helpful to start a job hunt support group if you know a few people who are also looking for jobs. You might meet regularly to exchange leads and air frustrations and successes.

Another good way to expand your contact network is to attend conventions and professional meetings in your area of interest, after first checking to make sure non-members can attend. As we mentioned in Chapter 12, newspapers and your Chamber of Commerce are good sources of convention listings.

Continue Information Interviews   Contact the people you spoke with in your previous information interviews, let them know of your job objective choice, and ask if they know of any openings. In addition, continue your job information interviews, with successful people in your area of interest, with friends of friends employed in your target industry, with anyone who is doing what you would like to be doing. Remember, people are usually more than happy to talk about themselves and their experiences in a relaxed atmosphere, which you will create when you let them know you are primarily looking for information. You *may* get job offers, but your primary aim should be gathering further information and uncovering potential openings.

In order to keep track of people you talk to during the course of your job search, use the Job Possibilities Log that follows. Make copies of it and keep them in your looseleaf job search notebook. Alternatively, you might consider starting a 3 × 5 card file. Write the name of each person you've talked to on a separate card, and include such information as who referred you, brief notes of your conversation, date of contact, phone number, names of other people to whom this particular contact referred you. Periodically you may want to check back with the people on your cards to see if they've heard of anything since you last talked to them.

The key to making contacts work is persistence and an assertive attitude. Rather than feeling ashamed or apologetic about looking for a job, make a positive statement about your goals. Respect your worth and be confident that people are glad to be able to help you. You won't give anyone the chance to help you get what you want unless you ask them.

Use Traditional Information Sources

While the best use of your energy during your job search is probably in cultivating your contact network, you will not want to totally ignore some of the more traditional routes. After we worked extensively with one client whose job objective was a sales position in building products, she rather sheepishly reported to us that she had accepted a position she found listed in the newspaper! The key to making these traditional methods work for you is knowing what they can do for you, what their limits are, and how to get the most out of them with the most economical effort on your part.

Classified Ads   The want ads probably identify less than ten percent of the published job market. When you rely on the newspaper you are competing with most job seekers for this small percentage, of which it's likely that only very few are of any interest to you at all.

It is important to remember that the classified ads describe what employers think they want, but the jobs often end up being filled by persons

JOB POSSIBILITIES LOG

Job Objective _____

Referral Source	Organization Contact Person	Address Telephone	Description of Job Opening	Date of Contact	Comments on Contact

who don't fit that description at all. An employer who advertises a position has to commit the company's resources to the unrewarding task of screening a deluge of resumes, telephone inquiries, and walk-in applicants. For these reasons employers will often choose to leave a position open or hire a convenient applicant rather than advertise the position. The converse can also be true—often few or no applicants appear for a job. "Never assume" seems to be a useful adage.

If you want to feel that you have covered every angle, play the classified ad numbers game with these guidelines:

- □ *Answer promptly.* Send your response and resume immediately after reviewing the Sunday newspaper. The peak of responses to these advertisements will usually arrive at the company on Wednesday. Better yet, add especially interesting potential employers to your personal call list, to be telephoned first thing on Monday. Scan the ads during the rest of the week and respond promptly.

- □ *Economize with your time.* Answering the ads can become busywork which is safer and easier than pursuing those crucial, but more intimidating, personal contacts. Make a plan, then stick with it.

- □ *Tailor your resume* and cover letter to the ad's specifications. Use your research to demonstrate knowledge of the company and product.

- □ *Omit* anything from your response that might screen you out. Let the employer contact you to find out more. You might feel more comfortable composing a chatty, friendly letter describing yourself, but you will risk including potential screen-out elements. Keep your letters, as well as your telephone inquiries, brief and professional.

- □ *Use personal contacts,* if available, to set yourself aside from the crowd. Call your friend at XYZ Company and say "I noticed your company is advertising for a _____ . Can you tell me anything about that? I'd like to call the supervisor of that department. Who would that be? Can I tell her that I talked with you and that I'm a friend of yours?" The fact that the job is advertised does not mean that you must pursue it through conventional channels. Buried by resumes and overwhelmed by telephone inquiries, most employers will have a more positive response to someone who appears to be recommended from within.

- □ *Beware of blind ads.* Ads asking you to reply to a box number are usually unrewarding and an uneconomical use of your time. They may be used by people who have no jobs to offer but want your name for promotional purposes, or by employment agencies who want to beef up their files of available applicants. Even if the ad is legitimate, you are severely limited in your power to promote yourself. If you are intrigued enough by the ad, send off a brief reply and see what happens.

□ *Avoid "invest in your future" ads.* They usually mean "invest in our company or product." They usually stand to make more money in this transaction than you do. Sometimes the investment you are asked to make is substantial, and the training and advice you receive is very minimal.

□ *Beware of "no experience necessary" ads.* A job that doesn't require any experience but needs to be advertised is probably difficult to fill because of poor salary, working conditions, or straight commission. Agencies pull in a lot of people with this kind of ad.

Position Wanted Ads   You can take the initiative to place an ad outlining your qualifications and job objective. Since employers are not in the habit of looking in the newspaper for employees, this strategy has not had a high success rate. If you want to increase your odds, you need to have fairly clear-cut qualifications and a specific job in mind. Your best bet is to advertise in trade or professional journals in your field. However, you may still receive a number of responses from employment agencies and "invest in your future" types, rather than legitimate job prospects. Whether you choose to use it or not, writing such an ad can be an excellent exercise in self-affirmation and goals clarification.

Clearinghouses and Registers   These are job banks and matching services which handle both employer and job seeker listings. They may be free or charge a fee. They may be general or for specific fields. Like employment agencies, these services are more oriented to finding people for jobs than jobs for people. Weigh the costs and benefits of each service and be selective.

Private Employment Agencies   All private agencies charge fees which are paid only if and when you are hired. These fees are tax deductible. You will be asked to sign a contract. Read it carefully and retain a copy. It is important to note *before* you go on an interview whether the fee is to be paid by the employer, by you, split between you, or is otherwise negotiable. Regardless of what the counselor tells you, once you are offered the job you can always choose to negotiate a better deal with the employer concerning your fee or salary. However, you may be better off paying the fee yourself than accepting the job at a lower salary to compensate.

Don't confuse a private employment counselor with a vocational counselor. Their loyalties lie in different directions. Private employment counselors are more loyal to their customers—the employers with whom they work regularly—than to you, the applicant. Agencies make their money on volume business and easy matches. "Counselors" essentially are salespeople who work for commission only or salary plus commission. Try to work with an employment counselor who appears to have strong contacts and experience in the business. Use the counselor's expertise to supplement your job search. Be assertive about your goals by refusing to go on interviews for positions which don't match your career direction. Don't expect counselors to spend any appreciable time looking for jobs for you, even if they request exclusive handling. They will probably ask, but we recommend that if you choose to use agencies, that you work with more than one.

Agencies usually don't know what to do with a re-entry woman because your expertise is less likely to be clear-cut and you are not likely to be an easy match except for entry level clerical positions. If you are bright, verbal, and assertive you may be offered a job as one of the agency's counselors. This can give you a good overview of the working world tapped by employment agencies. While many counselors have the hidden agenda of placing themselves in one of their own job listings, thus saving a fee and doing the job hunt on someone else's time, they rarely do. Your best bet is to work as your own agent/counselor and give yourself your exclusive and expert handling.

Public Employment Agencies. The United States Employment Service has over 2,000 local Job Service offices which offer a variety of counseling and placement services at no charge. You will be interested in checking their Job Bank, a computerized file of job openings which are revised and printed out daily. Many offices also have occupational registers—files of resumes of qualified workers in professional, clerical, and craft occupations, for employers to use.

All state employment service agencies develop detailed labor market data for local areas. These reports deal with future supply, characteristics of the work force, changes in state and local economic activity and the employment structure of important industries. While this information is pretty detailed and statistical, you may discover some good jumping-off points for your job search.

Executive Search Firms Employers use these firms to hire away executives and rising young stars from other companies. If you are already employed in a management position and looking to improve your position but not drastically change your work, these firms might be interested in you. They are generally not receptive to unsolicited resumes and are usually of little value to re-entry women.

Temporary Employment Agencies These agencies hire and pay you to work for short periods of time in other companies. You will have an inside track to talk with managers about the type of work you want and potential opportunities in that company, but you will have to assertively deal with your stereotype as a temporary worker. While you should have time between assignments to job hunt, you are likely to be quite tied up during the work day while you are on assignment unless you negotiate the time off.

Community Agencies A growing number of nonprofit agencies provide career development and job placement services, as well as counseling for personal, family, or other problems that may stand in the way of getting a job. Some agencies focus specifically on women, with re-entry women or displaced homemakers as a targeted group. Consult your yellow pages for names and numbers of agencies in your community.

College Placement Bureaus As we mentioned in Chapter 14, most schools offer career counseling and placement services to their students, including part-time students as well as alumni. They may offer or refer you to work-shops on resume writing, interviewing, and job hunting. Even if you do not choose to meet with on-campus recruiters, you can peruse old and current job listings to get the names of potential contacts and employers.

Company Personnel Offices While the personnel department usually knows of vacancies, it is reactive to the needs of the company. Thus, it is rarely attuned to potential jobs and has little power to redefine job descriptions to match the special skills and needs of the applicant. This ability lies with the person who has the power to hire you. The personnel department usually serves to screen out applicants and to refer the survivors to those who make the actual hire decisions.

Personnel departments should not be overlooked as good sources of information and the place to secure an entry level job, but they are likely to view their job as *not* including giving you contacts or referrals to people higher up. Again, your best strategy is to utilize your contact network to give you a personal referral to someone within an organization. If your referral network comes up empty-handed, call the company's switchboard, ask for the name of a department head for your area of interest, and then ask to be connected to that person.

Other Printed Sources of Information Professional, business, and trade association publications often have job listings. The same cautions apply here as to classified ads. It may be more useful for you to read these publications with an eye out for news of company relocations and expansions, and employee promotions and transfers.

The same goes for newspapers. Reading between the lines of the business section can give you clues to companies that may be hiring. And don't forget the phone book as a rich source of potential employers to interview for information.

Maintain Your Log

Remember to note in your Job Possibilities Log all information you glean from these more traditional job prospect sources. As you compare your entries, certain ones will undoubtedly stand out as more promising, because there is a position currently available that is attractive to you, a helpful contact person, or a company with a high likelihood of having a job that would fill your needs. Star these prospects in your log and make them the target of the next step in your creative job search strategy.

RESEARCH YOUR BEST PROSPECTS IN DEPTH

Your next step is to find out all you can about these best prospects, to get a better idea of your potential contribution and fit. What does the company do? What are its products or services? What is its general structure? Is it part of a conglomerate, incorporated, a partnership, or family-owned? Is it making money? Is it expanding or contracting? Where is it located? What is the company's reputation? What is the philosophy of its management? If you are researching a non-profit or social service organization you will want to know about its services, clientele, and funding.

Use a Variety of Information Sources

Use both printed resources and contacts to round out your picture of your best prospects. The Better Business Bureau and the Chamber of Commerce in your town can provide you with information about specific employers. So can placement agencies or executive search firms. And don't overlook the company's public relations department—they can provide you with brochures and annual reports that project the image the company has of itself.

In addition, college placement offices or occupational libraries have a variety of materials about specific employers. Particularly if you are looking for a job in business or industry, there are a wide variety of directories and manuals you can consult for specific information. Some of these are listed in the Resources section at the end of the chapter.

Stock brokers, college professors in related fields, and company employees or employees of related firms can all give you information about a company's reputation and direction.

Pursue More Contacts

In addition to information, you are looking for contacts who can aid you in pursuing your job objectives further with specific employers. Marion Smidt, working in public administration, wished to make a jump to private industry but was unsure how her general administrative skills would transfer. She considered a local multinational corporation a best prospect but was stuck about where to start. A co-worker offered to call a friend who worked in that company for advice. The friend suggested contacting the Vice President for Executive Personnel. An interview followed during which the executive, also a woman, explained how a person with Marion's background would best fit in the organization. She made suggestions for further contacts that would help further clarify her sense of direction.

Sandy Buchanan, more focused on her job objective, contacted a potential employer in the city to which she planned to move when her husband entered graduate school. Although the potential opening in this company did not materialize, the employer not only gave her the flavor of local opportunities in her field but picked up the telephone and arranged an interview for her at another company. Armed with information about the other company's reputation as well as the local norms for salary and job requirements, she received a job offer.

After this extensive research you are much better prepared than most job seekers to write a resume that displays your strengths and speaks to the needs of the few target companies you know you are interested in. We show you how in the next chapter.

HIGHLIGHTS

☐ The best use of your time while you are identifying potential employers is in cultivating a contact network.

☐ Traditional sources of job prospect information can be useful as long as they are kept in perspective.

☐ Research your best prospects in depth to get a better idea of your potential contribution and fit.

RESOURCES

National Directory of Women's Employment Programs: Who They Are; What They Do. Washington: Wider Opportunities for Women, Inc., 1979.

Contains information on organizations which serve women who are entering the work force. Describes 140 organizations, their services, and how to contact them.

Consult the following sources for information on publicly and privately owned companies. In general, directories will give brief information on company products and services, officers, size and sales, and address and telephone number. Some public relations and financial report material may be available free from companies you are interested in. Also check newspaper and periodical indexes, telephone directories, and clipping files.

College Placement Annual.

Published annually by the College Placement Council. This is worth looking through for information on jobs whether you are a college graduate or not. It contains the location of home and branch offices and a brief description of the company and the types of jobs it seeks to fill. Companies are also grouped by the type of job and by geographical location. Often the name of the person who recruits on behalf of the company is included.

Dun and Bradstreet Reference Book of Corporate Managements. New York: Dun and Bradstreet.

Published annually and arranged by company, this reference lists major executives and gives information on birth year, college attended, and employment data.

F and S Index. Cleveland, Ohio: Predicasts, Inc.

> *Consult this general business index when you want information on a company, product, or industry. Part one indexes articles about a particular product, business, or industry, arranged by Standard Industrial Classification (SIC) number. Part two contains periodical citations arranged alphabetically by company name.*

Jablonski, E., ed. *How to Find Information About Companies*. Washington, DC: Washington Researchers, 1979.

> *A guide to information sources about public and private companies. Includes information on local, state, and federal government sources, trade associations, data bases, and libraries. Telephone numbers for agencies are listed so that you can call for more information.*

Million Dollar Directory. New York: Dun and Bradstreet.

> *Information on products or services, amount of sales, number of employees and executive officers is presented for companies with a net worth of one million dollars or more. It is arranged alphabetically, geographically, and by primary business activity.*

Middle Market Directory. New York: Dun and Bradstreet.

> *This is similar to the* Million Dollar Directory *except that it lists businesses with a net worth from $500,000 to $999,000.*

Standard and Poor's Register of Corporations, Directors and Executives. New York: Standard and Poor's Corporation.

> *Volume 1 gives basic directory information for companies listed alphabetically. Volume 2 lists company officials and directors with brief biographical information. Volume 3 contains indexes to Volume 1 by Standard Industrial Classification (SIC) number and by geographical location.*

Thomas Register of American Manufacturers and *Thomas Register Catalog File*. New York: Thomas Publishing Company.

> *This register lists about 90,000 U.S. private and public manufacturing companies. Entries are arranged by product classifications and list manufacturers of each specific product. One volume lists manufacturers alphabetically.*

19

DEVELOPING YOUR RESUME

If you don't sing your song,
who will?
Anonymous

Y_{OUR} resume is a concise method of presenting key information about yourself to attract the attention of a potential employer and get you an interview. At best, it should present your skills and experience in a favorable and focused way so the person who has the power to hire you can immediately see that you will fill his or her need. It should also boost your self-confidence every time you read it.

In this chapter we show you how to put together such a resume. We also discuss situations in which a resume is *not* your most effective campaign tool, and show you an alternative. You will

☐ log experience related to your job objective

☐ select an appropriate format, draft, and polish your resume or resume alternative

☐ learn the best way to approach an employer

LOG RELATED EXPERIENCE

The first step in preparing your resume is to write down all the facts and figures about yourself so that you have a pool of data from which to select what's pertinent to your job objective. Even if you choose not to prepare a

244

resume, but to use the resume alternative that we describe later, you'll find the Resume Background Log useful in organizing your experience. At this point you will want to review the exercises in Chapter 10, in which you listed your basic transferable skills, personal traits, and work content skills. This information is an important part of your data pool. Fill out the Resume Background Log now.

RESUME BACKGROUND LOG

EDUCATION
List in inverse order, from most recent to past.

Name of Institution _____

Degrees Awarded _____

Date of Graduation (or Attendance) _____

Special Coursework _____

_____

_____

Name of Institution _____

Degrees Awarded _____

Date of Graduation (or Attendance) _____

Special Coursework _____

_____

_____

PAID AND UNPAID WORK EXPERIENCE
List all paid *and* unpaid work experience in inverse order from most recent to past.

Under "Job Description," use no more than three to four sentences to describe what you did in this work experience. Use action verbs . . . *organized, wrote, taught.*

Under "Accomplishments," list any concrete accomplishments you can. Brag a little! Attach numbers to your accomplishments if possible. . . "Cut $2,000 from supply budget," "Co-ordinated 3,000 walkers in WALK FOR M.S. FUNDRAISER."

Job Title _____

Name of Organization _____

Dates of Employment _____

Job Description _____

_____

_____

_____

Accomplishments _____

_____

Job Title _____

Name of Organization _____

Dates of Employment _____

Job Description _____

_____

_____

_____

Accomplishments _____

_____

Job Title _____

Name of Organization _____

Dates of Employment _____

Job Description _____

_____

_____

_____

Accomplishments _____

_____

ORGANIZATION MEMBERSHIPS
List in inverse order, from most recent to past.

Name of Organization _____

Membership Dates _____

Recognition (positions, awards, accomplishments) _____

_____

_____

Name of Organization _____

Membership Dates _____

Recognition (positions, awards, accomplishments) _____

_____

_____

SKILLS YOU WANT TO USE IN PAID WORK
Transfer your answers to here from the exercises in Chapter 10.

Basic Transferable Skills _____

_____

_____

_____

_____

Accomplishments in which you used these skills _____

_____

_____

_____

_____

Personal Traits _____

_____

_____

_____

_____

Accomplishments in which you used these traits _____

_____

_____

_____

_____

Work content skills _____

_____

_____

_____

_____

Accomplishments in which you used these skills _____

_____

_____

_____

_____

REFERENCES
Even though you will not list references on the resume, it's a good idea to organize these contacts now. Ask each person if they are willing to be a reference. Review your qualifications and objectives with them.

Name _____

Title _____

Address _____

Phone _____

Name _____

Title _____

Address _____

Phone _____

Name _____

Title _____

Address _____

Phone _____

Now you're ready to select *some* of the data from your background log and organize it around a job objective. List your job objective on the following Job Objective Experience Log. Make separate sheets if you have more than one objective. Then, reading over your Resume Background Log, jot down *any* experiences and skills which might relate to this objective. Don't worry about perfecting your language at this point. This is just a way to begin organizing your thoughts. Look at the example of Elizabeth Hilton's sheet.

JOB OBJECTIVE EXPERIENCE LOG

Job Objective: *to use technical writing and editing skills in a position with advancement potential*

Related Experiences and Skills:

1) recent coursework (Scientific and Technical Writing, Publications Editing, Technical Editing, Technical Graphics, Fortran).

2) training as x-ray technologist — medical terminology knowledge

3) editorial job — editing, technical writing, knowledge of technical language (mass transit).

4) edit church newsletter

5) research interviewing job — interviewing, technical language (vocational education).

6) x-ray technologist — communicate daily, oral and written in medical technical language.

JOB OBJECTIVE EXPERIENCE LOG

Job Objective: _____

_____

Related Experiences and Skills: _____

_____

_____

_____

_____

_____

_____

_____

_____

_____

_____

_____

_____

_____

_____

_____

_____

_____

_____

_____

_____

_____

_____

_____

SELECT AN APPROPRIATE FORMAT

Now you're ready to use information from your Job Objective Experience Log to put together a first draft, using one of a number of resume formats. Each of the formats we describe here is most appropriate to a particular set of circumstances. Read through each of the following to choose the style which best highlights your skills and experience.

Chronological Resume

This is the most accepted and familiar format. It's best for someone who has been steadily and sequentially employed without changing jobs more than once every few years. If you have job-hopped or had several employment gaps it will not show your qualifications to best advantage. This format also has disadvantages if your most recent jobs are ones which you would not want to emphasize. To use this format, list your jobs in chronological order beginning with the most recent. More recent experiences and accomplishments should be described in more detail. Build on your earlier experiences to show your growth and professional development.

We show as an example a typical chronological resume, showing no recent employment gaps. If Deborah Newhouse had more than one job objective or wanted to keep her options more open, she could delete the objective from the resume and add focused objectives to each cover letter.

Functional Resume

This format highlights skills and accomplishments while playing down specific dates and places of employment. It can help cover up employment gaps and de-emphasize recent menial or non-relevant employment. Consider this format if you are making a major career shift or if your skills are illustrated in a wide diversity of paid and unpaid experiences. The functional resume's disadvantage is that employers are less familiar with it and may be somewhat suspicious.

Jeanne Poole wrote the following functional resume with one particular job in mind. She described her skills in terms of a wide variety of paid and unpaid work experiences. Only two of her jobs were for pay (Elderhostel coordinator and high school teacher), but there is no need to make this

CHRONOLOGICAL RESUME

DEBORAH NEWHOUSE

412 Walker Street
Dayton, Ohio 45392
(513) 921-6043 (business)
(513) 962-8014 (home)

Job Objective: to develop and coordinate a volunteer program in a growing
  community organization.

Work Experience:

1977 - Present
Coordinator, Tutor Center
Southside Neighborhood Services
  . Build and expand program involving 15-35 junior
      high school students and their volunteer adult
      tutors.
  . Coordinate transportation and scheduling of
      tutoring.
  . Provide orientation and ongoing supervision.
  . Plan and carry out bimonthly tutor training
      workshops using community and school resources.

May 1974 - June 1977
Pre-school Teacher
Sunnyside Nursery School
  . Developed and implemented comprehensive curriculum
      for four-year-olds.
  . Initiated parent involvement teams.
  . Raised $2000 for Toddler Fun and Fitness Day.

September 1970 -
  February 1977
Office Manager
Oakridge Planned Parenthood
  . Scheduled and coordinated activities of paid and
      volunteer staff.
  . Oriented new staff concerning policies and
      procedures.
  . Wrote press releases and brochures to recruit
      volunteers.

Unpaid Work Experience:

1975- Present
Speakers Bureau, Women's Education Equity Coalition
  . Speak to community groups about need to eliminate
      sex-role stereotypes in educational curriculum
      and literature.

1979 - Present
Crisis Phone Couselor, SUPPORT for battered women
  . Actively listen and support women in crisis.
  . Make referrals to community groups for long-term
      help.

1973 - Present
League of Women Voters
  . Chair early education lobby group

Education:
Early Education Teachers Certification
  Wright State University, 1973
Associate of Liberal Arts
  Cuyahoga Community College, 1967

FUNCTIONAL RESUME

JEANNE   POOLE

123 68th Street
Kansas City, Missouri
(694) 830-8218

Job Objective: Communications Director, Kansas Science Museum

SELECTED ACCOMPLISHMENTS

Program Development: Designed and taught American History, French, and general science curricula to high school students. Coordinated program for American Foreign Student Exchange culture camp. Chaired program committee for Kansas City Girl Scouts Fitness and Fun Weekend.

Public Relations: Wrote brochures, press releases, and college bulletin copy for Elderhostel, a statewide summer college study program for senior citizens. Prepared press releases and posters for Bonne Bell 10K Race involving 1,100 women.

Research: Conducted evaluation follow-up study of Elderhostel participants. Designed and administered questionnaire; interviewed 35 participants. Analyzed data and recommended changes in Elderhostel program. Am an active member of the Research Committee, American Foreign Student Exchange Program.

Public Speaking: Have spoken on running and fitness, African folklore, feminist folklore, volunteerism, Elderhostel, to various professional associations, educational and civic groups, corporate seminars.

Writing: Published articles on regular basis in Daisy, national Girl Scout publication with circulation 250,000. Wrote individualized general science study guides for talented youth. Published scientific journal articles on women and running.

Liaison with Special
Interest Groups: Worked extensively with senior citizens, high school students, teachers and parents, Girl Scouts, foreign exchange students.

Education: B.A. from Grinnell College with major in History, minors in Education, French, and General Science.

differentiation in the resume. Transferring the job objective to the cover letter would allow her to use this resume for other job positions *if* the skills listed relate to other job objectives.

Combination Resume

This format is similar to the functional resume but includes dates, places of employment, and job titles in a later section. You spotlight your most relevant skills and accomplishments while also providing a chronology. Employers may be more accepting of this format than of a functional one.

Elizabeth Hilton's combination format spotlights skills she has developed through work and education over an extended time span. The recency of very relevant coursework is emphasized.

Resume Alternative

There are situations in which a resume is *not* your most effective campaign tool. If you have been out of the work force for quite awhile and don't have many paid or unpaid activities which you can relate to paid employment, your best bet is to write a letter which makes a direct pitch to an employer for your particular job objective. Such a resume alternative can get you an interview.

Career changers and women re-entering the work world after an extended absence will find a resume alternative advantageous. You can capitalize on extensive research into the organization and thorough assessment of your skills and goals. First, prepare a letter which outlines your objective and details what you can do for this employer. Address it to a specific person in the organization. Then, request an interview for a specific reason and offer a choice of times, following your letter with a telephone call to schedule an appointment. Insist on meeting with that person or another in the organization. Try not to be talked into discussing your qualifications over the telephone or into going through the personnel department.

Ann Belmont has been involved in many diverse volunteer activities in the past fifteen years. Having moved five times during this period, she has just arrived in the Eugene community. Her resume alternative describes only those experiences which relate to a prospective position. Her mobility and unrelated scattered experiences are not evident. She appropriately uses a referral to begin the letter. Mentioning a magazine article about the organization shows that she is knowledgeable and has done her homework.

COMBINATION RESUME

ELIZABETH HILTON

9432 Ashville Avenue
St. Paul, Minnesota 55402
(612) 228-3347

Job Objective: to use technical writing and editing skills in a position
                with advancement potential

Technical Writing: Wrote approved feasibility report, "Nutritious
                        Snackbar for Washburn Junior High School."
                        Successfully completed all projects for recent
                        college course, Scientific and Technical Writing.

Editing: Edited final draft of William Goodman's The Future
                        of Mass Transit. Successfully completed college
                        course, Publications Editing. Edited Twin Cities
                        Unite, Unitarian newsletter.

Technical Languages: Developed extensive knowledge of medical/hospital
                        terminology as x-ray technician. Became adept
                        with basic computer language. Learned terminologies
                        of mass transit industry and vocational education.

Research Interviewing: Interviewed counselors, instructors, and students
                        regarding the nature of sex stereotyping and dis-
                        crimination in vocational education.

Education:

1978-1980   University of Minnesota courses:
                    Scientific and Technical Writing
                    Publications Editing
                    Technical Graphics
                    Elementary and Intermediate Fortran

   1957   X-ray Technology Certification, Methodist Hospital

Work Experience:

1977-1979   Editorial Assistant for William Goodman, author of The Future
                of Mass Transit.

   1973   Data Collector, American Institute for Research,
                Palo Alto, California.
                Project: Sex Stereotyping in Vocational Education

1957-1964   X-ray Technologist, Children's Hospital
                Minneapolis, Minnesota

RESUME ALTERNATIVE

9241 Hillcrest Road
Eugene, Oregon 97401
26 April 19X1

Dr. Peter Hampton
Courage Center School
7432 Milton Road
Eugene, Oregon 97403

Dear Dr. Hampton:

Ms. Katherine Miller of the Eugene School for the Deaf suggested
that I contact you about a new position as fundraising coordinator.
I am aware of your faculty's outstanding reputation as educators of
the physically handicapped. A recent article about your creative
dramatics program in <u>Children's Theatre World</u> really sparked my
enthusiasm, since I have worked with the deaf in a similar program.

As a board officer of a children's theatre group, I have had a great
deal of fundraising experience. I coordinated a team which successfully solicited two hundred thousand dollars. My approach involved
making presentations to officers of local corporations and civic
groups, contacting foundations and endowments, and organizing a
public mail campaign. I used my organizational and delegating skills
to manage an efficient, enthusiastic team. I believe I can apply
these same fundraising strategies to expand Courage Center's quality
programs.

In addition to this experience, I co-authored and received a grant
to initiate an Arts Program for the Hearing Impaired. I became
familiar with many traditional channels of funding for the handicapped.
As the mime instructor in this program, I learned a lot about personal
strengths and obstacles of physically handicapped individuals.

I am eager to learn more about your school and this new position. I
will call you next Monday to arrange an interview. I would be free
to meet with you next Thursday or Friday. Thank you.

Sincerely,

Ann Belmont

Ms. Ann Belmont

POLISH YOUR DRAFT

Whichever format you use for your first draft, apply the following rules as you polish and finalize what you have written.

- ☐ Be sure to include your name, address, and most important, telephone number. This seems too obvious to mention, but we have been astounded by employers who have told us of being interested in applicants they're unable to contact for lack of this information.

- ☐ Keep it brief. One page is preferable, as any more is less likely to be read. Remember, your goal is to get an interview, not to provide an all-inclusive autobiography.

- ☐ Organize your pertinent data concisely. Be selective. Avoid over-writing and include only essential details. Give specific facts rather than general statements.

- ☐ If you indicate a job objective it should be clear and specific. Including a job objective is desirable but not essential.

- ☐ If you have more than one job objective, write separate resumes, each detailing skills and experiences appropriate for that objective. Or you can put the job objective in the attached cover letter, making sure skills and experiences in the resume still dovetail with each job objective.

- ☐ Describe your unpaid as well as your paid experience. It may not be necessary to separate your unpaid from the paid. Include dates, names of organizations, and job titles.

- ☐ Keep in mind your job objective or the position for which you are applying when describing your experience. Emphasize the aspects of your background which are most supportive.

- ☐ Use action language to describe your experience and qualifications. Instead of "my duties were" or "among my responsibilities were," state "I *managed . . . initiated . . . supervised . . . developed . . . designed . . . coordinated . . . implemented.*" Review the basic skills checklists in Chapter 10 for exemplary action verbs. Following is a general list of action/skill words from which you may wish to draw.

GENERAL ACTION/SKILL WORDS

adapted	established	planned
administered	evaluated	programmed
analyzed	expedited	proved
approved	founded	provided
coordinated	increased	reduced
conceived	implemented	reinforced
conducted	initiated	reorganized
created	improved	revised
designed	led	reviewed
delegated	managed	set up
developed	organized	solved
directed	originated	supervised

☐ Do *not* include: Personal data such as age, sex, marital status, number of children, height, weight, health, hobbies (unless very relevant to a particular job), or membership in religious, political, or social organizations. Do not include past salaries, salary expectations, or reasons for leaving past jobs. Do not include a photograph. Delete your grade point average unless it is excellent. You don't want to be selected *out* before you get into the interview.

☐ Indicate that "References are available on request" rather than listing specific names and addresses. Your references should be persons who are familiar with your work, not personal friends. Speak to these references about your objectives and discuss aspects of your skills and experiences that you would most like to have emphasized.

☐ Make your resume attractive. Stand out because of your preparation and professional manner rather than because of a resume on pastel paper or other gimmicks.

Paper: Use 8½ × 11 paper. Plain white, ivory, cream, off-white, or gray good quality paper are acceptable.

Layout: Increase eye-appeal with white space between paragraphs and along the edges. Do not fill the entire page with single-spaced typing. Use large or bold type, underlining, and centering to emphasize topic headings and important information. Use a quality typewriter or resume printing service.

Neatness: As with your application form, your resume reflects you— sloppiness, errors, and inappropriateness will be noted.

☐ Review your resume for grammar, spelling, and typographical errors. Have someone with the skills of a good editor proofread it to remove passive voice, wordiness, and awkward and unclear phrasing.

☐ Have enough resumes printed. But remember that you will want to continually update it and if possible, tailor it to specific job openings. Give copies to your references, friends, and others who can aid your job search so that they are well informed about you.

Finally, ask a couple of people to give your draft the one-minute readability test. That is, have them look at your resume for exactly one minute and then give you some instant impressions. After all, one minute is all the time some employers will spend before your resume goes into the wastebasket. Ideally, people employed in your prospective field can probably give you the most helpful feedback.

Updating your Resume Background Log from time to time will speed your updating or revising your resume.

PUT YOUR RESUME TO WORK FOR YOU

Now you're ready to use your resume to introduce yourself to potential employers and create a favorable impression even before the all-important interview. First you must identify the person with the power to hire you. You can get this information through leads from your contact network, or by simply calling a company and asking the name of the individual who supervises the department in which you wish to work. It's very important for you to address a specific individual when you send your resume.

Then, mail your resume with a cover letter pointing out how your skills and experience relate to the needs of the company or the particular opening for which you are applying. The letter should be brief—keep it to a page—and should close with a request for an interview. Following is an example of a cover letter which Elizabeth Hilton wrote in response to a lead from a neighbor. Note that she uses this referral to begin the letter and that she addresses the letter to the department director. She highlights skills most relevant to this company.

Keep a record of each resume and cover letter you have sent out in order to conduct an efficient follow-up campaign. Be sure to call when you indicated you would to schedule an appointment.

And remember to keep your resume in perspective. Although it is an important tool in your job search, it is limited in the amount of information

COVER LETTER

9432 Ashville Avenue
St. Paul, Minnesota 55402
15 February 19X1

Mr. John R. Peters
Technical Communications
  Department Director
Medtronics
4634 Wilford Boulevard
Wazata, Minnesota 55462

Dear Mr. Peters:

James Johnson, biomedical engineer at Medtronics and
a neighbor of mine, told me that you have an opening
for a technical writer.

As you can see from my resume, I have recent coursework and work experience in technical writing and
editing. In addition, I am quite familiar with
medical terminology as a result of several years
experience as an x-ray technologist. I am enthused
about an opportunity to combine my writing and medical
skills for a company with such an excellent reputation
in medical research.

I will call you this Friday to schedule an appointment.
I would be available Tuesday and Thursday during the
next week.

Thank you for your consideration.

                                    Sincerely,

                                    Elizabeth Hilton

                                    Elizabeth Hilton

about you it can convey. The interview is your opportunity to really express your strengths and impress your potential employer, and will count far more heavily in the employer's evaluation of you. So let's go on to that crucial next step in your job search strategy.

HIGHLIGHTS

☐ The purpose of your resume or resume alternative is to get you an interview.

☐ In your resume you should present only those experiences and skills that relate to your job objective.

☐ Draft your resume in a format that is advantageous to you and refine it to be concise and attractive. Use a resume alternative if appropriate.

☐ Send your resume with a cover letter to the individual who has the power to hire you, and follow up with a phone call.

RESOURCES

Brennan, L. D., Strand, S., and Gruber, E. C. *Resumes for Better Jobs.* New York: Monarch Press, 1973.

Over 200 example resumes in varied job classifications provide the reader with many alternatives, especially in format.

Faux, M. *The Complete Resume Guide.* New York: Monarch Press, 1980.

Model resumes keyed to over 200 job categories. Choosing a resume style, cover letter, asking for an interview. Special hints for housewives returning to work, over-forty job hunters, foreign-born, handicapped.

Lathrop, R. *Who's Hiring Who.* Berkeley, CA: Ten Speed Press, 1977.

One chapter contains excellent tips for composing a qualifications brief, rather than a traditional resume. Emphasis is placed on targeting the needs of employers plus personal abilities and achievements that will meet these needs.

Lewis, A. *How to Write Better Resumes*. Woodbury, NY: Barron's Educational Series, 1977.

> *A "special resumes" chapter gives tips and resume examples for: those over forty, minorities, returning housewives, handicapped, job changers, foreign-born, and returning service personnel.*

Resume Preparation Manual: A Step-by-Step Guide for Women. New York: Catalyst, 1976.

> *This excellent manual, geared especially for women, starts with analysis of both personal job targets and achievement. With this essential background, the reader learns to write chronological, functional, and combination resumes, plus resume alternatives and cover letters.*

20

MAKING
THE INTERVIEW
WORK FOR YOU

Always think in terms
of the needs and concerns of your interviewer
and you will be successful
in either getting a specific job or
getting a valuable referral which in turn
will lead you to another job.
Ann Miller, *Finding Career Alternatives for Teachers*

AT last we arrive at the interview—the culmination of your job search, when all of your weeks of self-assessment and research really pay off. The key to making the interview work for you is preparation—and you've got plenty of that. Pull it all together in this chapter as we describe to you

- □ the basics of how to leave a good impression
- □ what to expect in each of the parts of the interview
- □ how to follow through and choose among offers

PROMOTE YOURSELF

At this point in your creative job search strategy, you will be talking to the person who has the power to hire you, probably about an opening that's currently available. See this as your opportunity to actively promote yourself. Let the interviewer know what you want and do well, and why you would like to work for that company. You will come across as an interested and prepared potential employee. Even if a position is not available at this time, you will leave the favorable impression of being a well-prepared applicant, and will probably be the first person the employer thinks of when an opening does occur.

You can increase your effectiveness in promoting yourself if you keep the following considerations in mind.

Know Your Objective

Your objective in an interview is both to *convey* a good impression of your potential as an employee, and to *form* an impression of the position and the employer. It's very important for you to realize this. Too often job interviews are classic examples of one-way communication, where the interviewer asks the questions and you give the answers. The interview will work better for both of you if you remember that while the interviewer's job is to determine your qualifications and to predict whether you will be a successful employee, your responsibility is to make the same type of assessment about the organization and the job.

So remind yourself that an interview is not a win-lose situation but simply one way of predicting if you are right for a particular job and if the job is right for you. The interviewer's goals are nearly the same as your own—to place you in a position in which you are competent and satisfied.

Prepare yourself to elaborate on information in your resume or on the application by outlining beforehand the points *you* want to cover—your strengths, what you uniquely can bring to this position, and questions you have about the job and the company. Since a few interviews are conducted by panels of three or more, make sure to ask about this. You'll be much more likely to maintain a self-confident manner if you anticipate a panel.

Be aware that the most important information an interviewer gets out of an interview is a subjective feeling. Your application and resume provide the hard facts useful for screening your qualifications. Your enthusiasm, assertiveness, sincerity, self-confidence, and courtesy present an image that will convince the interviewer he or she ought to offer the job to you.

Dress to Impress

First impressions really do count. Research studies indicate that many interviewers make at least a basic pass/fail decision within the first few minutes of the interview. If you are sloppy, unclean, or dressed in an inappropriate or unprofessional manner, you are likely to be screened out in those first crucial moments. If the interviewer hasn't identified anything objectionable, you have the rest of the interview to build on your positive impression.

A lot has been written recently about dressing for success and the subtle psychological effects of colors. It can be pretty overwhelming to try to consider whether you should try to project an image of power or of a good team player, if this company's computer programmers should dress like office workers or junior executives, or if you would be better off wearing a conservative suit or a bright and cheerful outfit. These may be relatively minor issues that can distract you and contribute to your nervousness.

H. Anthony Medley, author of *Sweaty Palms: The Neglected Art of Being Interviewed,* gives some good, common-sense advice about dress based on his years of experience as an interviewer. He suggests that you should dress in accordance with consideration for three factors: (1) dress to your advantage; (2) dress to suit your interviewer; (3) dress appropriately for the position for which you are interviewing.

Usually your best bet is to dress conservatively. Avoid fads or new styles in favor of something that you like and in which you feel comfortable and self-assured. One woman's strategy is to dress for the position the next step up from the one for which she is interviewing. She likes to give the impression from the beginning that she would fit well in a higher position.

Get Off to a Good Start

Always arrive on time for your interview and be prepared to wait. See if you can put this time to good use. You can begin to get an impression of the company atmosphere while you wait. Since it would be awkward for you to ask questions such as "How conservative is this company?" or "How does this company treat women?", you will want to draw on your observations to supplement the picture you get from the conduct of your interviewer. Are the people friendly? How do they talk to each other? Is the atmosphere relaxed, businesslike, tense? How busy is the workplace? What ages are the workers? How is the place decorated? How do the employees dress? How courteously are you treated when you arrive? What jobs appear to be held by women?

When you arrive for the interview, you may be confronted with an application form to fill out. Even though you have a resume, fill out the application form completely and neatly. It's a good idea to bring extra copies of your resume and letters of recommendation.

Know the correct pronunciation of the name of your interviewer. If necessary, write it out phonetically. Repeat the name after introductions and a couple of times during the first part of the interview. After greeting the interviewer by name (last name, not first, unless suggested), shake hands with a firm grip. Wait until you are offered a chair before you sit down. Don't chew gum or smoke.

Although it is normal for you to be somewhat nervous, try to behave in as relaxed and friendly, yet businesslike, a manner as possible. It may help you to remember that interviewing is rarely a role that comes naturally to a prospective employer.

Communicate Assertively

As pointed out above, you and the interviewer share similar objectives, and your reaching these objectives will be facilitated if you both communicate assertively. You both have certain rights that go along with your responsibility to communicate assertively. Keep this list, adapted from *Responsible Assertive Behavior* by A. Lange and P. Jakubowski, in mind to enhance your confidence during the interview:

RIGHTS OF THE INTERVIEWEE

Right to be listened to.

Right to be nervous.

Right to make mistakes and be imperfect.

Right to be yourself, with your background, experience and personality.

Right to make your own choices.

Right to make positive statements about your qualifications and accomplishments.

Right to feel self-confident and good about yourself, whether or not you are qualified for the job.

Right to ask for clarification or specification of a question.

Right to ask questions in order to make the best decision for yourself.

Right to decide if you will answer a question.

Right to refuse to give information about yourself if you feel a question is unlawful or unethical.

Right to provide only job-relevant information about yourself.

Right to expect honest and accurate information from the interviewer.

Right to be treated honestly and fairly.

RIGHTS OF THE INTERVIEWER

Right to be listened to.

Right to make mistakes and be imperfect.

Right to expect honest and accurate information from the interviewee.

Right to make positive statements about the job and the company.

Right to ask questions about your qualifications, interests, attitudes, goals, and preferences.

Right to give information about the job and the company.

Right to expect that fair questions will be answered honestly.

Right to decide nondiscriminatory criteria for hiring.

Right to be treated honestly and fairly.

HOW THE INTERVIEW UNFOLDS

Interviews usually unfold in four stages from the interviewee's viewpoint: establishing rapport, giving information, getting information, summarizing and closing. The following will help you anticipate how the interview is likely to flow, and to prepare yourself by thinking about your answers to certain typical questions ahead of time.

Establishing Rapport

Most interviewers will start off with small talk to break the ice. This gives both of you a chance to relax, and facilitates communication. The opening remark often refers to some facet of your background that is of mutual interest, such as a community activity or a hobby.

After this small talk the opening question is often one which explores your job expectations or the events that led up to the interview. Your answers should invite further exploration of your capabilities and interests. If you feel that a question is too general, narrow your answer according to your knowledge of the company or ask for more specification.

Opening questions are often just that—open, and thus really block-busters to answer. If you have rehearsed some possible responses, you should not be at a loss for words or find yourself rambling.

"What can I do for you?" Tell the interviewer that you would like to apply for a job in some facet of the organization. Say something that will show you are interested in the company's products or services and in your progress with them.

"Tell me about yourself." Ask yourself, "If I were in the interviewer's position, what would I want to know about an applicant for this job?" Think of the most relevant points of your background, training, and interests. Be informative without boasting or offering excuses for past problems. Never make a slighting reference to a past employer.

"Why are you interested in this company?" Since you have given consideration to your interests and done research on the company, you can give an intelligent answer that should lead the interviewer to other questions. Remember, the interviewer will be thinking "What can this person offer my company?" The better you can fine-tune your answer, the better your chances.

The interviewer ought to take primary responsibility for initiating these opening questions. However, if you come up against an interviewer who throws the ball back to you, keep in mind a few openers of your own:

- □ *What interests me about your company is . . .*
- □ *What attracts me to this job position is . . .*
- □ *Do you have any questions about my qualifications I can answer?*

Maintaining eye contact is essential in creating a positive image and establishing rapport. When responding in a panel interview, maintain eye contact with everyone on the panel, even though one person asked the question. Eye contact is a simple, concrete strategy for building rapport with one interviewer or more.

Giving Information

In this phase, generally the interviewer will share some information about the overall organization and the particular job opening, and then will look for some baseline data to see if you match with the bedrock requirements of the job. He or she will want to make sure that you are willing to work the required hours, accept the salary range, and other basic go/no-go elements.

Next, the questions will pursue broader areas of information: your general background, education, work experience, and personal qualities. In addition to expanding on the basic information provided by your resume and application, the interviewer is looking for signs of instability, untruthfulness, or other characteristics that would negatively influence a decision to hire you.

To relieve their own tedium and identify individual differences, many interviewers explore your personal goals, aspirations, and work values. Think about answers that would highlight your individuality. Some interviewers will toss out a shocker such as "Tell me a story" to see how you will cope with it.

Reply Tactics   Under the stress of being interviewed, many people don't listen to the question being asked. You may be so involved with what to say next or your own state of tension that you partially tune out the interviewer. This is especially true in a panel interview in which you may feel barraged with a string of tough questions. *Listen carefully to the question.* Take time to think over your answer and if necessary ask for clarification.

You will want to draw the interviewer out about the special needs of the position in order to specify how you could fill them. Dovetail your qualifications to these needs by highlighting *only* those skills and experiences that clearly apply. When you talk too much, you risk saying something that may hurt your chances.

Be prepared to discuss your strengths and weaknesses as an employee. Try to outline your strengths as concretely as possible. Saying "I increased the contributions to this charity by one-fourth the year I was fund-raising chairperson" is more effective than saying "I'm a hard worker and a good organizer." The challenge is in describing your weaknesses in such a way as to encourage the interviewer to discover that they are really hidden strengths. For example, "I get bored easily" can be interpreted to mean "I enjoy challenging work." Try not to overdo this, however, so that you sound phoney.

Take the time now to think through your answers to the following common interview questions. Better yet, ask someone to mock interview so that you can practice your responses. Remember these questions aren't asked against you, but to gain important information; therefore, *never be defensive.* Keep your replies brief. Long answers are usually defensive.

YOUR INTERESTS

What type of position interests you most?

What interests you about our company/products/service?

What caused you to choose this job field?

What other occupations have you seriously considered?

Which school subjects did you like best/least? Why?

Have you changed your major field of interest? Why?

What community activities have you been involved in?

What social, civic, or professional organizations do you belong to? Why did you join? Have you held any offices?

How do you spend your spare time?

If you could be successful at anything, what would you choose to do?

What would you like to be doing five years from now?

If you didn't have to work, what would you choose to do?

Questions about your hobbies and spare time activities generally are asked to give you a chance to relax and warm up. Nevertheless, you will want to choose answers that have a purpose. Don't despair if you don't belong to any organizations other than your babysitting co-op, or pursue anything regularly enough to call it a hobby. Scan your major interests in Chapter 8 and the skills short stories in Chapter 10. Pick out job relevant activities, such as planning and organizing trips, developing a physical fitness program, and learning a new skill. Look for unusual answers or combinations that will help you stick out in your interviewer's mind, such as writing poetry and learning auto mechanics, or knitting and coaching softball.

Choose answers that support your interest in the job field, that highlight desirable personal attributes, and that will help the interviewer remember you positively.

YOUR MOTIVATION

Why do you want to go to work?

Why do you think you want to work for this company?

Why did you decide to apply for this job?

What job in our organization would you like to work toward?

Why did you leave your previous jobs? Have you ever been fired or asked to resign?

Why were you out of work so long?

Do you have plans for more school/training?

What is important to you in a job?

What motivates you to do your best work?

What have you done that shows initiative and willingness to work?

Looking back over your life, which years would you say were the most difficult?

What are your long-range career goals and what are you doing now to achieve them?

Outside of your career, what goals have you set for yourself? What are you doing about them?

Do you expect to be on this job five years from now? What else might you be doing?

Have a ready answer to the question "What do you plan to be doing in ten years?" You will want to emphasize your ambition, your ability to plan, and the soundness of your thinking. Are you vaguely hoping to get ahead or do you have a particular place you want to go? Avoid giving the impression that you are not sure of what you want and are just looking over the possibilities.

If the job sounds as if it matches your personal motivations and aspirations, convey this to the interviewer. On the other hand, if the company is looking for a "lifer" for the job, and you are looking for a job that will allow you to move ahead with ambition and fresh ideas, you may not be offered the job regardless of your qualifications. You may need to give careful thought to whether you choose to be aboveboard about your motivations if they do not match the company's needs but you nevertheless really want the job.

YOUR QUALIFICATIONS

What jobs have you held? What have you learned from these jobs?

Describe a typical day on your last job.

How have your supervisors complimented/criticized you?

How are you qualified for this job?

How can you make a contribution to this company?

What are your three greatest strengths/limitations for this job?

What were you doing during the periods not covered in your resume?

What equipment are you qualified to use?

How many people have you supervised? What were they doing?

What special training, if any, have you had for this job?

What is your educational background?

What were your best grades/best subjects?

Describe two of your most satisfying accomplishments.

Would you show me samples of your work?

What were your starting and ending salaries for your last three jobs?

Can I get recommendations from your past employers?

Why should we hire you?

Whether your past jobs were paid or unpaid, emphasize any responsibility you took and innovations you made (e.g., learned to deal with irate customers, revamped the filing system, learned an unfamiliar job in a brief time, trained several new employees). Use active verbs and "I language" by saying "I organized," "I initiated," "I developed." Mention how many workers you have supervised. Point out that you worked independently. Emphasize your career growth by indicating any responsibilities you assumed and any special training you sought. If you don't have the exact background for a specific job, pull together the best job-relevant aspects of your training and paid and unpaid work experience to amplify your qualifications.

Think now about how you want to deal with your sensitive or weak areas ("Why do you think you can do this job when you haven't been employed for several years?"). Anticipate objections that the interviewer might raise ("We prefer older/younger/more experienced/college graduates/ someone who has worked in this industry before/people who live nearby" . . .) and have some ready answers. Acknowledge your limitations briefly and honestly, then move on to issues you can relate to positively.

For example, you might say "I know that I don't have much recent experience in this industry, but my position as chairperson of the Fine Arts Committee for the Evening Women's Club required that I coordinate the activities of over fifty people and be responsible for many major decisions." Or, "I know that I'm more mature than the typical image of a receptionist, but I think what is important is for the person in that position to project the appearance of an attractive individual who can competently deal with your customers."

PERSONAL QUALITIES/ATTITUDES

Describe the biggest crisis in your working life.

Describe a major problem you have encountered and how you coped with it.

What is important to you in life?

Who has exerted the greatest influence on you? How?

What types of people rub you the wrong way?

How do you react to criticism?

How well do you take instructions?

How well do you work under pressure?

How do you plan your work?

What are your strengths/limitations as a supervisor?

What are your special abilities? Outstanding qualities?

How would you describe yourself? How would a co-worker describe you?

What do you anticipate might be your greatest problem with this job?

What do you do to keep in good physical condition?

What techniques do you use to manage stress? What makes you uptight and nervous?

Do you have any medical conditions which would limit your ability to perform this work?

Review your list of personal traits in Chapter 10. Often people are hired because their personality meshes well with the supervisor or the department, rather than on the basis of qualifications alone. You also may want to query the interviewer about what personal attributes or work styles would be most advantageous in this position—an assertive go-getter, a good team player, a planful organizer? If the interviewer will not be your boss, ask when you can meet this person.

PREFERENCES

What salary would you like to make?

What is the minimum pay you will accept?

Would you be willing to start at a lower salary and work up?

What kinds of people appeal most/least to you as work associates?

Do you prefer working alone or with others?

Do you like routine work? Regular hours? Travel?

Are you willing to relocate?

Do you prefer any specific geographic location? Size of city?

How much are you willing to travel?

Are you willing to work overtime?

Would you be willing to spend at least six months as a trainee?

What criteria do you use to evaluate whether a company or a job is right for you?

Look back over your answers in Chapter 7 on work values to develop your replies to questions about your preferences. When asked about the salary you expect, quote a reasonable estimate or salary range based on your knowledge of the going rate in your field. If you have some iron-clad salary requirements, or if pay is more important to you than the type of work you do, this is important to share in the interview since it will vitally affect your satisfaction with the job. Otherwise you may want to qualify your salary request by saying "depending on my duties and responsibilities" or "I'm primarily interested in advancement at this time."

A Word About Your Legal Rights   Each state has fair employment practices laws that forbid employment bias based on race, religion, sex, marital status, age, disability, color, national origin, or arrest record. This information may be requested on application forms for data-gathering in accordance with the company's affirmative action plan. However, there should be a clear statement that providing this information is voluntary.

As far as the interview goes, you should have a general feel for what kinds of questions are prohibited by your state. You can get this information by calling your state office building and asking for the Fair Employment Practices Commision, the Division of Human Rights, or the Equal Employment Opportunity Commission.

It is normal for the interviewer to ask some questions about your personal life, but you may get the impression the interviewer is biased if the questions develop in some of the following directions: Are you married? If not, do you have plans to marry? Do you have children? How old are your children? Who will take care of them while you are working? What kind of birth control do you use? How does your husband feel about your going to work? Will your husband mind if you travel or work overtime? What does your husband do for a living? How long do you plan to work?

Ask yourself if any of these questions would be asked of a male applicant. If not, they are potentially discriminatory and you need to decide how to cope with them. If you have decided that you don't want the job (and this discriminatory attitude may have clinched that decision), you may want to show your outrage before closing the interview and leaving. A more moderate stance would be to point out the illegality of many of these questions or at least emphasize your discomfort with them. If you want the job, you might wish to raise the interviewer's consciousness more subtly. Think about what the interviewer is really asking, and try to answer those hidden questions.

Questions about your children and child care probably indicate that the interviewer is concerned that you might have an absenteeism problem. Impress the interviewer with how well you have anticipated and resolved any child care problems. The question "What does you husband do for a living?" may contain several hidden questions. Anticipate and clarify them. The interviewer really may be trying to find out "Is your husband due for a transfer?" (translate: "When will you quit and move away?") or "How much money does he earn?" (translate: "How badly do you need the job?"). Try to give the impression that he is securely employed with an adequate salary, then attempt to clarify the hidden questions by saying, "I'm wondering if you're concerned about my commitment to this position." Move the interview in a more appropriate direction by then talking about your interest in and qualifications for the position.

If your reply to a possibly discriminatory question is one that can't hurt you, then answer the question. Then let the interviewer know that it was an unlawful question. On the other hand, if you think that an honest answer might hurt you, avoid the question by treating it humorously, telling the interviewer that of course he or she must be kidding because everyone knows that the question is prohibited. Even though you might suspect differently, give the interviewer the benefit of the doubt. Many interviewers ask these kinds of questions out of genuine interest and naivete.

If you honestly feel that the interviewer was asking you the questions in order to discriminate against you, then consider filing a claim with your state and the EEOC. Taking your case through the courts is usually a long and frustrating process which may award you damages and improve the lot of women in employment. On the other hand, you may develop an ulcer and be required to pay the other party's attorney's fees if you lose your case. Discrimination won't change if it is not confronted, but before you take this course of action, get information and emotional support.

Getting Information

Remember, in addition to convincing the interviewer that you are right for the job, you are also trying to decide if the company or the position is right for you and avoid what could be a costly mistake. While you are answering questions, you should be asking some. Before reporting to the interview prepare three or four questions that you will ask, such as:

- ☐ What is the nature of the work? What will be my specific duties? Approximately what percentage of time will be spent in each activity?

- ☐ What will be expected of me? How soon?

- ☐ Where does this position fit in the hierarchy of the organization?

- ☐ For whom will I be working? To whom will I report?

- ☐ How many people will I supervise? What are their duties?

- ☐ Is this a new position? If not, why did the last employee leave? Could I speak with this person?

- ☐ What kind of problems will I be likely to face?

- ☐ Are there any unusual requirements associated with this job (e.g., extensive travel, overtime, physical hazards, unusual hours)?

☐   What is the salary range? When would I first be reviewed for an increase?

☐   What kind of training will I receive (orientation to the job, in-service training, and outside education on a tuition-reimbursement basis)?

Taking an active role in the interview by asking questions will further an image of you as an active, interested, potential employee. Yet this is not the time to ask for specific information about benefits, raises, vacations, or hours. The time to ask these questions is after you have an offer.

Summarizing and Closing

Often, at the end of the interview, you will receive only a "thank you" instead of an offer. The interviewer may need time to review all the applicants or may not be able to make an independent decision without some consultation.

If you would like the position, *say so*. While thanking the interviewer for his or her time and mentioning that you enjoyed the interview, make a positive statement of your interest in the job. A comment such as, "I am intensely interested in this job and would like the opportunity to join your company" may give you the competitive edge you need. Many employers have told us "I would have given her the job, but the other applicant seemed more interested."

Be sure to thank the receptionist as you leave. Often receptionists have the opportunity to observe all applicants and may be asked to informally share their opinions.

FOLLOW THROUGH

One of the most essential steps in the job search process, and one that is commonly overlooked, is the thank-you note. Write a professional-looking note to your interviewer. Briefly repeat your skills and experiences that meet the needs mentioned in the interview. Thank the interviewer for his or her time and mention that you are hoping to hear from the company soon. Mail your note the following day. If you don't hear anything, follow your note with a telephone call in about three days to a week.

"Your goal is to extract an offer from the organization," writes Lidia Smith in *Women's Work* (January/February, 1978). She continues, "Whether or not you accept it is an entirely different matter. After all, you seldom know the opportunities (or lack thereof) that lie behind an opening until the organization is truly interested in hiring you. . . . Only then can you intelligently analyze the position and decide whether it will advance your personal career goals."

If you *are* offered the job, find out when you need to commit yourself, and try to keep your options open for as long as possible so that you can ideally have more than one offer from which to choose. Now is the time to approach the employer to discuss and negotiate salary and other job benefits.

Then sit down with each offer and plug it into the Alternative Comparison Chart we provided for you in Chapter 17. Weigh your alternatives on the basis of the information available, and make your tentative decision. If you choose to turn down a job offer, respect the employer's needs with a timely and courteous reply. You don't know when you might be dealing with this employer again.

If you *don't* get the job, contact your interviewer and tactfully express your disappointment as well as pointing out your positive feelings about the interviewer and the company. Ask if the interviewer has any feedback on your performance in the interview which might help you improve in the future. Also ask to be considered for future openings and ask for referrals in the same way you would in a job information interview. Request permission to cite your interviewer's name when making future contacts.

And simply persist. Even for the most skilled and best prepared, the lights do not always turn green immediately. Often when you are not selected it is for reasons outside your control. Your persistence is what ultimately makes your job search work.

HIGHLIGHTS

☐ Actively promote yourself during the interview by letting the interviewer know what you want and do well, and why you would like to work for that company.

☐ Remember your responsibility to assess the job and the organization while your interviewer is appraising you.

☐ Anticipate and prepare for the questions your interviewer is likely to ask.

☐ Follow through in a way that conveys your strong interest in the position, and aim for an offer.

RESOURCES

Bower, S. A. and Bower, G. H. *Asserting Yourself.* Reading, MA: Addison-Wesley Publishing Co., 1976.

One of the better assertiveness training guides on the market. Sharon Bower has worked extensively with re-entry women. We have found their DESC scripting system a helpful approach for dealing with stressful situations. The sections on assertive body language and "downer detours" are particularly helpful for job seekers.

Jakubowski, P. and Lange, A. J. *Responsible Assertive Behavior.* Champaign, IL: Research Press Co., 1976.

While this book is geared more toward professional trainers, the lay reader will find an excellent discussion of the fundamental concepts of assertion training. They deal well with the "me first" misinterpretation of assertive behavior and focus on assertion as a skill in interpersonal communication which involves knowing how to express your needs in responsible and appropriate ways. Chapter 12 focuses on assertion training for job interviews. The reader will want to learn to discriminate aggressive, assertive, and passive ways of responding.

Janis, I. and Wheeler, D. "Thinking Clearly about Career Choices," *Psychology Today.* May 1978, 67–75 and 121–122.

Acknowledging the personal stress associated with career decisions, the authors present a useful balance sheet approach for weighing alternatives. Sub-categories covered in this "pro-con" approach are: tangible gains and losses to self, tangible gains and losses to others, self-approval or disapproval, social approval or disapproval.

Lynch, J. S. and Smith, S. L. *The Woman's Guide to Legal Rights.* Chicago: Contemporary Books, Inc., 1979.

This book gives readable information on a wide variety of legal rights which have particular importance to women. Pay particular attention to the sections on job discrimination and workers rights.

Medley, H. A. *Sweaty Palms: The Neglected Art of Being Interviewed.* Belmont, CA: Lifetime Learning Publications, 1978.

Considers the job interview from the interviewee's point of view. Goes into different types of job interviews—individual, group, panel, as well as the logistical differences between screening and selection interviews. Examples and the author's sense of humor make this informative and enjoyable reading.

Morgan, H. H. and Cogger, J. W. *The Interviewer's Manual*. New York: The Psychological Corporation, 1973.

> *Job interviewees will benefit from reviewing the interview and evaluation techniques which are taught to personnel interviewers. An understanding of the process from the viewpoint of "the other chair" may help you relax and come across as a confident and competent applicant. On the other hand, remember that few interviewers have professional training. You may come in far more prepared to cope with a professional interview than your interviewer is prepared to conduct one.*

SECTION VI

CONTINUING TO GROW

21

CONTINUING TO GROW

In this, the closing years
of the Twentieth Century, there will be
five to seven occupational changes
in a typical lifetime, some authorities predict.
Certain occupations even now have a life
of only three to five years.
You'll either have to manage your career
or be carried helplessly by the tides of change.
Sylvia Porter

*D*ESPITE the old admonition about staying in one job because it implies stability, people serious about their careers change jobs, and they change jobs surprisingly often. They do so with a plan, to take an active part in the change that is all around us, and for the positive reason of getting a better job.

You now know a strategy you can repeat at any time you feel it's necessary to make a change to further your growth, to make a better match between your self and your environment. You know the steps: assess yourself, evaluate your opportunities, conduct a creative job search. You can adapt the exercises to appraise and revamp your present job when you have outgrown it, or you can go through selected parts of the process again when you want to move on.

ASSESSMENT IS A CONSTANT PROCESS

The process of assessment is really a continuing one in any life, and starts anew on the first day of your new job. Many times, on the first day of a new job people experience some regret. "Did I make the right decision?" There are trade-offs in any change; you both lose something and gain something. Stand firm against that first week or two of a sense of loss—the loss of free time, a friend, a long lunch hour. The sense of how much there is to learn on the new job can be exaggerated at this time also. Shirley Zimmerman confided to a friend that for the first month on a new job she went to bed every night at eight.

You can start evaluating your new job almost immediately by asking yourself these questions.

☐ Does it allow you to use the skills you most want to use?

☐ Does it meet your values, interests, abilities?

☐ Are you learning the new skills you wanted to learn?

☐ Does it fit well with your family, personal, social life?

☐ Do you have the support and contacts you want and need to maintain yourself on this job?

Most importantly, what are the chances for growth and advancement for yourself in this work environment?

☐ Are there clear lines of advancement?

☐ Are there people available to advise you and serve as mentors?

☐ Do you know how to increase your responsibility and earn a higher salary?

While assessing yourself, the job, and the work environment you may want to consider the need for you to brush up or develop career management skills.

☐ Would a workshop on identifying barriers to advancement on the job be beneficial?

☐ How about an assertion training course directed at job-related issues?

☐ How do you maintain and expand those all important people contacts in this work setting?

Once this constant assessment and awareness becomes a habit, you can control the direction and pace of your growth. There's little to be left to luck in this process. But luck has been defined as what happens when preparation meets opportunity.

Therefore, good luck!

APPENDIXES

APPENDIXES

APPENDIX A

SELECTING INDIVIDUAL OR GROUP COUNSELING

As you move through *Every Woman Works* there may be several points where you feel emotionally blocked by anxiety or the need to evaluate too many choices at one time. If you feel trapped by painful life issues or merely stuck, consulting a helping professional such as a psychologist can help you explore methods to free yourself. Counseling can give you a fresh perspective on recent or recurring problems—a revealing perspective that you might not discover through self-contemplation or through discussion with an involved relative, friend, or co-worker. Through counseling you can clarify your feelings, needs, and goals, scrutinize new options and learn action tools for dealing with yourself and others. Best of all, you can fine-tune your self-listening capacity. Thus, you can uncover *your own* answers, not the counselor's or the culture's answers.

CLARIFYING YOUR
EXPECTATIONS ABOUT COUNSELING

Before seeking information about various counseling options, spell out your own expectations. Your answers can be evaluative criteria for weighing various services. And knowing what you want will facilitate communication in your counseling relationship.

☐ What do I want help with? What are my most urgent concerns? What do I *not* want help with?

☐ What changes would I like to work towards in myself or my life?

☐ What *kind* of help am I seeking? Do I want short-term assistance with a crisis? Do I want long-term help with debilitating patterns in my life?

☐ With what kind of person or in what situation typically do I feel stronger when I need help? In what situations do I feel weak?

☐ What are my concerns or questions about counseling? How do I feel about asking for or needing help from another person?

☐ How much can I comfortably pay? Will my insurance cover counseling fees?

SURVEYING COUNSELING OPTIONS

Depending upon your needs, you may choose career or personal counseling, either of which may be in a one-to-one or group setting. While the goals of these various kinds of counseling overlap greatly, comparing the advantages of each is important.

Career Counseling

Career counseling benefits women whose most urgent concern is improving their work, women who desire job advancement or a job change. Typically, the goals of career counseling are similar to the objectives of *Every Woman Works*.

Personal Counseling

Personal counseling or therapy may be useful to those seeking personal growth or improvement in relationships. You need to know whether your desired counseling focus is personal or career or *both,* since some professionals specialize in one area while others are adept at both.

Group Counseling

Group counseling is advantageous for those who feel isolated from others who experience similar concerns. Facilitated by a trained leader, groups provide constructive feedback from several individuals rather than just one. In a group setting you can try out assertive ways to describe your feelings, strengths, and goals, and practice ways to communicate with others. Best of all, you can experience support from group members.

The advantage of one-to-one counseling is that you and the professional can concentrate your energies on your unique concerns. Some people find it easier to take risks and to be open with one individual than with ten.

ORGANIZATIONS OFFERING COUNSELING

With this broad categorization of counseling in mind, you're ready to survey resources in your community. Call these organizations for information about groups, counseling services, and referrals to other agencies or professionals:

> women's centers
> YWCAs
> college continuing education programs
> community mental health agencies
> crisis counseling centers
> displaced homemaker centers
> outpatient mental health units of hospitals, clinics

Look in the yellow pages under Psychologists, Counseling, Career counseling, or Marital/family counseling.

Two national organizations can help you identify additional career counseling services in your location. Catalyst, a nonprofit organization dedicated to helping women choose and advance their careers, publishes a free list of 100 career resource centers. Write:

Catalyst
14 East 60th Street
New York, NY 10022

The Displaced Homemakers Foundation can refer you to counseling and job training programs in the 25 states that have passed legislation providing assistance to displaced homemakers. Qualified clients include any woman who, through divorce, separation, widowhood, or midlife crisis, has been displaced from her job as homemaker and forced into the labor market. Write:

Displaced Homemakers Information
Business and Professional Women's Foundation
2012 Massachusetts Avenue, NW
Washington, DC 20036

SELECTING A HELPING PROFESSIONAL

Contact several counseling services and contrast their offerings. Request written literature and then read the fine print. In your initial phone contact ask these quesions:

- ☐ What kinds of counseling services are offered?

- ☐ What training, experience, areas of specialization, have the staff? Do they typically work with women with my concerns?

- ☐ What are the fees for various services? Are fees fixed, on a sliding scale, or negotiable? Do the staff qualify for fee reimbursement from insurance companies?

- ☐ What are the goals and agenda of a particular group? What kinds of individuals benefit from this group? What is the size of the group? Is there a possibility of individual counseling as a follow-up to the group?

A couple words of warning: cost is not a valid gauge of quality services. Some lower-priced offerings at nonprofit organizations or colleges are just as adequate as those offered by profit-making businesses or professionals

in private practice. For individual counseling through a profit-making organization or from a private practitioner, you can expect to pay $25 to $60 an
hour. Group counseling in these settings costs between $10 and $35 per
session. Again, your insurance may cover fees, or there may be a sliding fee
scale according to income.

Not all individuals offering career or personal counseling services are
qualified to do so. Consider a professional's training, state certification or
license, years of experience and areas of specialization. Unfortunately, there
are no clean-cut formulas for evaluating a professional's effectiveness. If possible, talk with previous clients or group members about their reactions to
a counseling service or staff member.

Once you've surveyed a few counseling services your best bet is to
listen to your own reactions. Trust your judgment and feelings. Then make
an appointment for an initial individual or group session. It is quite appropriate to make appointments with more than one professional. Being a cau-
tious consumer can benefit you *and* the counseling organization.

YOUR INITIAL COUNSELING SESSIONS

Use your first few sessions to further clarify expectations and goals for counseling. In some agencies, you'll first meet with an intake interviewer who
will then decide which counselor is best for you. In other cases, you will
begin working with your helper in the first session. Most initial group sessions involve definition of expectations and goals, but if you're joining a
group already in progress you'll need to find out whether your expectations
match those of the group.

Here are some additional questions to consider:

☐ What is the professional's attitude toward women?

You have a right not to be forced into any particular role—either a
traditional wife-mother role or a less traditional career-centered role.
Your roles are your own choice.

☐ Does the professional have time to see you on a regular basis? How
available is she or he for phone calls or extra sessions?

☐ Would it be appropriate to contract with the professional for a certain
number of sessions to work on a specific goal? Certain problems are
conducive to this arrangement. However, counseling is often open-
ended.

You need to find a professional you trust, respect, and can work with on your concerns. However, you don't need to like or agree with all of his or her feedback. Counseling can be a catalyst for change, but in the end, you are the one who must provide the motivation and take the not-so-easy action steps.

RESOURCES

Your Bill of Rights as a Consumer of Therapy. Available from New York NOW, 84 5th Ave., New York, NY 10011.

Detailed description of 17 of the client's rights in therapy. Helpful to read before selecting individual or group counseling.

APPENDIX B

INDUSTRIAL, TRADE, AND PROFESSIONAL ORGANIZATIONS

Accountants, American Institute of
Certified
666 Fifth Avenue
New York, N.Y. 10019

Accountants, National Assn. of
919 Third Avenue
New York, N.Y. 10022

Accoustics Society, American
1001 E Street N.W.
Washington, D.C. 20010

Actuarial Society, Casualty
200 East 42nd St.
New York, N.Y. 10017

Advertising Federation, American
1225 Connecticut Ave. N.W.
Washington, D.C. 20036

Advertisers, Assn. of Industrial
41 East 42nd St.
New York, N.Y. 10017

Advertising Bureau, Radio
555 Madison Avenue
New York, N.Y. 10022

Advertising Federation, American
1225 Connecticut Ave. N.W.
Washington, D.C. 20036

Air Line Employees Association
5600 S. Central Ave.
Chicago, Ill. 60638

Air Transport Association of America
1000 Connecticut Ave., N.W.
Washington, D.C. 20036

Airline Pilots Assn.
1625 Mass. Ave., N.W.
Washington, D.C. 20036

Anatomists, American Association of
Department of Anatomy
University of Arkansas Medical
Center
Little Rock, Arkansas 72201

Anesthesiologists, American
Society of
515 Busse Highway
Park Ridge, Ill. 60068

Anthropological Assn., The American
1703 New Hampshire Ave., N.W.
Washington, D.C. 20009

Appraisers, American Society of
Box 17265
Dulles International Airport
Washington, D.C. 20041

Appraisers, Assn. of Federal
Box 466
Silver Spring, Md. 20907

Archaeological Institute of America
260 W. Broadway
New York, N.Y. 10013

Architecture, The American
Institute of
1735 New York Ave.
Washington, D.C. 20036

Archivists, Society of American
The Library, Box 8198
University of Illinois, Chicago Circle
Chicago, Ill. 60680

Art Education Association, National
National Educational Association
1201 - 16th St., N.W.
Washington, D.C. 20036

Astronomical Society, American
211 FitzRandolph Rd.
Princeton, N.J. 08540

Auditors, Institute of Internal
5500 Diplomat Circle
Orlando, Fla. 32810

Author's Representatives, Society of
101 Park Avenue
New York, N.Y. 10017

Auto Trim Shops, National Assn.
129 Broadway
Lynbrook, N.Y. 11563

Automobile Dealers Association,
National
2000 K St., N.W.
Washington, D.C. 20006

Automatic Merchandising Assn.,
National
7 South Dearborn St.
Chicago, Ill. 60603

Automotive Service Industry Assn.
230 No. Michigan Ave.
Chicago, Ill. 60601

Aviation Adminis., Federal
800 Independence Ave., S.W.
Washington, D.C. 20591

Bankers Association, American
Personnel Division
1120 Connecticut Ave., N.W.
Washington, D.C. 20036

Bar Association, The American
1115 East 60th St.
Chicago, Ill. 60637

Barber Schools Inc., Nat'l. Assn. of
338 Washington Ave.
Huntington, W. Va. 25701

Beauty Career Center, Nat'l.
3839 White Plains Rd.
Bronx, N.Y. 19467

Biological Sciences, American
Institute of
3900 Wisconsin Ave., N.W.
Washington, D.C. 20016

Botanical Society of America,
New York
Botanical Garden
Bronx, N.Y. 10458

B'nai B'rith Career and Counseling
Services
1640 Rhode Island Ave. N.W.
Washington, D.C. 20036

Bricklayers, Masons & Plasterers
International Union of America
815 – 15th St., N.W.
Washington, D.C. 20005

Broadcasters, Nat'l. Assn. of
1771 N St., N.W.
Washington, D.C. 20036

Broadcasters, National Assn. of
1346 Connecticut Ave., N.W.
Washington, D.C. 20036

Business Equipment Manufacturers
Assn.
1828 L St., N.W.
Washington, D.C. 20036

Business Officers, National Assn. of
College and University
One DuPont Circle, Ste. 510
Washington, D.C. 20036

Carpenters and Joiners of America
United Brotherhood
101 Constitution Ave., N.W.
Washington, D.C. 20001

Central Intelligence Agency
Office of Personnel
Washington, D.C. 20505

Chamber of Commerce Executives,
American
1133 – 15th St. N.W.
Washington, D.C. 20005

Chamber of Commerce of the U.S.,
International
1615 H St., N.W.
Washington, D.C. 20006

Chemical Engineers, American
Institute of
345 East 47th St.
New York, N.Y. 10017

Chemical Society, American
1155 – 16th St., N.W.
Washington, D.C. 20036

Chemists, American Assn. of Clinical
1155 – 16th St. N.W.
Washington, D.C. 20036

Chemists, American Society of
Biological
9650 Rockville Pike
Bethesda, Md. 20014

Chemists Assn., Manufacturing
1825 Connecticut Avenue N.W.
Washington, D.C. 20009

Child Welfare League of America
67 Irving Place
New York, N.Y. 10003

Children, Council for Exceptional
1920 Association Dr.
Reston, Va. 22091

Chiropractic Assn., American
2200 Grand Ave.
Des Moines, Iowa 50312

Churches, National Council of
Professional Church Leadership
475 Riverside Dr.
New York, N.Y. 10027

City Management Association,
Internat'l.
1140 Connecticut Ave., N.W.
Washington, D.C. 20036

Communication, Women in
8305-A Shoal Creek Blvd.
Austin, Texas 78758

Communication Workers of America
1925 K St., N.W.
Washington, D.C. 20006

Communications and Technology
Publications,
Assn. for Educational
1201 - 16th St., N.W.
Washington, D.C. 20036

Communications, Inc., Society for
Technical
Suite 421, 1010 Vermont Ave., N.W.
Washington, D.C. 20005

Computer and Business Equipment
Manufacturers
1828 L St., N.W.
Washington, D.C. 20036

Contractors of America, Inc., Assn.
of General
1957 E St. N.W.
Washington, D.C. 20006

Correctional Assn., American
4321 Hartwick Rd. Ste. 208
College Park, Md. 20740

Criminal Justice Educational
Consortium, National
Arizona State University
Tempe, Arizona 85281

Credit Union National Assn.
1617 Sherman Avenue, Box 431
Madison, Wisc. 53701

Cytology Program, Clinical
229 Forsyth Bldg.
360 Huntington Avenue
Boston, Mass. 02115

Data Processing Management Assn.
505 Busse Hwy.
Park Ridge, Ill. 60068

Deaf, Convention of American
Instructors of the
5034 Wisconsin Ave., N.W.
Washington, D.C. 20016

Dental Assistants Association,
American
211 East Chicago Ave.
Chicago, Ill. 60611

Dental Association, American
Council on Dental Education
211 East Chicago Ave.
Chicago, Ill. 60611

Design and Drafting, American
Institute for
3119 Price Rd.
Bartlesville, Oklahoma 74003

Designers Society of America,
Industrial
1750 Old Meadow Rd.
McLean, Va. 22101

Dietetic Assn., American
620 North Michigan Ave.
Chicago, Ill. 60611

Direct Mail Educational Foundation
230 Park Avenue
New York, N.Y. 10017

Economic Assn., American
1313 – 21st Avenue South
Nashville, Tenn. 37212

Economists, National Assn. of
Business
888 – 17th St., N.W.
Washington, D.C. 20006

Electric Sign Association, National
600 Hunter Drive
Oak Brook, Ill. 60521

Electrical and Electronic Engineers
Institute of
345 East 47th St.
New York, N.Y. 10017

Electrical Contractors Association,
National
1730 Rhode Island N.W.
Washington, D.C. 20036

Electrical Institute, Edison
90 Park Avenue
New York, N.Y. 10016

Electroencephalographic
Technologists, Registration of,
American Board of
Cleveland Clinic, 9500 Euclid Ave.
Cleveland, Ohio 44105

Elementary, Kindergarten, Nursery
Educators
American Assn. of
1201 – 16th St. N.W.
Washington, D.C. 20036

Elevator Constructors, International
Union of
12 South 12th St.
Philadelphia, Penn. 19107

Employment Counselor Association,
National
1607 New Hampshire Ave., N.W.
Washington, D.C. 20009

Engineering Education, American
Society for
Suite 400, 1 Dupont Circle
Washington, D.C. 20036

Engineering in Medicine and Biology,
Alliance for
3900 Wisconsin Ave., N.W.
Suite 300
Washington, D.C. 20016

Engineers, American Society of
Agricultural
2950 Niles Rd.
St. Joseph, Mich. 49085

Engineers, American Society of Civil
345 East 47th St.
New York, N.Y. 10017

Engineers' Council for Professional
Development
345 East 47th St.
New York, N.Y. 10017

Engineers, Metallurgical Society of
the American Institute of Mining,
Metallurgical and Petroleum
345 East 47th St.
New York, N.Y. 10017

Engineers, Mining Society of the
American Institute of Mining,
Metallurgical and Petroleum
345 East 47th St.
New York, N.Y. 10017

Entomological Society of America
4603 Calvert Rd.
College Park, Md. 20740

Farm & Industrial Equipment Institute
650 Wrigley Building, N.
Chicago, IL 60611

Financial Analysts Federation
219 E. 42nd St.
New York, N.Y. 10017

Finance Association, National
Consumer
100 - 16th St., N.W.
Washington, D.C. 20036

Firefighters, International Assn. of
905 - 16th St., N.W.
Washington, D.C. 20006

Flight Engineers International Assn.
905 - 16th St., N.W.
Washington, D.C. 20006

Florists and Ornamental
Horticulturists, Society of American
901 N. Washington St.
Alexandria, Va. 22314

Food Service Industry, Nat'l. Institute
for the
120 So. Riverside Plaza
Chicago, Ill. 60606

Food Technologists, Institute of
Suite 2120, 221 North LaSalle St.
Chicago, Ill. 60601

Foreign Trade Council, National
10 Rockefeller Plaza
New York, N.Y. 10020

Forest Products Assn., National
Wood Industry Careers
1619 Massachusetts Avenue, N.W.
Washington, D.C. 20036

Foresters, Society of American
1010 - 16th St., N.W.
Washington, D.C. 20036

Foundrymen's Society, American
Golf & Wolf Rds.
Des Plaines, Ill. 60016

Funeral Directors Assn. of the U.S.
Inc., Nat'l.
135 W. Wells St.
Milwaukee, Wisc. 53203

Genealogists, Board for
Certification of
1307 New Hampshire Ave., N.W.
Washington, D.C. 20036

Geographers, Assn. of American
1710 - 16th St., N.W.
Washington, D.C. 20009

Geological Institute, American
2201 M St., N.W.
Washington, D.C. 20037

Geophysical Union, American
1707 L St., N.W.
Washington, D.C. 20036

Graphic Arts Tech, Foundation
4615 Forbes Avenue
Pittsburgh, Penn. 15213

Health, National Institutes of
Personnel Office
9000 Rockville Pike
Bethesda, Md. 20014

Health, Physical Education and
Recreation, American Association for
A div. of the National Educational
Assoc.
1201 - 16th St., N.W.
Washington, D.C. 20036

Historical Assn., American
400 A St., S.E.
Washington, D.C. 20003

History, American Assn. for State and
Local
1313 Eighth Ave.
Nashville, Tenn. 37203

Home Appliance Manufacturers,
Assn. of
20 North Wacker Drive
Chicago, Ill. 60606

Home Economics Association,
American
2010 Massachusetts Ave., N.W.
Washington, D.C. 20036

Hospital Administrators, American
College of
840 North Lake Shore Dr.
Chicago, Ill. 60611

Hospital Assn., American
840 North Lake Shore Dr.
Chicago, Ill. 60611

Hotel-Motel Assn., Educational
Institute of American
77 Kellogg Center,
Michigan State University
East Lansing, Mich. 48823

Hotel, Restaurant and Institutional
Education, Council on
1522 K St., N.W.
Washington, D.C. 20005

Household Employment, Nat'l.
Committee on
1625 I St. NW
Washington, D.C. 20006

Humane Society of the United States
2100 L St., N.W.
Washington, D.C. 20037

Humanities Education, National
Assn. for
Box 628
Kirksville, Mo. 63501

Industrial Engineers, Inc.
American Institute of
25 Technology Park
Norcross, Ga. 30071

Industrial Hygiene Assn., American
66 S. Miller Rd.
Akron, Ohio 44313

Information Processing Societies Inc.
American Federation of
210 Summit Ave.
Montvale, N.J. 07645

Instrument Society of America
400 Stanwix St.
Pittsburgh, Penn. 15222

Insurance Information Institute
110 William St.
New York, N.Y. 10038

Insurance Institute of America,
American Institute for Property and
Liability Underwriters
Providence and Sugartown Rds.
Malvern, Penn. 19355

Insurance, Institute of Life
227 Park Ave.
New York, N.Y. 10017

Insurance Management, American
Society of
10 E. 49th St.
New York, N.Y. 10017

Interior Designers, Inc., National
Society of
312 East 62nd St.
New York, N.Y. 10021

International Development,
Agency for
Office of Personnel and Manpower
Washington, D.C. 20523

Jewelers and Silversmiths of
America Inc.
Sheraton-Biltmore Hotel, Room S-75
Providence, R.I. 02902

Journalism, Assn. for Education in
118 Reavis Hall
Northern Illinois University
DeKalb, Ill. 60115

Journalists, Society of Professional
Sigma Delta Chi
35 E. Wacker Dr.
Chicago, Ill. 60601

Laborers' International Union of
North America
905 - 16th St. N.W.
Washington, D.C. 20006

Landscape Architecture, Inc.,
American Society of
1750 Old Meadow Rd.
McLean, Va. 22101

Language Assn. of America, Modern
62 Fifth Avenue
New York, N.Y. 10011

Lathing and Plastering, International
Council for
221 No. LaSalle St.
Chicago, Ill. 60601

Libraries Assn., Special
235 Park Avenue South
New York, N.Y. 10003

Library Assn., American
Office for Library Personnel
Resources
50 East Huron St.
Chicago, Ill. 60611

Library Assn., Medical
919 N. Michigan Avenue
Chicago, Ill. 60611

Library Committee, Federal
Room 310 Library of Congress
Washington, D.C. 20540

Linguists, Society of Federal
Box 7765
Washington, D.C. 20044

Locksmiths of America, Associated
11 Elmendorf St.
Kingston, N.Y. 12401

Machinists & Aerospace Workers
International Association of
1300 Connecticut Ave., N.W.
Washington, D.C. 20036

Magazine Publishers Assn.
575 Lexington Avenue
New York, N.Y. 10022

Management Association, American
Management Information Services
135 W. 50th St.
New York, N.Y. 10020

Marketing Association, American
230 North Michigan Ave.
Chicago, Ill. 60601

Mathematical Society, American
P.O. Box 6248
Providence, R.I. 02904

Mathematics, National Council of
Teachers of
1906 Association Dr.
Reston, Va. 22091

Mathematics, Society for Industrial
and Applied
33 S. - 17th St.
Philadelphia, Penn. 19103

Meat Institute, American
59 East Van Buren
Chicago, Ill. 60605

Mechanical Engineers
The American Society of
345 East 47th St.
New York, N.Y. 10017

Medical Assistants, American Assn. of
One East Wacker Dr., Suite 1510
Chicago, Ill. 60601

Medical Education, Council on
American Medical Association
535 N. Dearborn St.
Chicago, Ill. 60610

Medical Records Assn., American
John Hancock Center, Suite 1850
875 No. Michigan Ave.
Chicago, Ill. 60611

Medical Technologists, American
Soc. for
555 West Loop South
Houston, Texas 77401

Metal Finishers, National Assn. of
248 Lorraine Avenue
Upper Montclair, N.J. 07043

Metals, American Society of
Metals Park, Ohio 44073

Meteorology Society, American
45 Beacon St.
Boston, Mass. 02108

Microbiology, American Society for
1913 I St., N.W.
Washington, D.C. 20006

Modeling Schools, information from
State Department of Education

Music, National Assoc. of Schools of
One Dupont Circle, N.W.
Washington, D.C. 20036

Musicians, American Federation of
(AFL-CIO)
641 Lexington Ave.
New York, N.Y. 10022

New York Life Insurance Co.
Career Information Service
Box 51, Madison Square Station
New York, N.Y. 10010

News Directors Assn., Radio
Television
WKAR, Michigan State University
East Lansing, Michigan 48823

Newspaper Fund
Box 300
Princeton, N.J. 08540

Newspaper Publishers Assn.
Foundation, American
Box 17407 Dulles International
Airport
Washington, D.C. 20041

Nuclear Society, American
244 East Ogden Ave.
Hinsdale, Ill. 60521

Nursing Careers, ANA Committee
on American Nurses Assoc.
2420 Pershing Rd.
Kansas City, Missouri 64108

Occupational Therapy Assn.,
American
6000 Executive Blvd.
Rockville, Md. 20852

Oceanic and Atmospheric
Administration, National
6001 Executive Boulevard
Rockville, Maryland 20852
Attn: AD 411

Oceanographic Foundation,
International
10 Rickenbacker Causeway,
Virginia Key
Miami, Fla. 33149

Office Occupations
State Supervisor of Education
State Capitol

Operating Engineers, International
Union of
1125 – 17th St., N.W.
Washington, D.C. 20036

Opthalmologists, American Assn. of
1100 – 17th St. N.W.
Washington, D.C. 20036

Opticians of America, Associated
1250 Connecticut Ave., N.W.
Washington, D.C. 20036

Optometric Assn., American
7000 Chippewa St.
St. Louis, Missouri 63119

Osteopathic Assn., American
212 East Ohio St.
Chicago, Ill. 60611

Painters & Allied Trade, International
Brotherhood
1925 K St., N.W.
Washington, D.C. 20006

Pediatrics, American Academy of
Box 1034
Evanston, Ill. 60204

Personnel Administration, American
Society for
19 Church St.
Berea, Ohio 44017

Personnel & Guidance Association,
American
1607 New Hampshire Ave., N.W.
Washington, D.C. 20009

Personnel Management Assn.,
International
1313 East 60th St.
Chicago, Ill. 60637

Pest Control Assn. Inc., National
250 W. Jersey St.
Elizabeth, N.J. 07207

Pharmaceutical Manufacturers' Assn.
1155 – 15th St., N.W.
Washington, D.C. 20005

Pharmacology and Experimental
Therapeutics,
American Society for
9650 Rockville Pike
Bethesda, Md. 20014

Pharmacy, American Association of
College
Office of Student Affairs
8121 Georgia Ave., Suite 800
Silver Spring, Md. 20910

Photogrammetry, American
Society of
1515 Massachusetts Ave. N.W.
Washington, D.C. 20005

Photographers' Assn., National Press
Box 1146
Durham, N.C. 27702

Photographers of America,
Professional
1090 Executive Way,
Oak Leaf Commons
Des Plaines, Ill. 60018

Physical Therapy Association,
American
1156 – 15th St., N.W.
Washington, D.C. 20036

Physics, American Institute of
335 East 45th St.
New York, N.Y. 10017

Physiological Society, American
9650 Rockville Pike
Bethesda, Md. 20014

Piano Technicians Guild Inc.
P.O. Box 1813
Seattle, Wash. 98111

Placement Council, Inc., The College
P.O. Box 2263
Bethlehem, Penn. 18001

Planners, American Institute of
917 – 15th St., N.W.
Washington, D.C. 20005

Plant Physiologists, American
Society of
Box 5706
Washington, D.C. 20014

Plumbing & Heating Contractors,
Nat'l. Assn. of
1016 – 20th St., N.W.
Washington, D.C. 20036

Police, Fraternal Order of
National Headquarters
G– 3136 W. Pasadena Ave.
Flint, Michigan 48504

Political Science Assn., American
1527 New Hampshire Ave., N.W.
Washington, D.C. 20036

Psychological Assn., American
1200 – 17th St. N.W.
Washington, D.C. 20036

Public Affairs Pamphlets
381 Park Avenue South
New York, N.Y. 10016

Public Health Association, American
1015 – 18th St., N.W.
Washington, D.C. 20036

Public Relations Society of America
845 Third Avenue
New York, N.Y. 10022

Publishers, Assn. of American
One Park Ave.
New York, N.Y. 10016

Publishers, National Assn. of
Greeting Card
200 Park Avenue
New York, N.Y. 10017

Purchasing Management, National
Assn. of
11 Park Place
New York, N.Y. 10007

Quality Control, American
Society for
161 West Wisconsin Avenue
Milwaukee, Wisc. 53203

Radiologic Technologists, American
Society of
645 North Michigan Ave.
Chicago, Ill. 60611

Radiology, American College of
20 North Wacker Dr.
Chicago, Ill. 60606

Railroads, Association of American
1920 L St., N.W.
Washington, D.C. 20036

Range Management, Society For
2120 South Birch St.
Denver, Colo. 80222

Realtors, National Association of
Department of Education
155 East Superior St.
Chicago, Ill. 60611

Recreation and Parks Assn., National
1601 North Kent St.
Arlington, Va. 22209

Recreation Association, National
Industrial
20 North Wacker Dr.
Chicago, Ill. 60606

Refrigeration Service Engineers
Society
2720 Des Plaines Ave.
Des Plaines, Ill. 60018

Rehabilitation Counseling, American
Personnel and Guidance Assn.
1607 New Hampshire Ave., N.W.
Washington, D.C. 20009

Respiratory Therapy, American
Association for
7411 Hines Place
Dallas, Texas 75235

Retail Merchants Assn., the National
100 W. 31st St.
New York, N.Y. 10001

Retarded Citizens, National Assn. for
Box 109
Arlington, Texas 76011

Roofing Contractors Association,
National
1515 North Harlem Ave.
Oak Park, Ill. 60302

Sales and Marketing Executives
International
Student Education Division
630 Third Ave.
New York, N.Y. 10017

School Counselor Association,
American
1607 New Hampshire Ave., N.W.
Washington, D.C. 20009

Science Writers, National Assn. of
Box H
Sea Cliff, N.Y. 11579

Secretaries Assn., National
616 E. 63
Kansas City, Missouri 64110

Service Employees International
Union
900 - 17th St., N.W.
Washington, D.C. 20006

Sheet Metal Workers International
Assn.
1000 Connecticut Ave., N.W.
Washington, D.C. 20036

Social Work Careers Information
Service, National Assn. of Social
Workers
2 Park Avenue
New York, N.Y. 10016

Social Workers, National
Association of
15th and H St., N.W.
600 Southern Bldg.
Washington, D.C. 20005

Sociological Assn., American
1722 N St., N.W.
Washington, D.C. 20036

Speech and Hearing Assn., American
9030 Old Georgetown Rd.
Washington, D.C. 20014

Speech Communications Assn.
Statler Hilton Hotel
New York, N.Y. 10001

Statistical Assn., American
806 – 15th St., N.W.
Washington, D.C. 20005

Student Personnel Administrators,
National Assn. of
Portland State University, Box 751
Portland, Ore. 97207

Superintendent of Documents
U.S. Government Printing Office
Washington, D.C. 20402

Surveying and Mapping, American
Congress on
Woodward Building
733 – 15th St., N.W.
Washington, D.C. 20005

Teachers, American Federation of
1012 – 14th St., N.W.
Washington, D.C. 20005

Television and Radio Artists,
American Federation of
1350 Avenue of the Americas
New York, N.Y. 10019

Terrazo & Mosaic Association, Inc.,
National
716 Church St.
Alexandria, Va. 22314

Theatre Assoc., American Educational
1317 F Street N.W.
Washington, D.C. 20004

Traffic and Transportation, Inc.,
American Society of
547 West Jackson Boulevard
Chicago, Ill. 60606

Translators Assn., American
Box 129
Croton-on-Hudson, N.Y. 10520

Travel Agents, Institute of Certified
148 Linden St.
Wellesley, Mass. 02181

Trucking Assn., American
1616 P St., N.W.
Washington, D.C. 20036

TV and Electronic Service Assn.,
Nat'l Alliance
5908 So. Troy St.
Chicago, Ill. 60629

Underwriters, American Institute for
Property and Liability
Providence and Sugartown Roads
Malvern, Penn. 19355

University Professors, American
Association of
1 Dupont Circle N.W.
Washington, D.C. 20036

U.S. Civil Service Commission
Washington, D.C. 20415

U.S. Dept. of Agriculture
Forest Service
Washington, D.C. 20250

U.S. Department of Commerce
Employment Information Center,
Room 1050
Washington, D.C. 20230

U.S. Department of Commerce
Personnel Officer, Operations
Division
Office of the Secretary
Washington, D.C. 20238

U.S. Department of Health, Food and
Drug Adm.
Rockville, Md. 20852

U.S. Dept. of Health, Public Health
Service
National Institutes of Health
Clinical Center
Bethesda, Md. 20014

U.S. Dept. of Health, Social and
Rehabilitation Service
Washington, D.C. 20201

U.S. Dept. of the Interior
Director of Personnel
Washington, D.C. 20240

U.S. Dept. of the Interior
Geological Survey, National Center
12201 Sunrise Valley Dr.
Reston, Va. 22092

U.S. Dept. of Justice
Federal Bureau of Investigation
Washington, D.C. 20535

U.S. Dept. of Justice
Immigration and Naturalization
Service
Washington, D.C. 20536

U.S. Dept. of Labor
Bureau of Labor Statistics
Washington, D.C. 20212

U.S. Dept. of State
Employment Division
Washington, D.C. 20520

U.S. Dept. of State
Language Services Division
Washington, D.C. 20520

U.S. Dept. of Transportation
Federal Aviation Administration
Washington, D.C. 20591

U.S. Dept of the Treasury
Internal Revenue Service
Director, Administrative Intern
Program

1111 Constitution Avenue, N.W.
Washington, D.C. 20224

U.S. Dept. of the Treasury
U.S. Bureau of Customs
2100 K St., N.W.
Washington, D.C. 20226

U.S. Securities and Exchange
Commission
Director of Personnel
500 N. Capitol St., N.W.
Washington, D.C. 20549

Veterans Administration
Central Office Personnel Service
Washington, D.C. 20420

Veterinary Medical Assn., American
600 S. Michigan Ave.
Chicago, Ill. 60605

Wall and Ceiling Contractors,
International Assn. of
1775 Church St., N.W.
Washington, D.C. 20036

Watchmaker's Institute, American
P.O. Box 11011
Cincinnati, Ohio 45211

Welding Society, American
2501 N.W. 7th St.
Miami, Florida 33125

Wholesaler-Distributors, National
Assn. of
1725 K St., N.W.
Washington, D.C. 20006

Writer's Digest
9933 Alliance Rd.
Cincinnati, Ohio 45242

Zoologists, American Society of
Box 2739
Calif. Lutheran College
Thousand Oaks, Calif. 91360

INDEX

ABOUT THE AUTHORS

Bonnie L. Gray has had ten years of experience in teaching, counseling, and leading workshops for women re-entering the workforce or experiencing career and personal changes. Dr. Gray holds a Ph.D. in Counseling Psychology, is a Licensed Consulting Psychologist, an Assistant Professor of Continuing Education at the University of Minnesota, a member of the University's Extension Counseling staff, and a Consultant with Psyche, Inc. She is married and has two preschoolers.

Dorothy R. Loeffler has had many years of experience counseling re-entry and job-changing women. She has developed and presents local and national workshops for women in areas of identity, personal growth, and career development. She is a Fellow of the American Psychological Association, a member of the Committee on Women in Psychology of the American Psychological Association, Executive Officer of the Minnesota Psychological Association, and founder of the Minnesota Women Psychologists. Listed in *Who's Who of American Women,* Dr. Loeffler has a Ph.D. in Counseling Psychology, is a Licensed Consulting Psychologist, an Associate Professor at the University of Minnesota, and Executive Officer of Psyche, Inc. She is a single parent with a very active daughter.

Robin King Cooper became interested in and familiar with the problems of women re-entering the workforce while she was managing a temporary employment agency. She now teaches classes and workshops in women's identity, personal growth, and career development. She is an Instructor of Continuing Education at the University of Minnesota and a Consultant with Psyche, Inc. She is married and balances caring for a young son with work and school, as she completes a Ph.D. in Counseling Psychology.

Psyche, Inc. is a consulting and educational organization offering programs in career development, personal growth, and communication skills, both to individuals and organizations.